Just Keep Pedaling

Just Keep Pedaling

A Corner-to-Corner Bike Ride Across America

T. E. Trimbath

Writers Club Press
San Jose New York Lincoln Shanghai

Just Keep Pedaling
A Corner-to-Corner Bike Ride Across America

Writers Club Press
an imprint of iUniverse, Inc.

For information address:
iUniverse, Inc.
5220 S. 16th St., Suite 200
Lincoln, NE 68512
www.iuniverse.com

One man's bike ride across America.

ISBN: 0-595-22100-9

Printed in the United States of America

CONTENTS

INTRODUCTION

Eat less, exercise more. I have been trying that for years. Except for a brief spell where I lost a lot of weight and gained a surly disposition, that mantra has never really worked for me. Finally through some saving, some investing, and lots of lucky timing I was able to retire early. Of all the benefits of not working, one of the big ones was finally having enough time to workout enough to hopefully make a difference. Almost every year I make an event of taking on some physical feat that forces me to get into shape. I've stayed in shape but haven't liked the shape I've had. Each year I was able to accomplish the feat but my waistline kept getting bigger even while the diet got leaner. The burgers and fries were down to, at most, a once a week event and it can take us months to go through a pound of butter. I switched to no fat milk and gave up potato chips and still the waistline would not recede. Getting my diet even leaner was possible but cutting down even more would start to make food such a chore that I would dread each meal. I had the time so I could finally concentrate on the other side of the phrase. I decided to exercise more.

I had just turned 40 and was the heaviest I had ever been. Granted I had a 6 foot 2 inch frame to carry it all around on but why did the extra weight have to show up as more belly than I wanted? Within a few years I had gone from a 32 inch waist to rapidly approaching 36 inches at a pace that was unsettling. That was not helping my wardrobe. I wasn't bummed because my wardrobe was expensive; it wasn't. I was bummed because it meant I had to go shopping, which I am not good at. To make it worse, it would be the first time that I would have to buy pants where the waist was bigger than the legs were long. I felt huge. I definitely didn't want the situation to get worse.

My exercise schedule got much busier. At least four days a week I worked out for an hour and a half: weights, calisthenics, aerobics, karate, and stretching. At least one other day of the week I did stuff outdoors that I could spend all day at: hiking, skiing, or bicycling. I was out there for hours. It was really nice being in the mountains in the middle of the week when the trails were empty and I could set my own pace. The Cascade Mountains are less than an hour from our house and Mt. Rainier is about two hours away. That is an awesome and aerobic playground.

After about a year of that I still wasn't noticing any change. According to the scale, I was holding my weight down. According to my pants, my waist size was still growing. That was frustrating. There I was devoting at least twelve hours a week to exercise and eating a diet far leaner than before and yet I wasn't making progress. What hope do most people have if even that much effort didn't produce results? It was ridiculous. Lots of times I had heard news reports about the benefits of good diet and exercise. They make it sound so simple. Throw away the potato chips and lose weight. Walk each day and lose weight. I was busting my buns out there and still having to trade up to fatter pants. What chance did anyone have if they had to spend most of their day working a desk job and raising a family?

I knew that drastically cutting back on my diet could work but I also knew that in the past it had made me so grouchy that I don't think I was nice to be around. My concern for my weight shouldn't overshadow the way I treat my family and friends. At the time I didn't realize how surly the diet had made me. That is one of those things that are easiest to see in hindsight. I didn't want to go back there if there was some other way of losing the fat. Maybe twelve hours of exercise a week just wasn't enough. Maybe I had to break through or clear some major hurdle to reset my body's metabolism. I started cooking up ways of getting out there for hours on end. It had to be something aerobic. If I was going to do it for hours on end with a forty year old's body it had better be low impact. Forrest Gump had run across America in the movie but my knees didn't think that was a good idea. I also knew that it would have to be something that I could do for weeks. Enough of my annual events had been week long trips and none of them had changed a thing. What got to me emotionally was that my waist size hadn't changed. So I knew I might have to do this for a lot longer time. At one point I considered just finding some cheap motel where I could ride out on my bicycle every day. If I tried it at home I knew that I would be too distracted by mowing the lawn or pulling weeds. Getting control of my body was and is a higher priority for me than having a manicured lawn or weed free flowerbeds. Finding a motel with that many good bike trails would be tough so I considered biking from one motel to another. I figured that if I could exercise for hours a day for about six weeks there would bound to be an obvious benefit. Six weeks of riding for about six hours a day should clear any physiological hurdle that my body may have. Some quick math made me realize that I would have cycled over two thousand miles with a workout like that. That's when I started planning to ride across the country. That should take care of any boredom.

I've done a fair bit of biking for fun. There've been a few long trips thrown in. My wife and I had gone on a bike trip to Austria a few years earlier and that was a fairly affordable venture. She still liked her job so she wasn't coming along on this trip. None of my other bicycling friends were available. At least going solo would allow me to set my own pace. My goal sounded like getting from one coast to the other, but to me the main goal was to get control of my body's weight. Getting to the opposite corner of the country was the carrot.

I like travelling. So much of the media seems to show the extremes of life. The reality shows focus on how ugly life can be. The other end of the spectrum are the stories about people who are portrayed as saints and angels. Channel surfing can bring up a show on abusive people and switch immediately to some story about some child saving the family from fire. Those are fascinating stories but for me the really appealing stories are in people's everyday lives. There are a lot of stories out there. The lives people are living in downtown Seattle are a lot different than the lives of people living only an hour east over the mountains. Seeing how similar and how different our lives are is one of those things that can make me just sit back and ponder for hours on end. We talk about cultural diversity, but frequently it is the diversity of ethnicity that folks have in mind. Someone may see someone from another country and smile at some odd habit they have as a sign of their culture. That same person may sneer though if the person with the odd habit was born and raised in another part of town. This is one enormous country and I am fascinated by the cultures it contains. I have wondered whether I should have gotten a degree in Anthropology or Sociology. The job market in Aerospace Engineering seemed brighter at the time.

I wasn't ignorant of the problems out there though. Despite the progress we have made in Civil Rights, I knew that the person least likely to have problems would be a white middle aged male. Of course a white middle aged male riding around in skintight Lycra has to realize that some people won't feel comfortable seeing all of a body's contours. Clothing matters and that is always such a strange fact for me to deal with. I carried some other frumpier riding clothes just in case someone got too upset by the sight of me in something that showed my gut and other features.

It was also a good way to see the land: how it gradually changes from one environment to the next and how the way we use it changes too. There are lines on maps between city and country, desert and forest, but reality is much more gradual and much less well defined. I not only wanted to see it, but also be out in the midst of it without the protective cage of a car filtering my senses.

The money would be a bit of a problem but as long as the stock market held up I would be alright. Back in 1994 I had some money saved up and had the lucky timing to invest it in a company called "America Online". I wished I had invested more, but there was at least enough to pay for a bicycle trip. I set myself a budget for the ride and decided to stick to it.

I've been told that there is really no training for a trip like this. There is no way to get used to sitting in the saddle for hours on end except to sit on a saddle for hours on end. Getting some long rides in ahead of time is a good idea to get into some general shape, but the more important task is making sure the equipment works, fits, and does the job. Actually it helps to at least get some start on the calluses and sore spots that long rides will generate. Those pains are the best measure of whether you have the right equipment and attitude.

If you are lucky and there aren't any schedule pressures, you can just start the ride in an incredibly leisurely fashion without any training. Start the ride knowing that each day you will do just what you can. At the start it might not be much, but eventually you'll get into shape and your daily mileage will improve. Why spend those miles training when you could be out there actually making progress and getting to watch the world go by? Of course, you'll get lots of miles in right off the bat if you are already in good shape. All bets are off though if you have a schedule to keep. Then make sure you're either in good enough shape to finish or don't mind stopping short when you run out of time. I tend to be somewhat conservative on solo ventures so I made sure I got out there on the bike for progressively longer and longer rides. I also started replacing some of my runs, hikes, and ski trips with bike rides. Every week I would get in two or three good rides. The shortest were about an hour and a half and I would try to keep the speed up on those. The longer ones were usually about four or five hours long but I would take them at a more normal pace. The shorter ones frequently ended up being shopping trips. That was how I stocked up on some of the items like the panniers and emergency equipment. It was an excuse to get out on the bike and get something done too.

Getting the gear ready was a big issue. My biggest gear decision was made for me when I trashed my road bike. Usually I just ride from home. There is a lot to see around where I live and I know a lot of routes. Occasionally though I throw in some variety by starting from somewhere else. For that I have a bike rack on top of the car and that is right where the bike was when I drove back into the garage one day. I was so tired after that ride that as the garage door went up I drove right in without thinking. I heard the crunch and stopped the car but it was too late. My faithful road bike that I had bought back in the early eighties was turned into a bent frame wonder. It had over ten thousand miles on it and it would never be ridden on the roads again. The frame was buckled in two places and wasn't coming back. I felt stupid and sheepish.

Being somewhat frugal, or possibly stingy and naïve, I realized that I still had my mountain bike. It wasn't an extreme beast with shocks and springs and stuff. It was an old hardtail that I had sometimes used as a commuter bike. Road bikes are faster and quieter but lots of the roads out there are so broken up that a mountain bike can be a nice reliable alternative. It isn't as fast as a road bike but a bike loaded down for touring may not get much of a chance for getting up to speed. Besides, it was the bike that I had used in Austria. That time I had picked it because I thought it would survive the airplane ride better than my road bike. It wasn't very fast but it sure was nice when we came across the road construction and the time that the bike path turned into a strip of mud along an orchard. It hadn't been my first choice but maybe it would be the better choice.

Originally I had planned a Springtime tour. I wanted to start sometime in March after most of the snow was out of the local mountain passes. Hopefully I could make it to Florida before the RVs came out of hiding. I took that to be around Memorial Day. If I had to take more time, then I would still be on the road before the heat of July and August. Life interrupted those plans. While this trip was important for me, it wasn't as important as my wife and I relinquishing our roles as landlords. We had decided it was time to finally sell her old house from her single days. Even with a property manager tending it, we didn't like being landlords so we decided to sell. So much for me riding in the Spring. I didn't want to ride in the Summer because of the traffic and the heat. Some of the places that I would go through could get very hot and very busy. That left riding in the Fall or waiting for the next Spring. One of the reasons for doing it sooner rather than later is age. The longer I put off the trip the older I would be. Being in my early forties didn't make me feel decrepit but I did realize how priceless time is. It was not hard to imagine one thing after another getting in the way of the ride season after season. There is no knowing when things will change. My body can have troubles. Accidents can happen. If I didn't do it in the Fall, then something else may come up in the Spring that would keep me from doing it again. Besides, leaving Kaye to tend the house while I was going felt bad enough. This trip was essentially a selfish act even though I was trying to get her a thinner husband as a Christmas present. There is a lot less yard and housework to do in a Seattle Fall than in a Seattle Spring. A Fall trip would be tougher though. I wouldn't count on the herds of RVs retreating until after Labor Day but I would have to get across the Rockies before the Winter storms hit. Even if I got across the Rockies okay I would be trying to go south faster than the change in the seasons. I didn't want Winter to catch me. I also didn't want to catch up to hurricane season. To top it off, I didn't want to be out on the road as the holidays approached. There is a lot to do at home for the holidays so I gave myself the arbitrary limit of being home by the beginning of November.

Once my friends heard about my ride all sorts of advice started to flowing in. A lot of it could be classified as queries about my sanity. People dredged up horror stories from places along the route or passed along dire warnings of every ilk. At the same time they were encouraging as well. That was definitely a mixed set of messages. They cared. Kaye and I talked a lot about it. In amongst all of the noise I had also heard from a couple of people who had actually gone on similar trips. The people who had actually gotten out there and ridden were the ones with the stories about how good it was. The down sides were just cautions and caveats. None of the riders had run across any of the horrors that lots of people had warned me about. What I kept in mind was that this was something I was choosing to do. I didn't have to go out there and ride. If I wanted to turn around and come home all I had to do was find a bus stop, train station or airport and I could be back home within a few days or even a few hours. Coming home early would only wound my ego and pride. That would be painful but not bad considering the trials some people are forced to go through in their normal lives. This trip wouldn't feel luxurious but I recognized that being able to go on it was a luxury and nothing else. If it was tough, it was still something that I was bringing on myself. If it was too much I could just tell my ego to stuff it and then give up and come home.

Even though my route planning was very simple and straightforward it took a lot of time. It came down to finding a way across the Rockies and across the Mississippi while keeping the motels less than one hundred miles apart. I usually didn't make any reservations because I didn't know how my body, spirit, bike or the weather and terrain would change how far I went each day. One risk I took was to only carry the simplest emergency shelter and gear. For everything else, I planned on using my credit card a lot.

In addition to the credit card, another bit of civilization that I would take along would be a cell phone. I had never owned one before but I had to admit that it was cheap insurance. A solo bike ride without one was possible but there was no good reason to take on that unnecessary risk. I even told the regular Friday lunch crowd that I would call them every Friday to join in. I also decided to send out emails on a regular basis just so folks could read what was happening. I didn't know if anyone would really care but I did know that Kaye's job was busy enough that she wouldn't have time to continually field questions about my ride.

The italics that follow are the emails that I sent out from the road. I've cleaned up the most egregious typos. But mostly they are left here the way everyone received them. Each day was a separate email but the emails went out in batches. There weren't very many computers out there to work with so I sent out emails from Bellevue, Boise, Ogden, Price, Grand Junction, Pratt, Russellville, and from back home. The emails only brushed what happened each of those days and showed what was on my mind at the time. The rest of the words are the rest of the story that my friends didn't know about. The story of each day is what I have been able to recollect and sift through after finishing the ride and thinking about it. The story of the whole trip is one I am still trying to figure out and am still learning from everyday.

SHAKEDOWN

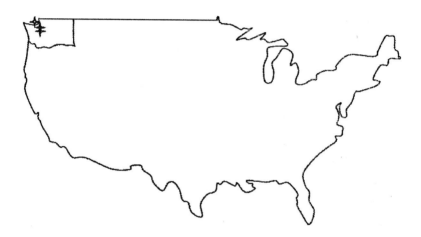

September 4, 2000 Roche Harbor Resort (base camp)

Kaye and I drove up to Roche Harbor. It seemed like a good place to start a corner to corner trip across the United States. Beautiful place. Lots of money. Surprisingly noisy. This has to be the biggest collection of monster yachts that I've come across. One in particular was about 110 feet as I paced it out. I figure there are lots of big boats when I am frequently looking up to see the anchor. There was also a really cool hull that was only there to have four engines strapped to it. The two outboards were 300 horsepower each and then we noticed the two jet exhaust ports below the waterline. All of this on a boat that was smaller than the dinghy from the 110 footer. It had lots of decals for "America's Cup 2000, New Zealand". They need this for a sail boat race?! So you can see where some of the noise *came from. Another source was the airport adjoining the resort. Lots of private planes and little charter jobs. Diesel and Av Gas. Oh boy, lots of toys.*

Unfortunately for me, they celebrated the end of the tourist season for this quiet resort by having a rock band play until midnight. After getting such poor service in the restaurant that I had to go to the grocery for dinner you can imagine how happy I was to be on my way the next morning. Really it was a nice place. I just don't expect to go back anytime soon.

I am a romantic at heart. Some say altruistic. Some say an idealist. Some say I just ain't normal. It must have been the romantic side of me that figured it would be good to start a ride like this from someplace nice. That was especially true because my wife, Kaye, would be there too. Chances were that along the ride I would find enough places that weren't nice so I might as well start from a comfy spot. Besides, it would act as a small vacation for Kaye and I without having to worry about the house and the cats. If things went well, my route would pass through our house in a few days so I'd see her again soon, but that wouldn't be the same. I wanted to have one last night someplace where we could just relax and be with each other.

There are a bunch of islands in the northwest corner of Washington State called the San Juans. They're a great place to get away to because if your troubles want to find you they'll have a rough time getting there. Most of the islands are uninhabited except for some starfish or maybe an eagle. The ones with people tend to have amazing homes in the midst of a marvelous setting. Only four of the islands are visited by the state ferry. The ferry ride was an hour long cruise through marine wilderness, small town America, and passed the homes of the rich and resourceful. You have to be resourceful just to get to some of those homes. Building them couldn't have been easy either. We were headed for a resort on one of the biggest islands: Roche Harbor Resort on San Juan Island.

We had been by the resort years ago when we were staying on the island for an extended weekend in Friday Harbor. At that time the resort had seemed quaint and quiet. The resort is one of the oldest buildings around; though in this part of the country that is only a bit over a hundred years or so.

When we got there this time it was a bit different. The hotel and all looked the same but there was a lot more activity than we had expected. The last time we were there had been in the off season. On Labor Day, folks were probably getting their boats or ships ready for Winter. Naturally that made the docks bustle.

The grounds were pretty though and the boats were amazing. I wonder if the late 1990's stock market had brought a lot more mega yachts to moor where there might not have been many before.

It was nice having some time for Kaye and I to walk the grounds and see the gardens and such. They have a fascinating old Masonic memorial for one of the founding families. It is up in the woods through an old cemetery. That monument and the ruins of the lime kiln business that became the hotel make for an interesting picture of how developed this area was. It is also very apparent how quickly it could all go to nothing if left to nature. Turning it into a resort is helping to hold back nature somewhat but oh, what a battle.

As pretty as it was, quaint does not always translate into comfortable. Between my nervousness, the noise and the lack of a real dinner, I was happy to get on with the ride.

September 5, 2000 Roche Harbor to Friday Harbor to Anacortes to Oak Harbor to Mukilteo

Time to start riding. Kaye took a picture of me touching the waters of the Pacific and then it was time to get on the bike. The ride to the ferry was about 10 miles so she got there first. At least we got to ride the ferry together. After that, she went shopping and I headed south.

The clouds had formed up overnight but it wasn't raining much. Cool weather for riding. Whidbey is a nice quiet place once you get past the

Naval air station. The A-6s were practicing flying around on edge a few
hundred feet off the ground. Quite impressive.

The island is nothing but rolling hills with some flat parts down by the
water. Traffic wasn't much of a problem once you account for the surge
when a ferry docks. My primary goal was to make it past Oak Harbor in
the North part of the island and get as far south as my aching butt could
get me. The legs were sore but the butt was complaining the most. One
town after another went slowly by and I realized that I could actually make
it to the mainland at Mukilteo. Luckily, I was able to get to the ferry
terminal right before they loaded. I was also lucky enough to get one of the
last rooms at the hotel by the ferry terminal. Waterfront costs but I wasn't
taking on the next hill until I had a night's rest.

We woke up to typically grayish Northwest skies. Luckily for me that
was a familiar sight. Besides, it was a great excuse for some awesome
French toast from the restaurant on the resort's dock. Breakfast can be
such a blessing. It would have been nice to linger because it was so quiet
in the morning but the ferries don't run very often and I didn't want to
miss the next one. I also wanted to have some extra time because there
is bound to be something that desperately needs adjustment on the first
day out. Simple things like fixing a loose fitting or finding that I had
forgotten something make me plan for a bit of extra time for the first
day's ride. This time it was the panniers. Luckily it didn't take too long
to adjust a them so they would quit hitting the spokes.

One odd aspect of this part of the trip was having Kaye and I leave
Roche Harbor at the same time heading for the same ferry in separate
vehicles. It didn't take her long to pass me. I actually got the headstart
because I took a shortcut along a gravel road that saved me about a
quarter mile. But unless I am in city traffic, even a slow car will catch
and pass me.

I was hoping to come across other cyclists on the ride. It is nice to
have someone else to talk to and if they know how to draft, then so
much the better. As I headed out I saw an organized tour group and

their guides coming along on their red bikes. I think they weren't nearly as comfortable in the gray skies and drizzle as their guides and I seemed to be. Besides, they were going the other way, which makes having a conversation hard. There were a few other cycling tourists going my way, but they were couples involved in their own conversations. Besides, they turned off onto a side road to one of the local attractions about the time they caught up to me. They were moving quicker because they weren't carrying nearly as much as I was. Day touring is so much easier than long distance touring.

It was good to be on the bike, but I was already worrying about whether I had trained enough and brought the right gear. Those little hills in the car had suddenly grown. Funny how that happens when you don't have a hundred horses helping you out.

Fortunately, Kaye and I caught the same ferry. The ferries only run a few times a day so missing one could have meant losing hours of riding time. At least the ferry traffic was acting like the off season. Bikes can almost always get on but you can't count on there being enough room for all of the cars. Kaye was able to get the car onboard. We went upstairs to the passenger deck. She read a book while I got some much needed sleep. The ride takes about an hour so I was able to take a good nap. The area is pretty but I needed the rest so I missed the sights.

I found more bicyclists! We were getting off the ferry at the same time. The ferry folks ask bicyclists to get off either before or after the cars so we tend to leave together. Well I found them but they were only going a few miles. They lived in the area. They were nice enough to give me better directions to a shortcut that Kaye and I found on a bike map of the area. That got me out of traffic and onto some nice backroads. The land is hilly but it has lots of nice views of the water. The stretch through the forests was quiet and green. Well it was mostly quiet except for the occasional car and my huffing and puffing.

At that point I didn't know how long it would take me to get to our house in Bellevue. If things went amazingly well I could make it by evening. If things weren't nearly as rosy I might not get there for a couple more nights. It was hard to know if I had trained well enough or if I had the right gear or if I would be held up by logistics, breakdowns, or ferry schedules. I decided that I had to push it the first day just to get my confidence level up. It is possible to go at a trip like this slowly and then build up. With me, that just gives me more time to think up things that might go wrong. I can worry myself to the point that I might just give up. Giving up really wasn't an option. I had mentioned this ride to so many people that my ego wouldn't let me stop unless I had a gut wrenching excuse. Quitting because I was wet and tired wouldn't get me much sympathy in Seattle.

Deception Pass is an awesome sight to take in while driving. It was even better as I approached on a bike. I still was not on the mainland, but the islands are close enough to be linked by bridges. It just so happens that the bridge is narrow, a few hundred feet above the water, and carries a lot of the truck traffic destined for the island. The sidewalks have railings on either side so there wasn't room for my panniers. That didn't matter because there were tourists blocking the sidewalk as they snapped pictures of the awesome tidal surges going by beneath the bridge. Between the truck traffic and my fear of heights, I had a hard time enjoying the view from the bridge. It really is quite impressive when you are not fearing for your life.

I like Whidbey Island. It is supposedly one of the longest islands in the United States. For me that was a good thing and a bad thing. I decided to ride along it because the mainland roads are awfully busy nowadays. Whidbey was much quieter and more rural once I got away from the Navy's Airbase but it is also hillier than the main route over on the mainland. The big difference was the better traffic on the island. I used to ride out there almost every weekend when I first moved out to the Pacific Northwest. Have the hills gotten bigger since then or have I gotten older or do panniers really make that much of a difference? Maybe someone else can do a scientific study.

For most of the island the road was a hilly two lane that sometimes has a shoulder. There were even parts with a bike path beside the road. It was a pity that I didn't know where the bike paths went and a shame that they were frequently much hillier and rougher than the shoulder.

The surprise came when I found the construction site. I hadn't expected one so large on the island. It looked like Whidbey was growing up and needed a four lane highway. That meant that they were felling trees on both sides of the road and the traffic was down to one lane for more than a mile. The trees grow big on Whidbey so the crews were working up high and there was no shortage of pine needles and boughs down below. Of course that happened on a long uphill grade where there was no shoulder. That was one of the things they were trying to fix. One lane was closed and covered with branches. In the meantime it put me at the head of a bunch of traffic pedaling uphill as fast as I could. Eventually I decided to ride in the lane with all of the fallen and falling branches just to keep from being more of a traffic hazard. One motorcyclist who was stuck back in the traffic shouted some epithet. The funny thing to me was how motorcycles used to be considered targets. Maybe they still are but I thought they were in fashion now. They used to get the epithets. Now they hand them out. I can't imagine bicycles being so generally accepted. Of course I wouldn't mind being proved wrong.

Whidbey may be hilly but the ferry had to be at sea level so eventually all of that up and down had to treat me to a downhill run. It happened sooner than I expected but later than my legs appreciated. It was late. I was tired and I didn't know where I would sleep that night. So out came the web enabled cell phone and I went hunting for a motel. After a frustratingly slow trial I gave up and called directory assistance. I found a human voice who found a motel phone number. There was a new hotel right on the water where the ferry docks on the mainland. I got one of their last rooms. What a way to end the day: a long downhill ride to a nice ride on the ferry and with a short walk to the hotel at sunset. I was within fifty miles of home and on the mainland.

That night at dinner I had the first indication of how much my journey would put me outside of normal people's lives. As I sat there with my dinner I watched various dramas unfolding in the restaurant. Some of the staff were giggling over some piece of gossip. One of the tables was a bunch of folks who worked together having an after-work party with the obligatory gag gifts. Some of the laughter was genuine. Some seemed to be forced: like they had to attend and enjoy themselves to be accepted. There were also a couple of other individuals sitting there trying to keep themselves distracted with work or fluff while waiting for the chance to eat another dinner on the road. Such is life in a hotel restaurant. Whatever endeavor I was on was my own and I was alone with it. I would be watching all of these other lives without them knowing anything about mine. There was nothing wrong with that. So many people had made a big deal of me going on the trip that it seemed like I might be the center of attention. In reality, unless I was in the bike clothing there was no way anyone at dinner would have a clue that my trip might be different than most. In other words I was just like everyone else there. Everyone has a story unfolding and we tend to ignore that.

At least for me the hotel staff was very accommodating. They must have had other cyclists come through often enough. They suggested that I take my bike up to the room and were more comfortable with the notion than I was. That was a nice way to start.

September 6, 2000 Mukilteo to Everett to Bothell to Redmond to Bellevue

Wake up early and notice that the streets are wet. I guess I will be too. Actually it wasn't too bad. It had rained at night and all I got was a bit of road splatter. The first hill was long but well graded and most of the commuters had no problem getting past me. Of course for a while there I was passing them. Isn't our traffic wonderful? I wonder at it all the time.

I had a small problem finding the Bothell Everett highway. I used to live in this neighborhood. What was once a quaint little two lane through some farms and pasture has now been straightened, flattened, broadened and populated by low rise industrial buildings. At least it has a bike lane now. I was able to ride bike lanes almost all the way home from this point. I even ended up riding within a mile of Plexus. Any later in the day and I could have had lunch with Kaye.

Things were going fairly well. I know most of this area and when I got on the Sammamish Slough bike trail I was set. I was ahead of schedule enough that I stopped at a Starbucks in Redmond for an Espresso Brownie and a Vente Chai Tea Latte. How very Redmond-ish.

I got home just past noon and felt a little silly. The next day is supposed to be a rest day and I can tack another half a day onto that. Oh well. I guess I'll just get a bit more laundry done and pick up a few things. There are always chores to do.

Breakfast confirmed that I wasn't exactly fitting into most people's lifestyles. I went down to the lobby and joined the other guests at the continental breakfast bar. I was already in my bicycling gear. Everything else was already packed. Sitting all around me were the business travelers and such in suits and their version of travel clothes. I would get the occasional side glance from someone but no one would say anything. Of course, what would they say? On my business trips, breakfast was my time to get my head together for the day's meetings. Talking to me sure wasn't going to help these folks get ready for their day's events. I was part of their world but more like some painting: something to notice but nothing to interact with. That would get to be a familiar feeling on the road.

The first few days of the trip were all on familiar roads. That's why I knew that I had a long hill ahead of me. I lived near the top of it for about four years. That was one long haul and I had to do it during rush hour traffic. The bad news was that it was rush hour traffic and that the area has grown a lot since I moved. The good news was that the roads were so clogged that there were stretches where I made better time than the cars. It can even be safer. When things are so clogged up, the cars aren't very dangerous.

The roads were supposed to be familiar. The area had grown so much that massive chunks of it were unrecognizable. The only sure signs I had of familiar territory were the Interstate overpasses that had been there all that time.

Progress may mean that a lot of the country was paved over and not nearly as green as the farm that it replaced, but at least I found a bike lane. I could have sworn that the area was hillier when I lived there. Even though things didn't look as familiar as I had expected, at least I knew where the roads were generally headed. I trusted my intuition. I hadn't expected to find a route that took me right past my wife's office building. If I had worked the route out earlier I might have timed it for lunchtime. I tried calling her at work but as usual she was in a meeting of some sort. Busy, busy, busy.

Being so close to her office at Plexus made it that much more embarrassing to get lost at the next intersection. I knew how to get home on the highway from there but I couldn't remember how to get to the bike path that would get me most of the way home. Should I stop and ask for directions? Well yes. I had to practice bugging strangers because soon I would be going through places I had never heard of before. Pretty soon I was pointed off in the right direction. Within a few miles down a road I wouldn't have taken otherwise, I found the bike path. I'd ridden it a lot and it is where I do some of my longer training runs when I am getting ready for a marathon.

I took a break in the park where the road joined up with the bike trail. It was a nice park for a number of reasons but was possibly unique because of its chickens. There was a flock of show quality roosters and chickens living there. I don't know if they were escapees or were released by their owners. In any case they were living there and quite literally strutting their stuff. The part that convinces me that the area has become too citified is that the chickens are protected by law. Someone took the time, money and energy to get the local municipality to protect these birds. Evidently everything else in the town is working fine so that they could devote time to protecting undomesticated farm animals. It amazes me each time I go there. That day it meant I had some of the most colorful and odd road obstacles to ride through.

The area had not only grown recently but it had a lot of the new economy money running around it. There were some very nice places to take breaks for the next ten miles or so. That's why I knew I could find a Starbucks somewhere just off the trail. It turned out to be the only one I stopped at on the entire trip. They and their competitors are everywhere around the Seattle area but the next few thousand miles would have fewer coffee shops than I have within walking distance of my house. Of course I can walk a far piece so that might not be saying as much.

There were very few people who figured out what I was doing just by looking at me. Most folks didn't even notice me. One of the Starbucks customers guessed right away. She was an older woman who had very nice things to say and I really appreciated her encouragement. Bicyclists are common enough around Seattle that there is nothing odd about seeing one. They are part of everyday life and are generally ignored. In retrospect, it was nice to be able to blend in so well.

The bike path had to end eventually. Once I left the bike path I headed up through the neighborhoods and the suburbia along one side of Microsoft. It is a long hill without a bike lane but it got most of the climb out of the way all at once and early. This was when I got my first chance to play Good Samaritan. There was an early model Mustang stalled in the road. Nice car, but it wasn't being taken care of well enough evidently. Before my trusty cell phone and I could help out though, a local police car dropped on by. They didn't need me so I was on my way. As I passed by Microsoft I had to give at least some slight quiet thanks. Indirectly they helped make this trip possible. Kaye and I are fairly frugal folks and with some of the cash that we hadn't spent, we had invested in Microsoft as well as some other companies. None of those had made us rich but each had contributed enough that I felt comfortable quitting work. It gave me the opportunity to go on such a trip. It is amazing what frugal living and fortunate investing can do for one's lifestyle.

By the time I got home there was still half a day to work with. Somewhere else along the ride I would have found the next place to stay and kept going until I got there. I had decided early on though that I would swing past the house and take one full day of rest. Being over 40 there were enough body parts that could veto my plans for rides like this. That meant it was prudent to sit still for a day and see if any of them spoke up. I sat still for the rest of that day and the next, but it wasn't easy. I was antsy to get going and knew a storm was coming in. Going through the local mountain pass may not compare to others in altitude, but it makes up for it with bad weather. Sitting for a day while the storm got closer was not what I needed out of a rest day, but I had to make sure my body was not going to have a major problem.

Nature wasn't planning anything around my itinerary, but I can be a stubborn sort. I had a plan and I was going to stick to it. Besides, the normal lunch crowd was going to get together on a Thursday just for me, and it would be impolite to skip out on that lunch. It is interesting to see how priorities sort themselves out. There I was placing a night with my wife, a lunch with friends, and an itinerary at a higher priority than potential hypothermia in the mountains. There's some insight into my self there that I still don't understand. It is probably obvious to everyone else, but that is the way we work isn't it? We all have blind spots that everyone around us can see but we just can't focus on.

Now I'm Getting Somewhere

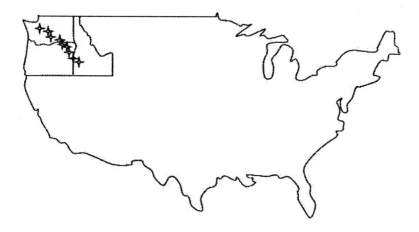

Sept 8, 2000   Bellevue to Redmond to North Bend to Snoqualmie Pass to Cle Elum

The first storm of the year and I get to go through the pass at the same time. I-90 was closed to bicycles for only two miles but it made me detour through Redmond. Just below Snoqualmie Falls I came across a wrecked semi that completely blocked the road. I only got past by following an access road until I was beyond the wreck. Then I had to take everything off the bike and carry it about 20 feet up through bushes. It took about four trips.

From there it was a cold slog up through the Pass as the storm came through. Luckily that meant I had a tail wind. It was 44 and raining in the Pass. It should be better further East shouldn't it? So I pressed on to Cle Elum. At least the Sun was shining when I got there. The storm caught up to me later that night. I'm glad I missed the worst of it.

Kaye went to AAA and has established a library of maps and directories that are impressive. She is now my remote personalized travel source.

This machine is about to tun off.

I wasn't able to get this email out until I Boise. The Internet may be ubiquitous but that doesn't mean that accessing it is easy. When I finally found a machine it was an expensive kiosk in a truck stop. The keyboard was sticky and it kept disconnecting before I was finished typing. I lost about six days worth of emails. When I finally got back on I was determined to be very concise. That day's description deserved much better because it was one of the more dramatic days that I had on the ride.

Interstate 90 goes within a couple miles of our house and is the nearest and shortest route over the mountains from Bellevue. The pity was that the state had closed a tiny section of it to bicycles for road construction. The irony is that the road construction was on the other side of a divided highway. There actually wasn't anything in my way but an overly reactive bureaucracy that didn't realize what they had done. By closing that one bit of Interstate to bicycles, they forced me to either play tag with the police or to take about a twenty mile detour on narrow roads in the name of safety.

I knew about the detour ahead of time and had already resigned myself to the fact that the first thing I would do in the morning was to backtrack through Redmond. There was a lot of growth along that route so the rush hour traffic had the extra flavor of construction equipment heading out for the day's work.

On my day off I had kept up on the progress of the storm coming into town. It was expected to be the first Winter storm and its rain started as I headed out. The early storms usually don't close the Pass but they sure don't make for optimum bicycling weather. That's why the detour I headed out on was slick. The road was wet enough and narrow enough that a tractor-trailer and a step-van had a head on collision that sent one driver to the hospital and closed the road. I was about the seventh vehicle to come across the scene. This was one of those cases where from guardrail to guardrail and even from hillside to drop-off, there was a continuous barrier of wrecked pieces of metal. I still don't know if everyone ended up alright.

I felt bad having to think about myself at this point. Here was evidence that some unlucky person could be in serious condition and all I had to think about was how I was going to get past all of it. I had just gained almost all of the altitude I needed to bring myself back up to the Interstate. If I turned around my only real option was to backtrack about ten miles, losing a lot of elevation, climb back up some other narrow roads, and hope that the storm wasn't going to get worse. As worried as I was about the drivers I was surprised to find that one of the firefighters was taking it all in stride. He gave me some directions on how I could possibly get past if I went through the bushes. I think he welcomed the opportunity to solve one easy problem. That and the fact that nothing seemed to have spilled or ignited might have given him the time to help me. Who knows? Maybe he was a bicyclist too.

He pointed out a path that led down to a stream. The path was actually a small access road for a water management gate of some sort. The path was beside the wreck but below it by about 15 or 20 feet. From there, getting back up to the road was no trail, just a tangle of blackberry bushes and thistles up a wet and sloppy slope. If the wreck had happened ten feet farther along the road, I wouldn't have been able to get past. The hill steepened too abruptly. Instead, I was able to get around it by hauling all of my gear up in pieces. There were some nervous moments as I worried that a slip on the rocks could end the whole trip right here. I didn't want to twist an ankle or worse. At least the paramedics were conveniently standing by. My gear didn't appreciate the route very much. I hadn't worn stuff for beating back bushes and such. Luckily the scratches and snags weren't too bad. The rest of the day would be so messy that no one could tell the difference.

It is odd how silver linings show up. The road was closed. Therefore it wouldn't have any traffic on it. At least that helped me but it was probably not a good trade off from the point of view of the people involved in the wreck.

I stopped at Snoqualmie Falls and watched a group of tourists snap away happily. The Falls were impressive during the rain. I would have been happier if there was less water for them to work with. Most folks weren't even aware that the road ahead was closed. All of these vignettes play themselves out so near to each other but are totally separate and ignorant of each other.

From the Falls it was a straight shot to the Pass. Once I left the last truck stop behind there was nowhere else to stay until the top of the Pass more than ten miles up the road. That part of the mountains is not even described as rural. It is wilderness. I like it but it makes it hard to find a dry and warm place to stop.

The next job was to climb up the Pass. Instead of taking breaks every few miles, I started taking breaks every few hundred yards. The mileposts went by so slowly that I would think that they had skipped one. Then I would come across it and realize how slow I was going. As I got closer to the Pass the wind and rain decided to pick up. Luckily they didn't get as serious about it as they could have. It was cold and wet enough that I definitely needed to get somewhere warm and dry.

It was Good Samaritan time again. Near the top I came across a family stuck in their car. It happened right at one of those bends in the road where a cell phone is useless. When I stopped to offer help I could tell that they were getting cold while they sat in their car trying to figure out what to do. I couldn't exactly tow them up the hill or give anyone a ride, but I pointed out to them that the next exit was within walking distance and that one of them should go for it.

There I was watching them get colder without realizing how long I had been out in the wind, rain and cold myself. About that time I might have been starting to get hypothermic. I couldn't think as quickly as usual and my energy level was dropping. Luckily I had given the folks some good advice. The next exit was the Pass and it wasn't that far away. I celebrated making it to the Pass with lunch at the mini-mart. It may not have been fancy but as messy as I was, I couldn't imagine going into the restaurant. I sat on the floor inside back by the ATM where they had some open floor space. It gave me a chance to get to some sort of dry, warm, and fed condition.

The afternoon decision process began again. Should I go on or stay in the local motel? Emotionally it would have felt good to make more progress but I was bushed. But then again, I was at the Pass, so it should be mostly downhill to the next motel. The storms usually don't make it much farther than the Pass. I probably should have stayed there but I decided to go on. I was trying to keep my spirits up by making progress.

I had packed for late Summer weather so the only eye protection I had brought along was a pair of dark sunglasses. They weren't very useful under all of those clouds so I was riding downhill with nothing protecting my eyes except my blinking eyelids and luck. Riding with my eyes shut didn't seem like a good idea. Lots of folks promised to include me in their prayers and maybe that is why I found a pair of clear eyeshields lying on the side of the road. I noticed them sitting there during one of my breaks that afternoon. They were scratched up and abandoned. They looked like the sort that the road crews use. There wasn't much style to them but I wasn't going to complain.

The next motel was about twenty miles farther. It was downhill overall, but there were enough flat stretches and uphills that I was dragging by the time I got into Cle Elum. I stopped at the first motel that I could find. Luckily, it was across the street from a supermarket.

Before I could change clothes for the walk across the street, the storm let loose with a downpour. All of my bike stuff was wet from the ride and all of my regular clothes were going to get drenched just walking across the street. While I had warmed up and had some food from the deli, I was still chilled enough that in retrospect I could tell that I was at least mildly hypothermic. I couldn't motivate myself to eat a normal meal, drink more than a glass of water, or even take a shower. I did have something of a dinner but it sure didn't compensate for what I had just been through. That night's phone call to Kaye was more evidence. She said I sounded so bad that she almost drove out to spend the night with me.

I think that day was the one that convinced me to not push it too close to nightfall again on the ride. That was one tough day. Only later did we realize exactly how much that detour added and how far I actually rode that day. I had done almost 90 miles with a mountain pass and an early season Winter storm thrown in. It was no wonder that I was tired.

Sept 9, 2000   Cle Elum to Ellensburg to Union Gap

Well the rain was mostly past but it was still cold and damp so I was wearing lots again. Most of the day I was off the Interstate. There are two nice canyon drives that aren't as hilly as the Interstate. Good advice from locals. The sky was still wet but the land is definitely drying out. By the end of the day I was in sunshine and warmth watching fly fishers floating down the Yakima River.

There hasn't been much wildlife though I am noticing rattlesnake skins on the road so I no longer turn down rest areas.

Kaye provided a pleasant surprise by driving out to meet me. She realized that this would be the last Saturday that I would be within driving distance. Without knowing my route or final destination she guessed pretty well. This is when we learned that my fancy cell phone does not prompt me about messages east of the mountains. She kept calling until finally I had the cell phone on when she called. She zeroed in on me and we got to spend the night together. That was spontaneous, persistent, patient and sweet of her.

Wearing lots was an understatement. I was so cold when I started out that I had to put on all of my rain gear just to stay warm. There was hardly anything left in the one pannier. It was the beginning of September and some of the hills had their first snow that night. I had hoped to catch the tail end of Summer, not the leading edge of Winter. What happened to Fall?

After the first five miles I was finally on unfamiliar roads. Up to that point I had been on roads that I had driven many times on the way to hiking and skiing trips. Heading out of Cle Elum I took the old highway that followed the river. There was hardly any traffic until I got near Ellensburg. Most of the traffic was over on the Interstate. The road was peaceful and pretty. I could see the Interstate on the opposite side of the valley. The road I was on was older, curvy, and fairly level. The Interstate was designed to be straight so instead of curves it ended up with hills. Climbing Snoqualmie Pass had been enough up and down for me for a while. A flat ride on a quiet road into Ellensburg and beyond sounded great.

The terrain really started to dry out. The road kill changed too. There was a lot of stuff that I am not used to seeing flattened: owl, skunk, and porcupine. Did that last one cause a flat for someone? Once the rattlesnake skins started showing up I started holding it until I found a bit of civilization and a rest room. It wasn't hard to give up the use of the bushes. Vegetation in general was disappearing so there wasn't anything to hide behind anyway.

Ellensburg looked like a nice place to stay. Without that construction detour and accident I might have made it that far the previous day. Instead it ended up being a way station between Cle Elum and Yakima and a place for me to buy some fruit. I also got some local advice that changed my route for the day.

Heading down to Yakima the Interstate drives up and over at least three good sized hills. The women in the fruit stand on the far edge of town steered me off onto a canyon road. According to them it got rid of a lot of the hills and was a pretty ride. Just to reinforce the notion, I was lucky enough to meet a cyclist coming up and out of the canyon as I was looking for it. Sure enough it was more curves than straight but it followed the Yakima River as the river flowed downhill. Downhill is good. That was such a nice ride that it kindled some hopes that the whole trip could be sweet with only a bit of sweat. I was a little behind schedule, but things were warming up and the scenery helped move me along through the afternoon.

The ride was more pleasant that I had expected. The only land I could see were the sagebrush covered canyon walls. There were a few rocky outcroppings as well. That all acted as a nice backdrop to the green ruff of bushes and trees lining the meandering river.

There weren't many people around. There were a few for the occasional farm or ranch. The ones I remember the most were the folks fly fishing. It looked like the guide services were busy. I suspected the guys grunting on the oars were not the paying customers. The other folks on the river that I recall were the three guys in truck tire inner tubes floating along and drinking beer. They were generous folks but I turned down their offer of a beer. The beer wouldn't help me stay hydrated and even that much alcohol would show me up to be a really cheap drunk when I was tired from so much riding. Besides, I was staying off caffeine and alcohol to see what would happen to my body. Supposedly I would be healthier mentally and physically.

The canyon seemed to be one of those places that won't know phone service until there are a lot more satellites, towers or cables laid. The road is pretty for all its turns and the steep walls but those are the same things that block signals and make it hard for any services to come to the valley. Instead the area is quiet and remote.

There was one rest stop, which was greatly appreciated. Besides the obvious reasons it was also the place where I was able to talk to a Forest Ranger. I love talking to people and asking them questions. He was one of the few that turned that back on me and peppered me with questions about my ride. It was hard for me to answer him. He was impressed with what I had set out to do. I was focussing on how little I had done and how many things could keep me from finishing. I don't think I started getting over that feeling until I had crossed the Rockies. Even then it wouldn't get much better until I had finally crossed the Mississippi. It's a point of view thing I guess. He saw the whole journey already completed. I noticed the things like my sore butt, tired legs, and doubts.

Downhill is a good thing and I ended up in Yakima in the early afternoon with a bit of energy left. Looking at the map I realized that if the rest of the road to the Columbia River was downhill like this, I could make it to Oregon in one more day. I pulled out the cell phone and got to work finding how far I could get and still have a place to stay. This was one of the few times that I followed a bike path and also partially why I rarely did again. Bike paths are usually built for recreation but not for actually getting anywhere. This one was pretty as it followed the river but it left me with very little indication that I was heading anywhere useful. Supposedly there was a motel at the end of it but it didn't look promising when it dumped me out at a wrecking yard. That was not the sort of feeling I wanted to have as I was hunting for a place to sleep. It worked out but I decided to skip that level of ambiguity whenever possible. It was good getting into town with enough time to shop for maps and postcards.

It had to be frustrating and uncomfortable for Kaye. While I was shopping she was sitting in some parking lot by a pay phone and calling me every twenty minutes or so. She had driven all of that way and had only a vague notion of where I was. She was there for two or three hours before she managed to call me when my cell phone was on. Because I had made it farther than expected, she was a few miles away. After some confusion over the name of motel we were able to get together. That was an impressive effort on her part. The desk manager at the motel loved the story too. She thought our story was so good that she made sure that her husband got to hear the story straight from us. Evidently Kaye also figured that because I had sounded so bad over the phone the previous night that maybe she should come check up on me.

Sept 10, 2000 Union Gap to Kennewick

Today was exclusively on the Interstate, where it is hard to get lost and you are never truly alone. You can however still get bad advice. Some of the locals told me the route was flat. Not quite. Horse Heaven Hills even has a Pass report radio station.

Since it was Washington I got rained on. The weather improved again but not quite as much. Between the weather in the hills and a seemingly unending climb outside Kennewick, I decided to stay in WA one more night.

The charcoal from the Hanford fires is very noticeable.

When Kaye and I were checking out of the motel, we were treated to a celebration. A different desk manager was on duty and she was so pleased with herself. We were more of an audience than a couple of customers to her. She had just refilled the juice machine on her own for the first time. She was so happy and proud that she would probably stay bubbly for hours. We even got a demonstration of what she had done. The previous night we had been the center of attention. The morning belonged to the queen of the juice machine.

I had really looked forward to the ride through Yakima and down to the Columbia River. This is part of Washington's Wine Country. It is supposed to have nice weather and the terrain is supposed to make its way downhill to the Columbia River. Of course it does so but not the way I thought it would. The river made a nice gradual progression downhill but the road wasn't so stately about it. I had hills to cross. The storm was still rinsing the state. The bit of dry weather the day before was busy leaving and I eventually got to ride in the rain. I suspect that at least the grapes were happy about the water. We both probably would have appreciated a bit more warmth though.

I was fairly sure about how to get to the next set of cities down at Hanford but wasn't sure about the area beyond it. One route went along the river but a shorter route went across something called Horse Heaven Hills. The night before I called a few bike shops in the area and asked them which way was best. Basically I was curious about how high those hills were. Surprisingly, the folks in the bike shops hadn't ridden out that way. Two of them did offer up that they thought the route was fairly flat and shouldn't be a problem. That helped pick the route but I kept in mind the comment that one passed along from a friend of his. Evidently his friend is a truck dispatcher who wanted to point out that I would really enjoy the ride down to the river because it was a long downhill run. If it was such a nice downhill wouldn't that mean that there was an uphill too? Well, I couldn't get any better information so I followed their advice and their route.

I can't say that it was the poorer route but I do know that it was bad enough for me. The Interstate was nice to travel on but it rolled with the terrain. Yes it is downhill overall but there were hills to climb along the way. There weren't many places for me to stop for most of the day. The road didn't seem to want to spend much time getting anywhere near civilization. By the time I got to Hanford I was getting concerned. Making it past Hanford and into Oregon was looking very doubtful. The fact that the highway was staying up on the hill above town made me wonder if I would come across any motels at the exits. I knew that there was a long stretch past Hanford that looked awfully empty. By the time I got to Kennewick on the outskirts of town, I was tired and no longer in sight of motels or restaurants. I finally got out my cell phone and called around until I found a place to stay just off the Interstate on the far side of town. I was feeling low. I knew I wouldn't make it to Oregon and my doubts about my conditioning were holding fast.

As the exits went by I noticed that I'd left the river and most signs of civilization behind. Then I started to climb. The Hills are really there and they made that exit with motels seem that much farther away. Again I was fooled by people's recollections of the road based on having their car's horsepower doing all of the work. The grade is not as steep as Snoqualmie Pass, but it was tough enough when I encountered it after having ridden for seven hours. As I climbed I noticed that the clouds were lower than the hilltops. When I reached the exit I was so glad that the clouds hadn't come down to meet me but I was so disappointed to not find the motel. Despite the desk manager's description, the motel which was supposed to be right by the Interstate was actually two miles away down a good sized hill. I didn't want to have to climb back up for breakfast so I went on to the next exit hoping to find another motel. All I found was a brand new police station and a freshly tarred road. Riding in the rain isn't too bad but riding on fresh tar was a long way out of my comfort zone. I headed back down the hill, found a motel, and checked in for the night.

As it turned out, the Hills act as a small mountain pass with their own pass reports and everything. I got great advice in Ellensburg and lousy advice since then. It was all free so I can't complain too much. It was more a measure of how hard it can be to notice the world around you when you're sitting in an air conditioned vehicle being pulled along by an amazingly useful engine. I do the same thing. Since the ride I have noticed how many roads I drive that I used to consider flat. Now I look at them and realize not only how hilly they are but I am impressed with what highway design and effort must have happened to smooth it out so well that a driver barely notices the change in altitude.

Sept 11, 2000 Kennewick to Hermiston to Pendleton

Finally out of Washington and the skies clear. Even after finishing yesterday with what I thought was a five mile climb, I still had a few more to go right out of the gate. Hills with their own pass report radios are not flat no matter what the locals say.

Oregon starts out with a visitor center that actually has bike maps. Very handy. After that there was a bit of truck stop traffic which quickly gave way to RURAL. For one long stretch of Interstate there was only one landmark: a grain elevator. This was on one long straight stretch of climb that I couldn't see the top because of the heat distortions. Hmmm, maybe some rain isn't so bad.

I end up in Pendleton a little early to prepare for what is rumored to be an agonizing climb right out of town. At least this gives me the opportunity to hit a bike shop and get my top gear fixed.

By the way I was so tired that I checked into the wrong hotel.

Gotta go but I have to remind myself to talk about the geography sleuthing that Kaye and I did that night. That pass was about as bad as Snoqualmie but not undoable.

The Sun flashed briefly for me when I started the climb the next morning. It came up and then the clouds came back in. They kept me company on the climb into Horse Heaven Hills. I didn't like having to start off with a climb but once on the road it became obvious that there wasn't another place to stop in Washington. The next motel was at least an hour away in Oregon. The next stretch of road was quite a few miles of open, rolling terrain in gray weather. It looked like it could live up to its name. A bunch of horses would have been in heaven running around those hills. For me though, being stuck up there with only a hammock in a storm would have been doubly bad because there weren't any trees for shelter or support.

Coming down the long anticipated run to the Columbia River, I had a Cinemascope moment. Sure enough the road does finally turn downhill and I could see Oregon and sunshine. Looking out from under a carpet of clouds I got an expansive view of an Oregon that was sunny and clear. Washington had kept me cold and wet for the most part and I was finally going to get a chance to dry out.

Crossing the Columbia River was a small emotional milestone for me. I was past another geographical barrier. It was easy for me. I used the bridge. I can't imagine how the pioneers ever got across. There was a bit of tarnish on the event. The bridge only has room for bikes on the one sidewalk. Unfortunately for me, the sidewalk was on the other side of the Interstate. To get to the other side I had to go through a pedestrian tunnel that passed under the road. The tunnel was a mess. The tunnel and the path were half covered in sand with a liberal spread of broken glass. I didn't want to stumble on the folks who hung out there. They seemed to make a hobby of breaking bottles and probably weren't the sort that would want to make friends with 40 year old bicyclists.

Washington had been unseasonably cold. Oregon suddenly turned unseasonably hot. It all started out unexpectedly pleasant. Someone planted one of Oregon's Visitor Centers a bit farther off the highway than most folks expected. They had even posted a sign on their front door apologizing for their inconvenient location. The building was far enough off the road that it was easier to find on a bike than in a car. That was fine by me. The people there were very friendly and had maps that I hadn't been able to find at home. Oregon has produced a nice bicycle map of the state showing which roads are steep or busy. This was such a help. It was also the first proof of how tough Oregon was going to be.

It was nice being able to sit there in the visitor center and relax while I warmed up, dried off, and scanned the new map for every possible detail. Originally I had considered finding some place past Pendleton to stop that night, but the map showed a potentially ugly hill just past town. It looked like I would have to pull up short for the day. By the end of the day I would think that I had pushed it too far. Eventually I had to get back out on the road. At least I had taken the opportunity to change out of rain gear and into something that I could get a tan in.

It felt good to be warming up again. Unfortunately it didn't stop at warm but went right past it to hot. I got off the Interstate for a while because there was a straighter way right through some of the towns down by the river. I tried getting some road advice from someone I thought was part of a road crew. He was actually an inspector of some sort so his road advice was vague at best. At least he was fun to talk to. When I got back to the Interstate the road straightened out and I saw a long stretch just heading up into a heat shimmer. That gave me a hint of what the pioneers may have gone through. It meant things were heating up and making it harder to see where I was headed. I wasn't going to be lost, but it was hard to know what places were up ahead where I could find some relief. Soon I was stopping under every overpass to cool off. I would know I had been there long enough when a passing breeze would finally feel cool rather than hot. It seemed to take me forever to catch the grain elevator that I saw in the distance. That and the mileposts marked my progress. For a long time there was no sign of Pendleton and I was wearing myself out.

When I finally saw Pendleton I understood what the motel manager in Kennewick had said. She cautioned me that if I didn't like losing elevation coming into Kennewick, I probably wouldn't like going through Pendleton. Pendleton is in a valley and around a ridge so I couldn't see it until I was right on it. Losing that elevation didn't bother me because the motel was right beside the highway. If it was any closer it would have been under it.

After I came to the first Pendleton exit I started calling around for a room. That was not as easy as I had expected. The big rodeo, The Pendleton Roundup, was starting the next day so almost all of the motel rooms were taken. So much for travelling without reservations. At that point I was seriously overheating and I knew it. I knew I was too tired to risk not having a room. So, I decided to make a phone reservation from the side of the road. Out came the cell phone again and I hit redial and got the room. When I got off at the exit and pulled into the motel they seemed somewhat confused but were glad to put me in the room. A few minutes later I realized that I had stopped at the wrong motel. I was so tired that I didn't know that I was in the wrong place talking to the wrong people. The world works this way sometimes. As it turned out while the motel may not have had the best amenities, it did have a great location.

My gears had started slipping a little while before this. I am talking about the bike's gears, not the ones in my head. I had planned on replacing the chain every 500 miles or so and this seemed like a good time and place to get the messy job done by someone besides me. Unfortunately, the gears were taking too much of a beating from the worn chain. I decided to replace both if someone had the parts for sale. The road from the motel to the bike shop was wonderfully flat. With the Pendleton Roundup rodeo preparations underway, the bike shop had very little business to worry about so they were able to fit me out with a new chain, saddle, and other supplies without a wait. My saddle was showing its age. I hadn't noticed it back home but my butt convinced me to try something new. A new saddle with new cushioning and a more ergonomic design sounded like a good idea. Switching saddles was not an easy choice to make. There was no guarantee that the new one would fit me. I decided to carry along the old one as a backup for a few days.

That was where the Cabbage Hill debate began. According to the bike map, the hill out of Pendleton was one of the steepest around. If I had gone farther that day I probably would have hurt myself. The shop owner was certain that I should take the old highway rather than the Interstate. Both roads climbed the same hill but at least the old highway didn't have the traffic and it spread the climb out over more miles. The problem I had was following the directions to get to the start of the route. I really didn't want to get lost in the backroads and wind up back in Pendleton without a room for the night. Back in the motel room I decided to call AAA and hear what they had to say. Lucky for me, they have an office in Pendleton. Unlucky for me, their office was getting ready to close and I still had other errands to run. The woman from

AAA was nice enough to mark out the route on a map and drop it off at the motel front desk. That was some excellent service.

I was glad for all of the information. It was the sort of local knowledge that I hoped to find. It still had to be filtered though. Everyone has slightly different skills and talents. One of my characteristics is perseverance and some talent on a climb. Mostly that is because I was brought up in a valley outside of Pittsburgh where the only way out was up. Hills and me get along better than most from what others tell me. So I had to temper all of this information with the knowledge that the next climb might be harder for some other folks than it would be for me.

Talking to Kaye that night I found out that she had picked up some great software that can do things like tell us what kind of ups and downs a road has to deal with. She plugged it in and fired it up while we talked. By the time we hemmed and hawed over it, I got the feeling that going up the Interstate might be formidable but the hill wasn't steeper than what I'd already ridden. It was just much longer. Logically I believed it, but emotionally it was a hard sell. Personal experience can have a hard time winning out over a never ending tide of other people's doubts and discouragements.

We decided that I'd take the hill on by going straight up the Interstate. Getting through Oregon was not going to be quick or easy. The staggering of the hills and the motels meant that the next day would be short and tough. It wasn't the kind of progress that I had in mind but I didn't have many options.

Sept 12, 2000 Pendleton to La Grande

To better understand everyone's warnings about the BIG CLIMB tomorrow, Kaye and I researched it and the alternate route that was supposedly better. Thanks to some topo software that Kaye bought we were able to figure out that the hill was about 50% longer than Snoqualmie but no steeper. This was such a relief. Rather than take some windy long side road, I ended up ignoring the local's advice and went right up the hill. It was a tough one but I got to do it first thing in the morning which helped a lot.

The climb also got me back up into the trees. Around Pendleton the trees grow above the treeline where there is snow to water them. The desert is down below. It was pretty up there. Trees and a few ranches made it very picturesque.

I got to stay up there for a few miles, but being a mountain pass, it had to go back down again. La Grande is on the opposite side of the hill. It isn't the desired 70 mile jump, but we decided that a short day was appropriate for such a steep day. I guess 3,000 feet is a bit much. It was a good thing that I quit early. One of the fasteners started to go on the chainring and I wasn't able to figure it out until I had the bike propped up in the hotel room.

Wildlife is mostly insects like grass hoppers and praying mantises.

La Grande also has a steep hill immediately out of town. Save it for the morning.

My climb through Snoqualmie Pass happened during the first Winter storm of the season. Heading out of Pendleton was an even longer climb on a day headed for record high temperatures. That was an amazingly rapid and dramatic shift in less than one week of bicycling.

I was able to plan ahead for the heat. I started out wearing my lightest clothes and carrying 60 ounces of Gatorade. There was no room left in my panniers. They held all of my clothes except for what I was wearing: one short sleeve shirt, one pair of bike shorts, my shoes, and a pair of socks. Everything else was stuffed in there along with all of those bottles of Gatorade. That would be the case on every hot day. The panniers were stuffed on hot days and nearly empty on cold days. When it was hot out I wasn't wearing much so everything was crammed into those bags. When it was cold out the bags were limp because I was wearing almost all of my clothes to stay warm.

I hoped to survive the heat better by starting early and staying very well hydrated. I am so glad that I went straight up the hill. I'm not going to call it easy but it was doable. The climb started out imperceptibly. The gain in elevation was so shallow that it looked like I was still on the flats. I thought that I could coast long enough to straighten out my back or get the blood flowing back into my palms. That didn't work. As soon as I stopped pedaling my speed fell off and the bike began wobbling. Evidently the grade was slight and significant. The start of the real climb was more obvious. Instead of being a straight shot across the fields, the road started switching back and forth and my eyes lost track of it as it hid itself behind the hills. I was so glad that I didn't try taking it on during the heat of the previous afternoon.

I may do well on hills but I'm not stupid about them. Tucking my head down and cranking up a few thousand feet of elevation is possible but a real pain. Instead, I played games with it. Count a hundred pedal strokes in English. Then count a hundred pedal strokes in Japanese. Then maybe count a hundred while standing up in the pedals. I didn't say it was a fun game. It is just a way of covering distance. As long as I didn't stop, I was getting closer to the top. Every half mile or so I took a break and tried to remember to eat, drink or at least get off the saddle and get my wind back. The truckers were great at this point. A fair number of them honked, saluted, waved or give me a thumbs up. Little things like that helped. It didn't make the hill shorter but it helped keep my spirits up.

Climbing something like that hill was a great opportunity to look back and see how far I had come. I was starting to get a different appreciation for how far away the horizon was. Everyday I was blowing past the morning's horizon and getting farther around the planet. Bicycling seems so slow and yet I would usually pass the morning's horizon far before noon.

For most of the climb the uphill lanes were far below the downhill lanes. The geography wasn't nice enough to allow them to be built beside each other. It must have been tough putting that road in. Near the top the summit started to show itself. The median was no longer a piece of the mountain but was just a bit of dirt between the guardrails. The summit wasn't some abrupt and spectacular point on the road so I just celebrated when I got to a spot with a nice view. After all of the discussions the night before, I thought that Kaye deserved a quick phone call so she could celebrate too. Standing by the Interstate was not the place for quiet background noise so it was more an event than a conversation. The call was short but it was fun to share the summit with someone. I gave her a quick description of the view and let her get back to work.

The view from the top confirmed that there is a whole lot of empty out there. That was ranch, timber and farm land so plants and livestock get to use most of the room. There are just a few humans sprinkled about to tend and harvest. Of course there might be more people out there if there was more water. The land looked very dry. Without water it is understandable why the folks on the Oregon Trail passed through and mostly settled in the river valleys. With more water there might be more urban sprawl. I haven't decided if that is good or bad. Cities are crowded but we need crops and open spaces too.

It was pretty up there. I was back in forest again. I do like trees. I can understand the appeal of the wide open plains. But I've always lived around trees, or better put, they've been around wherever I've lived. The top of Cabbage Hill was a nice mix of trees, open spaces and vistas. I wondered if anyone lives up there year round or if the ranch land is only occupied in the Summer.

The new bike seat was helping but still wasn't good enough. As I took my usual breaks, I would tweak the seat's adjustments. After enough breaks and tweaks I noticed some of the back and hip pain fading away. My butt, back and hips were never exactly comfortable but getting the seat position right meant that I didn't have to stop as often.

Even though Kaye and I figured that I would probably stop in La Grande, I also kept in mind that the possibility existed that I could make it to the set of motels in Baker City. Each day was like that. I would have a primary destination in mind, but all day long I wondered about whether I would have to stop short or could go long. There were so many variables that I could never be sure until the afternoon came around. The map showed another hill heading out of La Grande. I would either have to take it on in the heat of the afternoon and commit to a long jump to Baker City or stop in La Grande and tackle the hill the next morning.

As tired as I was coming into La Grande, my bike really drove home the point that I should stop early. It was really quite surprising that the bike waited that long to have a failure. All I knew was that the bike started to go clunk when I turned the pedals. One of the fasteners that held on the front gears was working its way free. I never would have thought to carry a spare of one of those. Gears usually don't fall off bikes. At that point I hadn't even had a flat and there was a chunk of metal trying to leave my bike. At least it happened close to town and in the flats. I didn't have to stress the bike very hard or for very long to get to the motel. It still took me about fifteen minutes in the motel room to pin down what was going on. Luckily it was an easy fix. I got a spare the next time I found bike parts for sale.

I was tired and overheated again, so it was a good thing that I stopped early. All of my strategies for coping with the heat helped but weren't enough. Nature was unrelenting and beat me down by the end of the day.

After the fiasco of checking into the wrong motel back in Pendleton I decided to have reservations and good directions for a motel in La Grande. It still didn't work right. When I got there they had no record of any reservations. No one else in town did either so it wasn't like I showed up at the wrong place. That was so embarrassing. I still managed to get a room but it took a lot of checking to make sure that I wasn't expected elsewhere. To make matters worse, the credit card company flagged my credit card. I had to call them up and tell them that everything was alright. They were worried about the sudden spurt of activity. I was nowhere near my credit limit. They were just worried that someone had stolen my card. I appreciated their vigilance but it didn't make my life easier. It was hard dealing with that rationally when I was so beat and just wanted to lie down for a while.

This was the first motel laundry that I had to deal with. After a nap I was reintroducing myself to how to use a Laundromat. I actually called one of those 1-800 numbers on the back of some laundry detergents. It took them about 30 minutes to answer my question. I wanted to know whether the detergent was alright for the fancy bike pants' fabric. Because there wasn't a pay phone by the laundry I foolishly used my cell phone. That load of laundry was much more expensive than I had planned. Next time I'd either guess or find a pay phone.

Sept 13, 2000   La Grande to Baker City

Here I go with another climb in the morning. To top it off, they are forecasting a string of days of record setting temperatures.

The climb wasn't as much of the problem as the downhill was. I got to go through a construction site near the bottom of the hill. They had reduced the traffic to one lane but I was on the shoulder so there shouldn't be a problem. One of the construction workers tells me to look over my shoulder. Sure enough here comes a wide load making it's way along the shoulder about a quarter mile back. I am just lucky enough to turn off onto an exit so I didn't slow it or any other traffic.

When I got back on the road one of the construction workers paces me in his pickup and invites me to ride in the lane they have blocked off. Sweet. I get to ride in the fast lane with LOTS of elbowroom.

Real craggy style mountains start showing up. The river has water in it and there is green stuff without irrigation. Things are still very dry but it is prettier.

The flora and fauna are predominately Black Eyed Susans and Magpies. There are even a few herons on occasion if I recall correctly.
Oh yeah, and it is hot.
People are very helpful and supportive. There are a lot of good people out there. And boy is it dry where they live.

The morning hill was not as bad as Cabbage Hill, but it still took a lot out of me. They all did. Going up was never easy. At least it was always doable. It could only be easy relative to some other hill, but it always took a grunt of effort. Doing it in hot weather was hard for someone like me who has acclimated to Seattle's weather. I used to think it wasn't hot until it got above 90. In Oregon I was having trouble when it got into the high 70s. Funny how we change.

I had been on the Interstate for a few days and liked it. There was lots of room on a smooth road and I didn't have to guess about what road to take. It is hard to get lost at 10 miles an hour on the Interstate. Interstates were even better than smaller roads when it came to road construction. Losing a lane of traffic on a four lane with big shoulders isn't nearly as severe as losing a lane on a two lane that had no pavement outside the white line. That time on Whidbey Island had driven that point home.

Having felt that way I still found that the wrong combination of traffic and construction was enough to give me a good shot of adrenaline. I thought that there wouldn't be much of a problem because I was riding on the shoulder and they weren't doing any work there. The wide load that came up behind me was a house. That was startling and definitely unexpected. I had never needed to get out of the way of a house before. For some reason this one was wider than most. The driver had to take up most of the remaining lane and a fair chunk of shoulder too. Fortunately it was still about a quarter mile back. Unfortunately, as slow as it was going, it was still going way faster than me. My choices were to make him slow down, hop over the guardrail and embankment with me, my bike, and my gear, or pedal my heart out and see if I could make the next exit. I was headed downhill anyway and am not graceful enough to leap over a guardrail with a loaded bike so I went for the exit. It had felt uncomfortably close but by the time I was up the ramp the house still took a bit of time to pass the exit. The adrenaline probably made me feel like it was right on me. At the top of the exit I just stood there and gasped for a while.

That left me at the bottom of the hill. From there on it was flat for miles. Standing above the highway near the overpass, I had a good view and thought I could see the end of the construction site. It was a long way off but there shouldn't be any more houses coming along, right? When the road crew's pickup truck pulled along side I was expecting to get screamed at for riding through his construction site. That is why I was so pleased and relieved to hear him suggest that I used the lane that they had closed. He thought I'd really enjoy riding on something better than the shoulder for a while. That was a real nice touch. It was only for a mile or two but it was a joy and a luxury while it lasted.

Before I left on this ride, lots of folks gave me dire warnings about bikes on the Interstates and people in general. I have to admit that their comments did give me a hesitancy towards some folks. I am so glad that they were wrong. There are lots of nice people out there.

Back down in the flat lands again it was nice to see some of the trees were down there too. They were following the river through the valley and were backdropped by some nice craggy peaks. The pioneers must have loved coming across this place.

Along that stretch of highway I crossed the 45th latitude line. I had entered the Southern Half of the Northern Hemisphere.

That was one of the chunks of the country that I didn't know much about before. I knew that Eastern Washington was dry and that Idaho was hilly. I hadn't known that Eastern Oregon was such an interesting mix of the two. The Blue Mountains were pretty and the signs for ski slopes intrigued me. Maybe I'll check them out in a car some ski season.

I didn't expect Baker City to be such a big place. It's not like it has skyscrapers and such, but it was big enough to have a real diversity walking the streets of a sizable downtown. One guy I talked to was of the spiked hair and earring crowd. Another was just in from the ranch. Maybe it is in cities like this that it is easiest to see how varied we are. In big cities, any minority be it genetic or social can be large enough to have their own neighborhood. They are diverse but they rarely have to deal with folks that aren't like them. In smaller places, there are so few people that anyone that is different may feel lonely and ostracized. In places like Baker City, each has some friends like themselves and also can't ignore the other folks running around. There's probably some sociologist who's already played with this idea. As for me, I just found it a nice mix.

I could have gone farther that day but Kaye and I weren't sure that I could find a better place to stay than in Baker City. They too had a hill right out of town. Oregon was hills in the morning for me. At least I had met my daily goal of "safe, sound, and sitting in my room by dark".

Sept 14, 2000   Baker City to Huntington to Annex to Ontario

After one small hill, relative to the last two days, the majority of the day was long run down a canyon. Nice. I got an early start to beat the heat and was actually chilly for the first three hours.

Canyon riding is nice. The scenery keeps changing and if the river goes downhill, so do you.

The road construction in such narrow places is more difficult to negotiate so when I got the chance to take a side road, I went for it. It was a good time to check out a little hotel that I could use if the heat got bad. About then the heat got bad. The side road was not flat, though supposedly it was better graded than the Interstate. Hard to tell while riding. I found the hotel. It was a bit better than some shacks I've seen in fairly desolate places. It felt that way there too. I continued on.

The Snake River shows up. Rafts of waterfowl are all over the place, the air is a little cooler, and I stay off the Interstate the rest of the way.

The route takes me through the onion harvest. Onions and potatoes line the shoulder. Interesting debris. About this point I am only 15 miles from Ontario but the temperature in town is about 95. I am having some trouble until I find a diner run by two wonderful women. The one is a grandmother and the other is her mother. For the price of a Mountain Dew and a bag of chips I get 30 minutes in the shade, some pleasant conversation, and an angel. The older of the two gives one out to each cyclist that comes through. Sweet and noble.

I remember climbing that hill in the morning thinking that I had better make a lot of progress early if I was going to beat the heat in the afternoon. Sure enough, even though I was chilly in the morning, when the world heated up it happened fast.

It was a pleasant ride once I got past the hill. While riding across the plains it had been easy to see where I was headed and I got to watch the scenery slowly change. Outside of Baker City though I was in the canyons where the scenery changed quickly. Canyons have rivers and having the river nearby meant there was always something to watch. The river made the breaks nicer and much more varied. Ironically even though the breaks were nicer, I didn't have to take as many breaks because I was headed downhill. I got to enjoy the scenery more as an in-flight movie than as a still life. The air was cooler there too. The hillsides provided some shade and the river did what it could to cool the air.

Unfortunately, road construction had essentially reduced the road down to one lane for fourteen miles. I had another close call as I passed one of the on ramps in the middle of all of that. The truck on my left distracted me and I almost didn't see the other truck coming up the ramp on my right. It seemed to come out of nowhere. Normally I would have heard it but the other traffic noise drowned it out. I had to cut in front of the one on the on ramp to get to the one patch of open shoulder that had enough room for a bike. Luckily the truck coming up the ramp was still building up his speed. I wished I had a CB radio along so I could apologize.

Oregon had one last set of hills to throw at me and a long stretch of highway with very few places to stay. It looked like the shortest route to Idaho would take me right up and over those hills into the heat of the late afternoon and wouldn't give me a chance at a motel until I was past them and on the Idaho border. Kaye and I had found a side road on the maps that seemed to have a motel. We couldn't find out much about it so it sure wasn't something I wanted to count on. If it was there, it would give me a place to stay in case the record temperatures or just fatigue pulled me up short. The side road also looked like it followed the Snake River so we guessed that it wouldn't be nearly as hilly as the Interstate.

By the time I got to the exit for the side road I was glad to take it. The road construction had been a problem. In the plains, when I came across a narrow spot, I could look over my shoulder and look for breaks in the traffic. In the canyons, I couldn't see far enough back to make a difference so I had to just go for it a lot. That is not my preferred way of reducing risk and it burned up a lot of energy in the sprints. The side road wasn't down by the river yet but it was headed that way. The traffic stayed up on the Interstate and I relaxed a bit.

The heat started to come on big time. I was out of the canyons and the area was dry so there were very few places to find any shade. There weren't any towns that I could see and I started to wonder about where that motel was. It was farther along than I thought it would be. After wondering if I had taken the wrong road and perhaps gotten lost, I found the town. It was small and would suffice but as I passed through it I realized that it might not be the place for me. That was true if for no other reason than the fact that I didn't know where I would get something to eat. Of course I was tired enough that I probably looked right at a restaurant and didn't notice it. By that time I hated the heat but after having to stop early for the last few days I really wanted to give myself a boost by getting to the border. As tough as it was I pushed on.

The road out of town headed towards the river but it wasn't going to get there without a few hills and turns thrown in. My choice of routes seemed poor until I caught a glimpse of the Interstate. It was a lot higher and it looked like it was probably a lot hotter. My route just felt desolate and dry. At the crest of one of the next hills, I saw the river. That big chunk of water looked wonderful. There was green along it and I wanted to get there. It was all downhill to the river. I wanted to take a break at the riverside park, but as I came to the entrance I noticed a sign cautioning folks that it was the site of a prison work detail. The park lost some of its appeal. I ended up stopping a mile or so farther in a restaurant's parking lot up by the Interstate. The day was wearing on and I felt too sweaty to park myself in a restaurant's booth. Instead I stood in the shade of the sign in the parking lot and prepped myself to do a few dozen more miles.

The Interstate looked like it was heading back up into hills that could be called mountains so I decided to stay down by the river. It was beautiful. There was a raft of birds floating on the water. They looked so peaceful and relaxing. I noticed that none of them were close to shore. That made a lot more sense when I heard the gunshots from the opposite shore. The middle of the river looked like the safest place to be. I was still hot as can be but it was nice to see such a cool image. The Sun was high enough that shade was hard to come by. There weren't any shade trees along the road. It was even rare to find some shade from the hillside at a wide point in the road. The road wasn't flat, but at least it didn't climb much and it had a nice view. That didn't last long.

The road left the river in a few miles. I missed the cooler air. Soon I was up in farmland and the route felt impossibly long. At least some folks had planted trees close enough to the road provide pockets of shade big enough to give me a break. Big old deciduous trees are so good at making a cool spot. But I couldn't stay there long. I had to make it to town by nightfall and the heat was slowing me down. I was running out of food and water as well. I was, however, treated to some new sights. I had never seen an onion harvest before. There were onionskins all over the road. I guess it is the area's version of autumn leaves.

It was hard to keep track of my progress through the jumble of roads and intersections. The mileposts kept changing every time two roads converged for a bit. I was tired and demoralized. Then I found the Angel ladies. They don't call themselves that but that's the name my brain affixed to them. At one of the turns in the road I found a mini-mart. It isn't part of some global entity with gleaming shelves and predictable experience. This is a real store run by a couple of women. I was so glad to see someplace where I could get out of the sun and maybe buy some supplies. Once I was in there I was discouraged. It wasn't the sort of place to carry much of what I had been surviving on: Gatorade and Powerbars. I bought some pop and some potato chips and only then found the little diner counter they had in the next room. It has five or six stools and no waiting. I asked the woman there if she minded me taking my break at her counter. She had no problem with that and was as friendly as can be. We sat there and started talking. It ended up being one of those conversations that only took a half hour but seemed to encompass everything under the Sun. I found out that she was working two jobs and that the other woman was her mother who sometimes works three. They found out about my bike ride. We found out about how different life, or at least prices, were between the onion fields in Oregon and the urban life around Seattle. At one point a travelling salesman came in to pitch his product. This was no slick high pressure dude that had been doing this forever. This was a guy who appeared to be right out of high school even though he may have felt that he had been doing this his whole life. Within five minutes he had sold her about a half dozen items that she planned on using for Christmas presents. She bargained a bit and they both seemed to come away from the deal satisfied. I was just sitting there thinking that she had more the look of charity than anything else at that time. Did she need that stuff? Probably not. Could she have gotten better stuff cheaper somewhere in town? Probably. I got the impression that she was more interested in helping him along with his hopes than in the stuff she gave him money for. He didn't buy anything in their store and she helped him out anyway. I sat there having only spent a couple of bucks and they're helping me get through the day. At this point they topped it off with the angel. The woman working the counter calls in the other woman, her mother, and told her about my bike ride. They get just enough bicyclists through here that she has decided to do what she can to protect them. She gave me an angel. This was sweet and in earnest. It is a refrigerator magnet angel and for the rest of the ride it lived in the tool bag on my bike. There were two women working five jobs between them and they were out there helping folks get by without cynicism or a Pollyanna attitude. I was so glad that they were out there.

Eventually I had to get going. I thanked them and they pointed out that I was on the right track and only had about a dozen miles to go. The day was no cooler but at least I was better off. Eventually I made it to Ontario, Oregon. As I walked into the motel, I was greeted by a couple of women sitting in air conditioned comfort in a pair of cushioned chairs who seem to be bored with the world and resigned to just dejectedly getting through it. I didn't think telling them to go meet the Angel ladies during a bike ride up through the onion fields on a hot afternoon would break them out of their funk. They seemed too set in their ways. What I had to do was get cleaned up, fed and ready for the next day. I hadn't made it to Idaho but it was only about a mile away.

The next day I found out that Boise had just set record high temperatures. I had ridden straight through it and the forecast predicted there was more to come.

Sept 15, 2000 Ontario to Boise

Yesterday I entered Mountain Time Zone. The day before that I crossed the 45th latitude. Today I cross into my third state.

And what do I find? Road Construction! Fourteen miles of it. This must be the season. Most of it is through a long uphill as I climb the Snake River plateau. The shoulder is narrower than usual so I pull over off the road whenever I think the traffic needs more room. I haven't made anyone slow down yet. Riding early helps since I get lots of miles out of the way before a lot of folks wake up. With two miles of construction to go I get another invite to ride in the closed off lanes. How much would I pay for this?

Idaho is definitely a desert, it is hot, between real mountains. More and more ski areas show up on the map. I doubt the hammock I brought will be useful any time soon.

Boise is my first real city to have to get around. I am staying on the far end of it to keep the next day's travel shorter. I decide to skip the Interstate for a while and make it through surface streets. The on ramps are busy and I am riding through rush hour type traffic. A bit of driving on the side streets with regular cars makes me appreciate the skill the truckers have when they pass me on the Interstate at full speed. Full legal speed in Idaho is 75mph.

The highlight of the day is finding a bike mechanic that makes house calls. For $35 I got my bottom bracket checked out and lubed, the brakes tightened up, the wheels trued and a few other items. I enjoyed the conversation and I think he enjoyed giving a hard ridden bike some good lovin. He would have liked it if I changed the wheels as well.

Gotta go. Log off time.

Crossing into Idaho was not like crossing into Oregon. I thought it might be similar because the map showed an Idaho visitor center just across the border. I looked forward to a fresh source of info and insight. Of course what the map couldn't show were the miles of construction that closed the visitor center and a lot of the other facilities too. At least they didn't seem to mind a bicyclist riding on the Interstate. As long as that was the case I didn't have to worry about getting lost.

It felt good to have passed some of the early milestones: climbing Snoqualmie Pass, crossing the Columbia River, crossing the 45th Latitude, a new time zone, and yet another state. On such a long trip, even the smaller milestones can be separated by a lot of time and distance and were wonderful to accomplish. If I had only focussed on the final goal I never would have gotten as far as I did.

The road construction was a real pain. Climbing up onto the Snake River plain was a lot of work too. The two made a terrible combination. First thing in the morning the traffic wasn't as bad, but it was moving awfully fast. That in itself hadn't been a problem, but I no longer had a nice wide shoulder to ride on. The road construction had closed the eastbound lanes of the Interstate so all of the traffic was running in the westbound lanes. The lanes hadn't changed width but the shoulder had. The side of the road became a lot narrower. The other side was fine but crossing the highway to get to the other shoulder didn't look safe. Whenever I found myself at a bottleneck, I would pull over where it was safe, look over my shoulder for a break in the traffic, and then pedal my heart out. That would've been a lot easier if I hadn't been going uphill at the same time. Originally I thought it would only go on for about a half an hour. My average speed was usually at least ten miles an hour and the construction was only supposed to be a few miles long. At the end of those few miles there was another sign saying that the end of the construction was only a few miles farther. By the end of it, the construction had gone on for about fourteen miles and an hour and a half of riding. Near the end of it I had to take a break. I noticed a couple of the road crew working in the median. That stretch of road was almost finished but it didn't have painted lines or signs yet. They were doing something simple like picking up debris so we got to talking while I took a break and they worked. I was so glad when they invited me to ride on the closed off portion of the road. This time I had even more elbow room because I had two lanes to myself. To top it off, the road was brand new so it was clean, smooth and fast.

Would there be enough bicyclists out there to justify putting in bike lanes like this? I can see why lots of folks wouldn't want to ride on the roads. Having bike lanes would make it more appealing, but I wonder if there would be enough people with the time and energy to take advantage of them. It seems to work in Seattle even with its rain and hills. But in places like the rural West there might not be enough people who want to get out there even if it is flat and dry. I do know that I started wondering how much I would be willing to pay for a nice coast to coast bike path. Ah well, that is only a dream.

The land really opened up once I was up on the plateau. I was in a broad flat area with the mountains in the distance. I don't know if the area fits some official definition of a desert, but it definitely fit mine. It looked lonely, dry, and windswept and I started to feel the heat again. That would be another day where the temperature was at, or near a record high. Stopping in Boise brought me up short again but the next jump was about forty or fifty miles long and I didn't want to tackle that in record heat.

The hammock that I mentioned was part of my emergency shelter kit. A hammock is a lot lighter than a tent and gets you off the wet ground. Most hammocks are for lazy day lounging. This one comes equipped with bug netting and a rain fly. Unfortunately, it also needs something to hold it up. While I had expected there to be stretches of road without trees, I didn't expect to come across entire states where I was out of luck.

I had decided to stay on the far side of Boise. If things went my way on the following day, I might be able to make that forty mile hop in the morning and have all afternoon to get to the next motel.

As I got closer to Boise the traffic got worse. That was not a surprise. Riding on the Interstate was fine as long as the exits were far apart or if there was no traffic. Near town the exits started coming more frequently and the traffic wasn't letting up. It got hard to cross the exits because there were so many cars running up the off ramps. I decided to take to the surface streets. It looked like I had a bit of extra time and at that point I still hadn't found anything like an open Visitor Center where I could get a bike map of Idaho. I passed signs for four of them and either couldn't find them or they were closed. Riding on the surface streets might have helped me find one. Maybe I'd even find a bike path or a bike lane.

What I found was an appreciation for the open Interstate. I was stuck in typical urban driving. There was no place for a bike to ride except out in traffic and I never knew when someone was going to cut in front of me or open a car door. In comparison, the narrow shoulder I had through the construction site with 75 mph traffic seemed a luxury. Luckily the roads were fairly easy to follow so I didn't get lost. I even found my first Starbucks since back around Seattle. I should've stopped but I didn't want to break my rhythm.

Once I got past the busy part of Boise I ended up back on the Interstate in search of the motel I planned on staying at. There was no choice. Road construction had closed the surface streets that I wanted to use. I was hot and wanted to stop. It seemed like the bike was tired too. It was starting to make a bit more noise with each revolution of the pedal. The cluster of motels that I was hunting for was near a college or business center. It had been days since I left Bellevue and the only person who knew what I was doing was Kaye. I really wanted to get to some sort of email connection so that I could write and tell our friends how I was doing and what had been happening. If for no other reason, it was to ease her burden so maybe she wouldn't have to answer the same question over and over. Eventually I got to the exit and found that there was one motel right there. The other motels and the business center where I might find email were at least two miles away back into town. That didn't meet all of my wants but it met all of my needs. There was a room and food here. The rest was just stuff that would have been nice to have.

There is also a truck stop. I wandered over there to get some food for the road and to check out the restaurant. Surprisingly I found a small Internet kiosk. It was expensive but it was the best thing going. Out came the credit card and then came the lesson. Not only was it expensive but I couldn't do much with it. There was no slot for a floppy so I couldn't access the email addresses that I had stored on the disk. There was a terminal, a small keyboard, an icky sticky mouse and a lot of grime. I figured that I just had to send the notes back to Kaye and hope that it wasn't too much of a hassle for her to redistribute them. After having typed up a few days worth of notes the terminal kicked me off. It seems that it would only run for about thirty minutes and then I had to start over again. I got back on and sent out each day's story as a separate email. Instead of Kaye getting one big email, she ended up having to collect one email for every day that I on the road, put them together and then ship them all out. She did so and I am grateful. The emails ended up being much shorter than I had expected and they cost a lot more as well.

I hadn't forgotten about the bike. I couldn't forget about the bike. Before I headed over to the truck stop I had the pleasure and surprise of finding a bike mechanic that does house calls. If he hadn't existed I might have had a lot more riding to do that day just to get the bike worked on. As it was, about the time I was done with the emails he called me back to tell me he was in the motel's parking lot. Such a deal. He is Steve Parrish the Dirt Dart. This is one energetic guy who has an excellent bike shop in his mini-van. Evidently he does a lot of work at the trailheads of bike races and such. That was excellent. That was the first time since Pendleton that I got to talk to someone who knew something about bikes. Of course he knew a lot more than I did. I think he felt very sorry for my bike. I don't treat my bike as well as I am supposed to. He usually saw the latest and hottest bikes being ridden hard and then replaced with the next year's model. My bike was about eight years old and had not had the tender care that some folks dispense on their toys. I don't abuse my equipment. If I had, the bike wouldn't have lasted this long. But I also don't keep it in pristine condition. I think he saw working on my bike almost as a charity case. He felt so sorry for it. All the while we were having a great time talking. He'd fix something. I'd ride it around the lot. He'd fix something else. He'd ride it around the lot. He fixed a lot of things. I don't know that we ever got rid of that squeak but I did end up with a bike that was running much better and was much more likely to stay together for me. At one point he pulled out one set of bearings and found that there wasn't any grease left in the casing. Maybe Seattle is so moist that they weren't drying out there but it sure looked bad in Boise. He also correctly diagnosed a problem that was to stop me cold later in the trip. I wasn't sure he was right but it didn't matter because he didn't have the replacement part. A mini-van can only carry so much. He was a real joy to talk to. Every once in a while we'd be pointing off to the mountains so he could try to show me various routes that he likes to ride. Boise does look like it is good for having the mountains nice and close. For a hiker and skier like me, that has a real appeal. For me it was a pity that it was so dry but it was obvious that he was in love with the place.

The ride had been short but I was tired and hungry. The heat sapped my energy. My butt was as sore as ever. At least the time between my breaks was increasing. I would go about ten miles between breaks instead of only four or five. That seemed like a good sign. I was starting to wonder if I had any chance of a nice relaxing 70 mile day on the west side of the Rockies. As sore as I was, I had it easier than the cyclist on the evening news did. That day a paraplegic was starting his ride from Boise to Las Vegas. That is incredible. I don't know if he made it alright. For me, the next day would either be just as short or much longer. The motels were thinly spread through there and the weather was not cooperating.

TAILWIND !

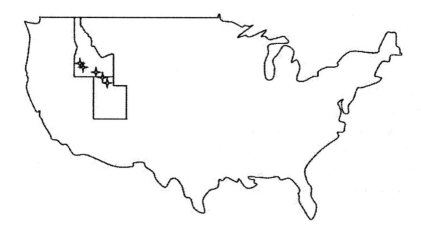

Sept 16, 2000 Boise to Mountain Home

  Welcome to more desert. Oh yeah and road construction. All along this route since about Pendleton I have been reminded of how easy I have it. In large part I am going back up the Oregon trail. The historical markers along the way remind me of how nice it is to have a road, maps, water, food, hotels, and marvel of marvels, a cell phone. These folks were no happy campers. What they would have given for a Holiday Inn.

  It ended up being a short day: only about 40 some odd miles. Staying in hotels constrains how far I can go each day. When I hit Mountain Home I thought the next hotel was about 40 miles away. As I hit Mountain Home, the winds switched around to a flag flapping head wind. Looks like a nice place to stop to me.

Long bike rides give me a lot of opportunities to find things to complain about. My butt and hands are very practiced at telling me how much fun they are not having. It is tough and it is easy too. Really, riding is a simple case of sitting down and moving your feet. This is not something that is relegated to young folks or extreme athletes. From what I can gather most bike tourists are older people. It is not an extreme activity. That doesn't mean that I didn't look wistfully at people going by with their cruise control, air conditioning, windshields, and cushioned seats. As a matter of fact it was hard not to notice how uncomfortable some part of me was at any one time. The people that went through there on covered wagons had it much tougher than me and they were more comfortable than the people who came out here on foot or on horseback. They couldn't count on water, food, or the local highway patrol. Living was a tough enough chore. I am amazed and impressed with the people that made that trip and built a life out of what they brought.

It would have been really nice to get farther than Mountain Home that day. Forty miles of cycling didn't seem like much. Even though I realized that it wasn't as far as I could have gone, I tried getting there early in case by some fluke I found someplace else to stay farther along the road. If I was going to travel past Mountain Home, I didn't want to have to do it in the afternoon heat. Well I got to Mountain Home early enough to actually eat lunch at a reasonable time. It was rare that I was getting to eat lunch. Having enough time to sit down to lunch in air conditioned comfort before noon was a treat.

I finally found an Idaho Visitor Center that was open. Unfortunately, they didn't have anything like a bike map of Idaho. Evidently there isn't much call for that. When I found the Visitor Center I also noticed that the winds had changed. The headwind was strong enough to make a flag stick straight out and point back to Boise. I can't remember what wind speed that happens at but it was more than I wanted to ride into. As I walked into the building my morale was fading. The last few days had really brought down my average mileage. The mileage had to stay reasonably high to get me over the Rockies before the Winter storms hit. I was in oppressive heat but I knew that within a few weeks the temperature had to drop and would change even more so as I gained altitude. But riding into a too strong headwind for too long a distance during record heat didn't sound prudent. A very useful event happened in the Visitor Center. I met another tourist who was browsing the racks of travel brochures. When he saw my bike clothes we got to talking about touring and his ride across the Northern Tier states from decades ago. He did a good job of pointing out to me that I probably could make it farther. But then he made sure that I appreciated that I was doing this ride because I wanted to; not because I had to. Risking life and limb for performance may have sounded okay when I was young but now I realize how little sense that makes. I was still frustrated and bummed that I wasn't making better progress. A more upbeat soul would probably have loved the excuse to kick back and relax. I kicked back and did laundry.

Despite my griping about my performance, the real culprit was logistics coupled with my conservative approach. Especially because I was on my own, I didn't want to be stuck out on the roads after dark. Instead I erred on the side of less mileage per day. Knowing how far to push it can be tough. The consequence of pushing it too far was too severe for me.

I got another lesson in bike touring at the motel front desk. When I told the desk manager what I was doing, she mentioned a news item I had heard months before. There had been a family of five riding from Maine to Alaska. They had stayed at her motel. I remember a bit about their story. They were doing about forty miles a day with a toddler along as I recall. Like I said, there is always someone out there doing it in a way that you'd never imagine.

Later that afternoon as I headed out to do the laundry I noticed that the wind had changed. The headwind would have been a problem for an hour or two at most. After that it had turned into a tailwind. Continuing probably would have been alright. Still I had to go with what I knew and know that I wouldn't always be right. I did not want to become a toasted tourist.

Sept 17, 2000 Mountain Home to Burley

Logistics lined up better today. There are a lot more places to stay along the Snake River. Two of my favorite names were Bliss and Eden. Each is a truck stop with a small hotel attached. The tail winds returned after I finished dinner last night and were still in force this morning. Each time I took a break I felt like I was letting an opportunity pass me by. By the end of the day I had done over 100 miles and was very tired. Fortunately this positioned me nicely for what could be a rough ride into Utah.

This part of the ride was a pleasure to watch. Whenever the land and the Snake River got together they either made broad appealing townscapes or impressive cliffs and canyons. There were a few clouds around to throw in some nice lighting and a bit of drama. I kept watching a few of them turning into thunderheads in the surrounding mountains.

This day ended up being such a kick. I got a good early start and barely stopped all day. I didn't have to worry logistics for once. There weren't a lot of places to stay but there were enough and they were spaced out just well enough. I didn't have to worry about being very far from a motel. I even found a couple of them just twenty miles down the road. They evidently don't advertise in a way that brought them to my attention but sure enough there they were by the side of the road as I came across a wonderful valley. If I had known about them the day before I might have pressed on despite the winds.

That slice of Idaho was beautiful. The road went down to the river and the land turned green. There were clouds building up in the mountains and the Sun was still coming through. That made for some wonderful lighting as I looked up the canyons and valleys that led down to the river. Some of the settlers must have just stopped there and been very glad. I was glad too, as long as the clouds stayed up in the mountains.

The terrain is rolling plains punctuated with precipitous notches. Some of the notches have rivers running through them. Some of the rivers even have water. I remember the Malad River as a long square channel of dirt. Flat land near the water was usually a green townscape that looked wonderful and comfortable. Flat land near a channel of dirt was usually just more dirt.

The winds that turned around the previous day had strengthened. I wasn't sure if they were an indication of a storm coming up but I wasn't going to complain about them. They were pushing me along on the flats so well that when I took a break I would quickly get nicely cooled down and would want to get back on the bike before they died. The winds were with me all day long. The motels that I could stay at just kept going on by and I kept rolling up the miles. It felt so good to be making progress. I realized that if I could make it to Burley I would be able to get into Utah the next day.

It took a long time but I made it to Burley. At about 113 miles that was the longest ride of the trip. My butt was sore and I was beat but I was glad to be one day's ride from another milestone: the Utah state line. A day off sounded sweet, but the weather reports encouraged me to get through before the next storm.

The weather had held and I found a nice motel room to flop down in. This was the first chance I had for room service and I went for it. Of course just because they offer room service doesn't mean that they are used to people asking for it. I still am not sure what exactly happened to my order but eventually I got some kind of food and I was glad. I was hungry enough to eat anything and so tired that I wouldn't complain about the flavor as long as it was safe and edible.

It was getting lonely out there. I missed having someone to talk to. Most conversations were only a few sentences long. They tended to be either the same old questions about my trip or the regular chitchat with the folks working in the motels and restaurants about my room or my meal. Even some of the folks at the rest stops were downright taciturn. That especially seemed to be the case on Sundays.

Having someone else along could slow things down a bit but maybe that could be balanced by having better morale. I probably would have been willing to ride later in the day if someone else was there. There really is safety in numbers. Maybe next time.

Getting set for the ride into Utah was not a simple thing. For the previous few evenings Kaye and I had been trying to find someplace for me to stay along my sketch of a route. So far I had found a place to stay every night. It looked like there weren't many towns along the way and we could only find one reference to a motel. It was in the town of Snowville just across the border. AAA and most of the people I talked to in town hadn't heard of it. It was a 65 mile shot to get there and involved going over some desolate and hilly terrain. If I couldn't find the motel, the next place to stay was another 70 miles farther. I had just done a 113 mile day and thought that trying a 135 mile day was not just pushing it but was absolutely too risky. Kaye found their phone number and we got in touch with them. It was a small place that only had the office open in the evenings. It was right off the Interstate and I shouldn't have a problem. Just because I shouldn't have a problem does not mean that I wouldn't worry about it. The alternative was to head north through Pocatello and add a day or two. That route wasn't a sure thing either. I decided to go for Snowville and hope that I didn't have to try hanging a hammock from a barbed wire fence.

Sept 18, 2000　Burley to Snowville

The first few signs on this road were all dire warnings of severe weather, dust storms, lots of doom and gloom. The land looks like it could hold all of that and just dump it on you at its whim. There is very little between Burley and Snowville except a truck stop and lonely ranches. Each ranch seems to get its own canyon. At least it provides some life to the landscape.

While sitting at one of the two rest stops worrying about the weather, I notice one of the highway workers. By the time I'm done talking to him I have road, weather, and all sorts of good information about the road ahead. There is stuff to keep an eye out for but he doesn't expect anything bad today.

The slow gradual climb typical of these parts is punctuated by steeper climb up to 5,500 feet: Sweetser Pass. I can tell I am getting near the summit when I see the cell phone towers beside me. The weather is starting to form up but never decides to get around to it. Nice thing about climbing to 5,500 feet is knowing that I won't have to pedal for a while.

A long downhill run brings me to the last rest stop in Idaho. There I meet two guys from Seattle. Evidently they are skipper and one of the crew from a boat owned by one of the McCaw's. It is a 150 footer moored somewhere in Lake Union in the Ship Canal. The name on their T-shirts was something like Lateon or some such. It was a fancy font so it was hard to read. It was odd and fun sitting in the Idaho desert talking about boats and ships. He recognized some of the ones that Kaye and I had seen in Roche Harbor. He likes his job and it is good to see he gets some time off.

Welcome to Utah and the town of Snowville. Kaye found a real gem by finding me a place to stay just inside the Utah border. It was right about 70 miles from Burley and there was no other accommodation for 40 more hilly miles. If you're used to hiking then the room was luxury. If you don't like a few bugs, a noisy air conditioner, a door that doesn't quite close and a TV that only mostly works, well, then don't stop in Snowville unless you have a tent. It was just right for me. I slept well and had some of the best food so far: chocolate sundae, breaded veal cutlets, and a very good omelet.

That really was a desolate stretch of road. The signs along the highway warning about severe dust storms and strong winds would be foreboding enough in a car. On a bike I felt quite exposed. The thickening clouds didn't help either. The weather was shaping up to bring in some nastiness. Of course I didn't know that it would hold off at the time. I was worried about all of it happening all at once on a stretch of road that might end up being longer than I expected and wanted. I knew Snowville was out there, but I couldn't get comfortable with relying on only one motel's dot in the midst of the next hundred miles.

When I came across a rest stop I was so glad to find a bit of civilization. I got to meet an interesting range of personalities even though there were only three people there. On the one end of the spectrum was the energetic and enthusiastic highway worker. He was more than happy to go on about the road, weather and what I could expect. He seemed like a good guy to sit down and have a beer with. At the other end of the spectrum was a couple who showed no interest in noticing anyone. They were a very conservatively dressed couple. Without knowing more about them it is hard to be sure but they seemed to be dressed as Mennonites. Except for maybe his white shirt, he was dressed totally in black including a great broad brimmed black hat. She was standing by his side with her head bowed and wearing a very long dress. As I recall she had some simple decoration to her blouse but I think it was the bonnet that really set her apart. They were standing by the phones while he earnestly devoted his attention to the person on the other end of the line. I really wanted to know more about them but knew it wasn't the time. Besides even if they wanted local help the highway crew was better suited to providing assistance and I don't think they would have been comfortable talking to someone dressed like me.

There sure isn't much out there along that bit of highway. Some of the reason must be that there didn't seem to be much water. There is a whole lot of lonely out there too. The climb wasn't too bad but it took long enough to make me wonder if it was ever going to end. The Pass was one of those where it twists and turns near the crest. I could never see how much farther I had to go. The only real gauge I had was to watch the cell phone towers. When I saw them beside me, I knew I was near the top. I was so looking forward to riding downhill for a while.

The ride down into Utah was not actually a coast all the way but it was easier than the morning's ride. It was very apparent that I was going from one basin to another. The views stretched out before me. It looked to be a big open land contained by mountains. Off to one side I even came across a group of cowboys rounding up some cattle. As I got closer though it looked more like a staged event. There were about two dozen folks on horseback but only about four of them were actually doing anything. The others were staying together in a bunch and watching. Is that what life is like on a dude ranch? I wouldn't be surprised to hear that the people outnumbered the cattle.

I came across another rest area, which surprised me. It was really appreciated because there was nothing else out there and because I hadn't expected it. Well, there was almost nothing in the area. Evidently that is a neat area geologically. The rest area has a lot of reader boards describing the old lakebed. I like that sort of stuff. What I really liked was having a nice place to sit down for a while. Talking to people from back home was a welcome break and a bonus. Talking with them about 150 foot ships in the midst of bone dry terrain was at least a bit odd and fun.

I had to get to Snowville so it was time to get back onto the road. Yes the road was still going downhill but after a while the grade lessened enough that it didn't help much. I'd probably complain mightily if I had to ride back up it though. I was tired and did not want to have to backtrack by inadvertently riding past the motel. The people running the place were nice enough to take my calls a couple of times as I got closer and reaffirmed my directions. I had already messed up reservations a couple of times on this trip by not double checking things when I was tired. I didn't want to slide past this one. As small as Snowville may be to some folks, it was looking large to me. Soon after I crossed the border, the road smoothed out and I found Snowville. It had the motel, two restaurants, a gas station and a mini-mart. That was more than I expected and needed and I was very glad and relieved to find it.

The motel was probably not going to make it into the AAA guides, but it was fine by me. I had gotten out from under the clouds so the air was heating up. Luckily the air conditioning was working too. The room had enough space for my bike but what was most important was how well I was treated. The people running the place must have another job in the daytime and only came by to take care of the motel in the evenings. As tired as I was, that worked out fine for me. When I got there I was happy enough to just plop myself down in the room that they had recommended over the phone. Nothing was fancy but they were so accommodating and put up with so many phone calls from me that I felt more relaxed in Snowville than I would in places that had more amenities and cost a lot more.

To top it off I had some of the best food of the whole trip in Snowville. Right after I got there I treated myself to a chocolate sundae which was piled high and dripping in good stuff. I felt a bit odd sitting down to a sundae before I'd had my shower. The waitress assured me that I couldn't smell anywhere near as bad as the guys who come in fresh from working the manure piles. Evidently ranching is big in Snowville. That explained the flies. That night I had a breaded veal cutlet that was better than most expensive dinners I've had in downtown Seattle, and breakfast was a great omelet that was large and tasty. Did this place look elegant? No, but it was classic.

My stop in Snowville was one of my most memorable. I don't think the town and its businesses could survive anywhere but in the midst of ranchland. The people wouldn't be the same. The buildings might look cleaner in town and the selection might be greater but this was one fine oasis. I am glad I got in there when I did. By nightfall the motel was full and the owners were doing a fine business. I was glad to see that too.

Sept 19,2000 Snowville to Ogden

Well as I was approaching Utah everyone told me to look out for the road construction. I still hear that it is pretty bad. Fortunately for me, I got here after this stretch was done. The shoulder was new and clean. Very sweet. That didn't make this morning's two hills any smaller, but it did make the downhill easier to negotiate. Steering through broken glass at 40 mph is a thrill to miss.

The land has changed considerably. The ring of mountains do look like an impregnable fortress that no road is going to snake through, but along their feet is a flat road that is old lake bed and a swift ride. I have been very fortunate with the tail winds lately. I've only seen the North portion of this area but it is worth looking at for sure. Are they sure those mountains don't fall down on occasion? If this lake ever refills, there won't be much room left for people.

Tonight Kaye and I will commiserate over my route. The expected route is still US-50 through Grand Junction and Pueblo, but it is VERY prudent for us to look at the busy bike route of I-70 through Denver, and the flatter routes that are way up in Wyoming. None are easy. Some are better logistically. Some have easier terrain. We'll work it out.

It had been an impressive fire season and I smelled the evidence in lots of places along the route. Up in Washington near Hanford and in Oregon by the Snake River the smell of charcoal and the sight of scorched fields couldn't be missed. In Snowville I actually got to see the smoke from a fire a ridge or two away from town. I was so glad to have missed the road closures that some folks had to deal with. A lot of the acreage that I saw was charred right up to houses. Amazingly, I didn't see any burned out shells. I suspect that changes one's gardening plans. Amazing and impressive, it is also sad when you realize that some of it was caused by people and some of that burned other people out of their homes.

The signs said, "The Olympics are coming to Salt Lake City!" I didn't care! Except that it meant that I had been hearing dire warnings about massive road construction projects all over Utah. I didn't know if that was why that bit of highway was pristine but I loved it. My introduction to Utah was a dramatic improvement in road conditions. That was the good side of the road construction. The shoulder was nice and smooth and so new that no one had gotten around to breaking a lot of glass on the side of the road. Where does all of that glass come from?

When I did find more glass it was during a downhill grade that was short, steep and very fast. I didn't have a speedometer on the bike but from previous experience I guessed I was going over 30 miles an hour. For all I know I may have exceeded my personal top speed of over 40 mph. This time though was different. I don't think I've mentioned rumble strips before. They were a big part of my life on the bike. Rumble strips are grooves carved in the shoulder of the road to warn drivers that they are wandering out of the lane. Being the land of the free, highway designers have been free to come up with lots of designs for rumble strips. There are some nice simple ones that are right by the white line and nicely separate the shoulder from the road. There are some that span the entire shoulder, which is like riding a bike across four inch ditches every ten feet for tens of miles. That day's rumble strips heading down that hill were of the nice variety. Unfortunately, it was past the area with clean shoulders. Going down the hill at over thirty miles an hour, I noticed parts of the shoulder that sparkled with broken glass from the white line to the dirt. That would not have been a big problem if I could have used the right lane of traffic. The trucks were using it though so I was rapidly being presented with some bad choices. I could slam on the brakes at high speed and hope nothing broke, I could jump over into traffic and hope for the best, or I could steer for the glass and hope that hitting the rumble strips at full speed would only jar every joint in my bike and body. The ride was a bit abrupt, but after hitting the rumble strips, I brought down my speed as best I could and used the gaps in traffic as best I could. Everything turned out fine, but while I was hitting those strips at that speed I was also pumping lots of adrenaline. So much for enjoying the downhill rush.

The mountains certainly looked young. They were steeper and craggier than most of what I had encountered on the ride. They were magnificent. I love mountains. That is one reason I stay in Seattle. So when I came across these ones I was thrilled to look at them. I was just hoping I didn't have to ride over them. Thank heavens for old lakebeds. I don't know for sure that it was what the road was built on, but it was a lot flatter than the rest of the terrain and seemed to be down low. Cruising on into Ogden was a joy. The winds were never as generous as they had been between Mountain Home and Burley but they had pushed me towards Ogden and I was glad.

I can see why folks move to the Salt Lake City area. The mountains are right there backing up the city and there is nothing blocking the view to the west. Some mountain settings can get to feel closed in but not there. The mountains were actually so close that I was wondering if they had to worry about landslides and such. Clouds were playing around the mountaintops and possibly generating weather for two things I worried about: hypothermia and lightning. They can make an awesome pair for anyone out there in the great outdoors. Luckily it was much nicer down along the lake.

I had made it back to my first large urban area in days. Between the cities the riding was usually simple. The road might go up and over mountains but there wasn't much route finding and, as long as there was a shoulder, the traffic wasn't a problem. Coming into a city meant dealing with the stress of traffic but at least I knew that there would be places to eat at and stay in.

"I could have gone farther", but that was a better refrain than "I went too far". My motel room in Ogden was a far cry from the one in Snowville. The motel was only a few months old and the room was large enough to be a suite. Lucky for me, they were running a special to get folks into the place. Those were two of the most comfortable motels on the trip and they had very little in common.

It didn't appear that I would have to worry about finding a place to stay for the next day or two. I settled into Ogden and started figuring out how I was going to get through Salt Lake City and Colorado. There was a AAA office in Ogden and I decided to visit them the next morning. The local tourist office hadn't gotten around to collecting any information about bicycling in and around Salt Lake City. They thought it was a good idea but couldn't help me at all.

Colorado was getting to be a long discussion each night for Kaye and I. There were plenty of ways through but they all involved various logistical issues and significant terrain. Calling the Rockies "significant terrain" is an understatement. The weather reports were predicting storms. I didn't want to get stranded near some pass during a blizzard. We spent a lot of time talking about each pass in terms of how high it was, how steep it was, and how much of a hop was involved to get to it and over it. Kaye worked the issue hard. She used the topographic and road atlas software at home and was great about faxing me what she had learned. I was getting concerned. The next stretch looked rough and I felt tired. We did decide at that point to forego the routes through Southern Wyoming. It still didn't sound like Wyoming wanted bikes on their Interstates. Their suggested detours were flat relative to Colorado but they weren't straight and they didn't have much in the way of lodging and food. Colorado seemed to be much more bike friendly.

It felt good to get caught up on the emails. I was becoming much more aware of how inaccessible the Internet was. There was still a lot of progress to be made in wiring up the country

STORMY WEATHER

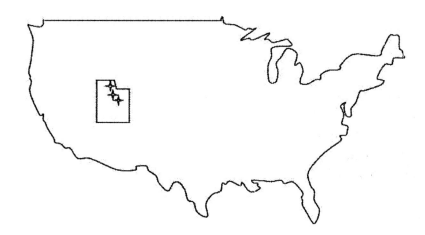

September 20   Ogden to Provo

Well Salt Lake City is right in the midst of this but if I stop there for the night I end up with two short days with a storm coming in. I decided to shoot for Provo (actually Springville) which is a slightly long day but gets me closer to the mountain crossings sooner.

First off is getting to AAA to grab some maps and books of Colorado. Even though there are nice flat roads around here, they have to be up on a hill. What a way to start the day. They were very helpful.

Leaving AAA put me on a road that was under construction. That is probably the closest I have been to a trailer yet. Let's not dwell on that. I'll just be thankful that those folks really know where their truck edges are.

Supposedly bicycles aren't allowed on the Interstate in downtown Salt Lake City. The road I was on dumped me back onto the Interstate and I immediately started looking for the signs directing me to leave. One road that I had planned on following had an exit on the left side of the road. Very inconvenient. Pretty soon after that the local constable pulled over and informed me that I was already past the signs and that I had to leave now. No problem. For the majority of the day I was off on a road of strip malls, light industry, and a few sections of town that the Chamber of Commerce usually doesn't include in their brochures.

This ended up being a LONG detour and a hot one too. I ended up stopping in Provo rather than Springville just because I started running out of energy and it was getting close to 6PM. This is of course when I got the flat where I even broke a tire iron. First flat of the trip.

According to Kaye, I have now done over 1,000 miles. I feel like it.

Despite the bad road conditions and all I can see why folks like Salt Lake City. It is too dry for me, but the mountains are always there as a fine backdrop. Very impressive and a great place to catch the sunset colors.

Heading to the AAA office meant that I started off the day with more climbing than I had expected. The effort was worth it though. The women in the AAA office were wonderful and helpful. One of the customers however deemed it important to sternly point out that the first A in AAA stood for Automobile. The people working there didn't seem to mind. Kaye and I have been members for quite some time so we have literally paid our dues. When she came out to meet me in Union Gap she brought along the AAA guides and maps for Washington, Oregon and Idaho. Ogden seemed a good place to pick up information for Utah and Colorado.

Everyone was still warning me about the road construction but it didn't make much difference. There was no way around it so I just had to go through it. The route I picked kept me off the Interstate for a few miles farther. Before I got back to the Interstate, I had to go through a road construction site that had reduced the traffic down to one narrow lane in each direction. There was no shoulder and the road was edged with concrete barriers. It was a busy street so the only breaks in traffic were when the traffic light cycled. There was no other way around that I could find. I went for it and almost got pinned and scraped between a tractor-trailer and the concrete barriers. It was over so quickly that I didn't have time to react or even look its way, but I am sure that the trailer passed within an arm length. So much for side roads being safer than the Interstate.

Eventually I came down off the hill and ended up back on the highway. Being back on the Interstate was so welcome after the morning's adventure. I even got to play Good Samaritan again. A young mother with her child was stranded on the side of the road. No one would stop for them. I couldn't do much more than offer the use of my cell phone but at least that was enough for her to get in touch with her mother for help.

Despite my visual vigilance, I hadn't seen any sign directing bicycles off the Interstate so I kept heading south. The road I had been on had merged with the Interstate and was supposed to peel off on its own again. I planned on following it until I noticed that it exited via the left lane. Crossing all of that traffic seemed fairly dangerous. That's why I was still on the Interstate when the police officer pulled me over. He was nice enough in telling me that I had to go find a side road and that the exit I had just passed was my best bet. It was obvious talking to him that he wasn't all that worried about me. His main problem was the time the police would spend answering calls from easily irritated cell phone toting motorists. It was easier to tell the bicyclist to get off the road than to deal with a never ending stream of cell phone calls. I had no problem with that.

Well I thought it would be no problem. The detour took me down roads that hardly ever had a shoulder. In the industrial areas I had to worry about the truck traffic. When I got down by the strip malls I had to worry about the chaos of suburban traffic. When I got south of all of that I had to worry about getting lost. If I didn't take the correct turn I would end up on the wrong side of a lake south of the city. As the day got hotter, the detour seemed to get longer. The detour was taking longer than I had expected. As I got farther south I couldn't see any places to stay. I felt that I was headed back out into the sticks far from my route and far from any motels. Finally and with great relief, I found the right intersection. It was late in the day and I was more tired than I wanted to be. I had hoped to get to the far edge of town to a place called Springville. It looked like I was going to have to pull up short and stop in Provo.

As I made my way towards Provo I came across a bike shop. I hadn't visited one in days so I thought I'd stop in and see if they had any good advice on the road ahead. Like a lot of bike shops I was to visit, these guys were mostly into dirt. They didn't actually use the bikes to get anywhere. It seems that very few folks do. When I got back on the bike it looked like I had about another hour's worth of riding ahead of me. That's why the first flat of the ride was so much more painful than usual. Somehow my tire had acquired a three inch screw. The tires were puncture resistant but they couldn't be expected to handle that much abuse. The tires were almost too stout. I actually broke a tire iron trying to get the tire off the rim. I didn't have to take those tires off the rim often but when I did it was an effort. To top it off, on my first try I managed to puncture the new tube. When I finally got going again it was without much in the way of backup supplies. Amazingly, I started to find more shops along the way. Stopping in two of them I found a good set of tire irons and more spare tubes. All of this was taking time though. I was getting more tired and the amount of light left was shrinking.

Finally I found myself in Provo. According to the maps the motels were somewhere nearby but I couldn't see them. Eventually I found out that the closest one was two miles away and off my route. The directions were too much for my tired brain to handle but I headed that way anyway, coasted downhill, and found the place. I got one of the last rooms available. Provo is a college town and there was a game there that weekend.

The day ended up being a lot longer than I had expected. The near miss in the morning, the long detour all day and the flat in the afternoon really drained me. My morale was running low. Part of it was the disappointment with the area. It is beautiful and they were going to host the Olympics. It looked great and sounded like a perfect place to have bike paths and bike lanes running through the city. The road behind me had not been kind and descriptions of the road ahead of me sounded formidable. There were mountains to climb and forecasts for bad weather. Before I went to bed that night I booked the room for another night or two. I needed to recharge my batteries before I could go on.

That evening the rains came in. Then and the next day there was rain and lightning. It was a good thing that I had finally taken a day off. I needed it and I am glad that I was able to sit out the foulest weather I had seen on the trip so far. That was my first day off since September 6.

September 21 and 22 Provo to Price

Well I finally took a day off. Mom Nature decided to have a lightning display after I got to Provo. Fortunately for me it gave me an excuse to stop for a day and load up prior to a significant climb: 3,000 feet to 7,400 feet, my highest yet and nothing compared to what is in Colorado.

The day started out looking like I might have to take two days off. Groan. It is hard to sit still when I know that the longer I sit the more likely I'll find snow in Colorado. The climb was a grind. None of it was as steep as Snoqualmie, but it was obvious and the majority of it was above one mile high. The country is impressive. It evidently gets just a little bit more rain than the stuff up by the Idaho border so there are a few trees filling in the gaps with nice Fall colors.

There is very little along this road even though it is a major way to
Colorado out of Salt Lake City. There is plenty of traffic and a shoulder
that is just wide enough.

As I got to the pass, the weather darkened but never really got around
to raining. Evidently yesterday was terrible. Good thing I missed it.

Over the pass the terrain changes quite a bit. The road starts descending
a canyon that is reminiscent of Zion Nation Park. Big red rock cliffs with
lots of sandstone and lots of geological features for rock hounds to play
with.

Unfortunately for me the other side of the pass had head winds so
instead of flying down 3%-5% grades, I had to get in there and pedal.
Bummer of a thing to do after riding that far and climbing that mountain.

Price is a nice town where the local Holiday Inn staff lets me use their
computer for typing these notes. Nice folks.

Getting going was something I did with mixed emotions. It would
have been nice to sit still and wait for better weather but the longer I sat
the greater the chance that I'd have even worse weather in Colorado.
The previous day's storm was bad. Staying inside had been an excellent
idea. It was Mom Nature telling me to sit still for once. If the weather
hadn't been so bad I probably would have kept right on going and worn
myself out. Instead I headed out on a day where the rains looked like
they could start up at any time. The clouds were not only eclipsing the
mountaintops but had almost reached the valley floor. I was heading
into one of the most desolate parts of the trip and hoping that the
weather would let me through. I had heard warnings about how tough
it was to climb Soldier Summit, which tops out at about 7,400 feet. Bad
weather, a long haul, little support, and a 3,000 foot climb didn't send
me off with a song in my heart. If there was a song it was more like some
dirge from the Middle Ages.

As I left town things got sparser as they always do. I was so glad to
finally find the right road. That leg of the trip would be on US
highways, not the Interstate, so things weren't quite as obviously

marked. When I found the road that led to Soldier Summit I was at the mouth of the valley. The rains hadn't done more than make a fine mist and the views up the valley surprised me with how bright they were. It wasn't sunny but it was odd to think that going into the mountains would be the way to escape the weather. It actually looked like the sun might poke through farther up the road. That was a surprise and a help. The other helpful surprise was the sign for a housing development at Soldier Summit. That was handy. Maybe the summit wasn't as desolate as I had feared and if nothing else, the sign gave me a guess as to how far away the development was.

The canyon was pretty. I love Fall colors and find it interesting how they vary from one part of the country to another. The rocks were a nice autumn set of colors that must be there year-round. The burnt reds and subtle browns of the rocks were accented by the greens of the foliage that was surviving there. Heading uphill for tens of miles gave me a lot of time to look at the countryside, that is when I was not looking out for glass. There wasn't much civilization out there. I suspect the folks living along the road like it that way. Of course I was going through there between the Summer tourist season and the Winter ski season so it probably wasn't always that quiet. An extra rest stop or two would have been greatly appreciated.

It wasn't just one long steady climb. Along the way there is a major portion of the road that has to climb to get around a bit of odd and difficult terrain. As I recall, the roadside markers describe how a landslide filled the valley and ruined a town. It is an impressive sight. Mom Nature does Urban Redevelopment. The road had been permanently detoured up, around, and through another hill. That meant I had done some climbing that was for naught. After I went down the other side I had to start grinding back up the main hill. That was tough. I only had a rough guess at how much farther it was and that was based on that real estate sign. Real estate developments do not have to be located at the place they are named after. If that was the case, then there are a lot of Shangri-La's out there that will have to change their names.

As I reached the summit the weather was gray, cold and threatening but never got around to raining. There I found the real estate development. It was a lot of land with a few signs. The only sign of activity was one guy on his horse who seemed to be checking out the lots. The summit may not have been very developed but there was one convenience store there and I was so glad to go inside, buy supplies and get warm. According to the people working in the store, the previous day had been extremely nasty: high winds, heavy rain, and lightning. They had even lost power for a while. I was so glad that I hadn't been caught up in that.

Some days that downhill run into Helper and Price must be an awesome ride. Not for me. While the weather hadn't been holding me back on the way up the hill, it did so as I headed down the hill. The winds had shifted and I had to pedal downhill. With the cold and wind I was getting chilled and did not like it at all. The canyon that I followed was gorgeous but was hard to take in. Fighting the wind and dodging glass through an area that should have been an easy coast through scenic country was disappointing.

At last I made it to Price. The area was dry but obviously got enough moisture for the occasional tree and forest. A few years earlier, Kaye and I visited Bryce and Zion National Parks and I could see more of that type of geology showing up. It was very impressive scenery. I was happy to just check into the motel and warm up. They had a restaurant there and a small convenience store nearby. It was nothing fancy but it was everything that I needed and more. From there the road tends downhill until Green River where I'd start the climb into Colorado.

Sitting still the previous day in terrible weather gave me the chance to psych myself out. My gut felt terrible all day long. Evidently I was not very good at relaxing. Of course, the weather and the desolation out on the road didn't help. They reinforced any vestige of gloom that I had about me.

By the end of the day, I was tired and beat. The pain in my right hip, knee, and hand had me wondering what it would take to make me quit. If a bit of adversity was enough, then I would never have made it out of Washington. Pushing into too much adversity could result in self-inflicted damage. The trip wasn't worth that price. I kept remembering that the main pain would be my bruised ego. Unfortunately my self-esteem would be bruised too. I decided that having some criteria for quitting was a good idea to keep me from giving up on a whim and also to keep me from pushing it too hard. Three consecutive days of showstopping weather with no relief in sight became one criterion. The other main criterion was any significant pain that was getting progressively worse and that didn't improve during a break. I also decided to not quit on a whim but to sit still for two nights before bagging the trip.

Kaye was very encouraging. She told me how she thought that I should keep going and that she trusted me to make the right decisions. We had at least made the right decision about not going through Wyoming. The bad weather may have been rain in Utah, but it was a blizzard in Wyoming. The Interstates were closed and people were stranded. It had snowed in Colorado as well but it would get a few days to melt off before I got there.

A WHOLE LOT OF LONELY OUT THERE

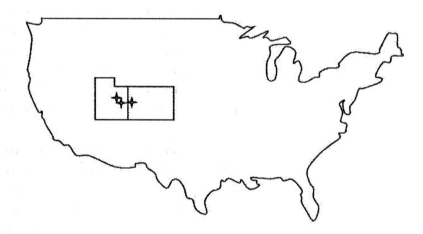

September 23,   *Price to Green River*

Riding along today and looking at the mountains to the East felt like a toddler wandering along the living room floor wondering how those adults ever get up onto that big couch up there. All along the route is a set of mountains that are easily 3,000 or more feet above the road surface. The winter storms that I have been dodging are dropping snow up there. I can see the clouds come in behind me, and I can see rain up ahead. I was lucky enough to miss all of that. That's not to say the weather was pleasant, but I did not get rained on in any significant amount.

There is a lot of lonely out here. I guess the desert is like that. It is a major event when I can spot a ranch or maybe even some small smoke stack miles off the highway. A 75 mph speed limit just seems pokey out here. Of course doing much more than that on some of these roads would be harmful to one's butt. I know my butt noticed the rumble strips that stretched from the road to the dirt. Not pleasant.

The road is busy but the traffic is not a problem. The rolling hills and a bit of headwind are more of an issue. That and the lack of anywhere to get more food or get out of the wind.

The day ends with a flat tire that I try to nurse into town. It almost makes it but I have to walk the bike the last quarter mile. These very tough tires are equally tough to get on and off. I lose a spare or two in the process and notice that the tire is losing integrity near the bead. Green River has nice views of the surrounding mountains and could be a destination in its own right, but it doesn't have a bike shop. I'll have to coax the bike into Colorado.

A whole lot of lonely out there really does describe how I felt at that time. After Price, the area gets very open and very vacant. There wasn't much vegetation and none of that was tall enough to get in the way of the views. The views were magnificent. The land was almost flat with the occasional rise to break the steady progress down to Green River. Off to either side the land didn't just rise up but was walled in by cliffs that seemed nearly vertical for thousands of feet. They were awesome and impressive and getting snowed on. The weather had stayed cold since Provo and the clouds were building up before me, behind me and on either side of me. I could see rain showers falling from some of them. At the same time that I felt so small in such big country, I also felt that things were closing in on me. Had I been driving through in a car I would have been enjoying the view and the power of nature. Instead I was wondering and worrying about what could happen to someone out there when a storm came through. Just to emphasize the issue, a head wind had kicked up which made it that much more difficult.

People do live out there. Every few miles or so there would be a road heading off to the side for miles. Occasionally there was a smoke plume or a building in the distance. That was some of the emptiest land I saw but it was still covered by man somehow. Even out there the road was bordered by barbed wire. Nearly the entire trip was on a fenced-in road. But out there I had a hard time imagining the fences holding in great herds of cattle. Maybe the fences were there to keep the wildlife off the road. There was enough road kill around to blast that notion. Whatever they were there for, they made me feel unwelcome. Barbed wire doesn't give me that good homey feeling. It looks a tough hard life for those living out there, especially when seen from an exposed bicycle on a day threatening storms. If you are familiar with it though, it might just be peaceful and majestic. I didn't get a chance to see, let alone ask, any of the residents.

The weather had either been extremely hot or extremely cold for too many days. Pleasant days of cycling along under Autumn skies were not happening. At one point I realized how much this was affecting me. Across a broad flat plain I could see an Amtrak train heading back the way I had come. Sitting in one of their nicer berths and watching the world go by seemed so tempting. There was no way I could get to that train but it made me realize how easy it would be to give up and go home. I had done a thousand miles. Surely that would be a significant enough achievement. But I was close to Colorado and reaching Colorado would be a nice milestone too. Without a doubt, the easy and enjoyable days were vastly outnumbered by the days of trials, but I would keep going on.

I am sure that I did not drink or eat enough that day because my mood ran downhill fast. The cold and the headwinds didn't help. I hadn't found any place to take a break from the weather for quite a while. So when my back tire started going flat about ten miles out of Green River, I felt like the world had just whacked me at the knees. The flat wasn't even that bad at the start. At first I thought that I could just pump it up and it would hold until town. I even came across a stretch of road where I was able to coast for a while. Soon enough I realized that town was farther than I thought and the tire was leaking faster than I had hoped. It didn't take too long before I had to pump the tire every mile. I just kept pumping the tires and the pedals. Green River was stretched out over a lot more land than I had expected, but why not? There is a lot of land to work with here. I finally realized that the motel I had been heading for was farther along than I wanted to go. The tires weren't lasting more than a few hundred yards at a time by the time I got into town. When a motel came into sight I stopped riding and walked the last little bit. They had a room and I took it.

Fixing the flat was a real pain. That was the same tire that busted a tire iron in Provo. I noticed that while its bead was strong, which is what made it tough to pry off, the rest of the tire was wearing thin. Somewhere along the line I had gotten cactus needles in the tread. Between working with a tough tire and missing a cactus needle or two, I ended up going through all my spare tubes. There wasn't a bike shop in town. I could either mail order some parts and wait there for them to arrive, or I could hope things would work long enough for the ride to Grand Junction the next day. If I rode, I would have to hope the tire was patched well enough and that nothing else went wrong. The road to Grand Junction was back on the Interstate so if anything went terribly wrong I would have to flag someone down for help. There were no motels or much of anything else until after the Colorado border.

My body could have used some patchwork too but all I could do was fuel it and try to rest.

I can't recall any of my dinners having a nicer view than the one in Green River. Looking back on those cliffs at sunset with a few clouds around was very nice to do while indoors where I was warm, dry and safe. Outside, the temperature was chilly and the winds were picking up. The next day was going to be uphill and it looked like it might be into a cold and nasty headwind.

September 24 Green River to Grand Junction

The weather has cleared and since this day's route is on a new compass heading, the wind shifts around to become a headwind again. Argh. The clearing sky has also allowed for record low temperatures. This is another day of lots of lonely. Most folks heading out this way are either going all the way through to Denver, or are heading south to one of the four local national parks. The Interstate is better than yesterday's road, but it has precious little in the way of support.

I actually got to see some wildlife today. They have a highway sign that warns "Eagles on Highway". Odd. I don't see any eagles on the road, but I do get to see one pronghorn antelope in repose, and one prairie dog like critter guarding his part of the shoulder.

Welcome to Colorado. I cross the border in mid-afternoon with some 3 hours of bicycling yet to go. I can get to Fruita and food in two hours, but Grand Junction is an extra hour along and more strategically positioned for heading North, South, or home. Besides it should have more bike shops and my bike needs help. The bad sidewall on my tire is giving out to the point that I can see a bulge developing. A bad sign.

The weather has cleared but is so cold that I am rarely warm throughout the day. I am starting to be concerned that Winter has come earlier to the Rockies than I had expected.

I was on the road as the Sun came up. Usually I would wait until about thirty minutes after sunrise before I would get going. Leaving at sunrise meant anyone coming up from behind would be looking east and might not see me because the Sun had blinded them. I'd rather be seen. That day though I preferred to be moving. It was past chilly to cold, but that was another day with very little support and no place to stay for about sixty miles. If I had to do anything drastic to the bike to keep it going, I wanted to have a lot of daylight to work with.

At least I didn't have the clouds to worry about. The wind had gotten a bit flaky but overall it wasn't helping me get to Colorado so I wasn't glad to have it around. Without the clouds the air had cooled off even more so than the previous day. I kept hoping that the Sun would eventually warm me up but it never happened. It looked to be a long day's trudge.

Late in the morning I was relieved to see a sign for a rest area. I realized that it was probably the only one on that stretch of road. It came on as a cruel joke. The person that designed it probably felt that it was skillfully positioned for a marvelous view. It did have that. It had that by being mounted on a hill to the side of the road. Having to ride uphill to get to a rest area was not the best way for me to rest. I didn't want to use the precious energy that I'd saved up. I climbed because I had to. The rest area was quite busy even if it wasn't tourist season. There were still people who were heading through to Canyonland and Arches National Parks. Some people wanted to know if I was going to go through there on my way to Colorado. A sixty mile detour is small in a car. It is a whole day's travel for me.

One of the groups of tourists was a group of three guys from one of the ex-Soviet Republics. They had saved their money for who knows how long and rented a car to see, climb and hike the United States. Their English was much better than my Russian. I am always so impressed with people who can command another language. I am also impressed with people like these guys who do whatever it takes to get themselves out there and see the world. They had done some bicycling in Europe where there is a lot better support for such things. They figured that Americans who can ride across spaces like Eastern Utah solo were impressive and nuts. At that time I hadn't made it across yet so I couldn't take credit for anything. They were off to Florida via Moab and I envied them. They seemed like a nice open minded group of guys who were out there enjoying the world. I was glad to see it.

Back on the road the day wore on. That was some of the loneliest country I had seen. The weather was not cooperating and even into the early afternoon I was cold. My mood was approaching the lowest point of the whole trip. I was climbing into a headwind and wincing every time I hit a rock or piece of glass because I never knew when the tire would blow out. Each successive hill drained me that much more. Late in the afternoon I nearly collapsed. It seemed like this ride was never going to give me a break. The road was messy and I was running out of food and water. I had to ration my sports bars, really fancy candy bars. I couldn't allow myself to eat and drink as much as I wanted. I could only have as much as I allotted myself for that hour of riding. At one point my mood dropped so low that I actually took to cursing the bike because it wasn't shifting gears well enough. I am not known for cursing so for me this was a sign that I should sit down and collect myself. I was almost crying. Riding against a noisy headwind all day had obliterated my morale.

The town of Fruita was my earliest hope for a motel and it was tens of miles away. Grand Junction was about another ten miles past Fruita, but from there I could catch a bus, train, plane, or maybe just rent a car and drive home. My morale was shot and it took me quite a while sitting there to decide to not flag down a car and hitch a ride into town. Maybe I had just picked the wrong time of year to do this. My mood was so sour that I didn't want to inflict it on anyone so I decided that if this was to be my last day on the road I might as well push on and not save any energy for the next day. It was time to use all of my reserves.

I had to grind away at pedaling for another hour or two until I finally found a sign welcoming me to the state of Colorado. At least I had met that milestone. The rest of the day's agenda was just a search for lodging and maybe a way home. After so much desolation, loneliness and parched terrain, it was a real pleasure to see the valley that Fruita and Grand Junction live in. It was green, there was water running through it and there were people living there. Not only that but they had restaurants and rest rooms. Oh joy. Near the end of the day I found myself checking into a motel near the Grand Junction airport. Maybe all I needed was a break. I made reservations to stay in Grand Junction for three nights.

That night my guess was that I was quitting. I spent the time getting price quotes for all the different ways of getting home. Getting me home wasn't the problem. Getting the bike home was the sticky point. At least if I drove I could make it back to Seattle in one long day or take two and thank some of the people that I had met along the way. Even if I did go back I decided that I would relax in Grand Junction for a day first. Getting the bike fixed was one way of getting out there and seeing the city. Besides, the bike needed a tire and even if I went back to Seattle I would still have to go shopping for one. I decided that I might as well shop in Grand Junction.

I went to bed with a severely damaged morale, and knee and hip pain that I could no longer ignore. The green spaces in the Colorado valleys may have picked up my spirits but my spirits had fallen so far during the day that it would take a lot more to get me back to even slightly sociable.

September 25 Grand Junction day off

Well Grand Junction has 9 bike shops and none of them can sell me 2 touring tires and replacement tubes. Even the REI here is no help. I manage to get one reasonable tire to replace the obviously bad back tire, but the only spare tubes are a bit too big for this type of tire.

The weather should improve, the bike might be okay, and maybe my knee and hip will feel better in a day or two but too many things in too many areas are riding close to the limit. Stay tuned. The engineer in me may abort the mission.

Grand Junction is a fine place. It reminded me of Seattle when I moved there in 1980. The area was just being discovered for its beauty and quality of life. Unfortunately, manners and traffic were both getting worse as the crowds poured in. Lots of people were moving to town and the locals wanted them all to go home. I heard the same things in Grand Junction. To me, Grand Junction had one of the politest set of drivers on the whole trip.

Thanks to one bike mechanic who knows more about scuba than bikes, I didn't have to visit all nine bike shops to find the tire that I needed. He was working in the second shop that I dropped into. He only had one tire that would work for my bike so he volunteered to get on the phone and call around to the other shops until we found just what I needed. For a scuba expert, he did a fine job on the bicycle side of their business. I sent some business his way by buying a chain from them and having them change it for me. I rode off to find the one shop that supposedly had good tires and found that there was a bit of miscommunication. It turned out that the only touring tire that would fit a mountain bike was back at the scuba shop. Grand Junction has nine bike shops but they are almost exclusively for dirt, tricks or racing. The area is gorgeous but it seemed that nobody went bike touring. Considering the wonderful bike maps that Colorado publishes I was surprised at that. I definitely lucked into the right time of year to visit. The Aspens were golden and people were taking long drives through to look at them. Evidently they weren't doing it on bicycles though.

Of course because I was taking the day off, the weather looked perfect for riding. A little improvement in my timing might have made a big difference in the ride. I really had to rest my body though. Even riding around on flat city streets with no panniers on the bike awakened the continual pain in my hip and knee. I was feeling better but the recovery was slow. My mood was improving too and I was able to get a lot of chores done. I got a haircut, sent off a slew of emails, and bought a book. Trying to relax by watching television was getting me nowhere. I found very little on television that was relaxing and enjoyable. Books are more restful and were out there but I was amazed at how hard they were to find. I have always had bookstores to browse through wherever I've lived and thought that everyone did. Lots of the small towns that I stayed in would only have what was in the mini-mart and sometimes the only literature available was the tabloids. Grand Junction had a nice used bookstore but I could only find new books at the airport.

Somewhere there had to be a mall but it didn't seem to be within easy walking distance for my bad knees. I had ridden enough already and didn't want to get back on the bike unless it was absolutely necessary.

Kaye and I spent those nights going over all of the possible routes through the Rockies. If I didn't quit and run home, then I had to know which way I was headed. Grand Junction lived up to its name for me. All of the routes that looked reasonable went through there. Picking a good route was no small feat. The Rockies are hard enough because they are steep, long and at altitude. They also had snow on them. Some of the routes had as much as six inches of snow dumped on them while I was in Provo and it hadn't all melted yet. The advice I had hoped to glean from the local bike community didn't prove to be of much use. What I relied on was Kaye and the software she had bought. She plotted out each of the routes to see how steep they were and how much elevation I would have to gain to get over them. She then compared that against climbs that I'd done on this and other trips. I started to appreciate just how hilly the Puget Sound region can be. Nobody was downplaying the difficulty I had ahead of me. The storm that just passed wasn't an encouraging sign so I turned much more conservative in my planning.

Another nice thing about Colorado was that all of the routes except one went right through ski resorts. Aspen was only twenty miles from a pass and Aspen also had lots of the same travel options that Grand Junction had. If I was going to quit, Aspen was as good a place as Grand Junction. I decided to try for it. If my hip and knee pain got to be too much I could turn around and ride back down to the Grand Junction airport for a flight home. If I made it to Aspen and went home from there, then at least I would have time to play tourist in Aspen. If I continued the ride, I was committing myself to a 12,000 foot pass. It was much higher than some of the alternatives, but at least I would get to tackle it early in the day when I was fresh, wouldn't have to be far from town when I climbed it, and had a chance at a good local weather forecast. Turning around after crossing the Rockies would make it much easier to return to complete the ride.

My mood was getting better but I still wasn't sure how much farther I wanted or was able to go. I could only think of the trip in short jumps. Florida was just too far away in just too many ways.

HEADING EAST INTO THE OLD WEST

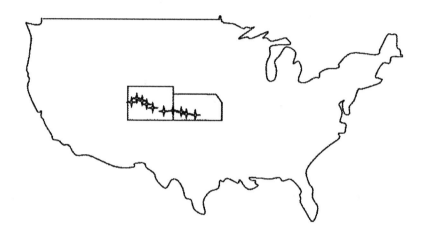

September 27   Grand Junction to Silt

The time off in Grand Junction was definitely beneficial. The joints aren't bugging me as much and my attitude improved. I decided to shoot for Aspen. Commercial flights leave from there so there is a good exit if necessary.

The ride is all uphill until I cross the Rockies. Heading to Silt the road is up a windy canyon where a rock falling from one side could make it to the other side if it wasn't for the river. The Sun has a tough time getting in here so the morning can be quite chilly. The wind in these canyons is also downhill in the mornings so the early going was tough.

The area is dry but getting less so. Maybe that happens with elevation. Below Silt the valley broadens and becomes much more appealing. This is definitely rural as opposed to the mix I saw in Grand Junction. The big news is the opening of hunting season in a few days. There are banners on the stores and such heralding the event.

The rumble strips on the Interstate get too much for me and the bike so it is time for the side roads and a view of small machine shops and some more small town America.

It didn't take long to find out that the new tire was not quite round. Every rotation of the wheel gave me a small lurch as the flat spot went by. Still it was better than having to nurse a tire that wanted to pop.

My aches and pains from the ride into Grand Junction had healed enough to be manageable. That was good enough for me. My main goal was to get to Aspen. Once I was there, I would let all of my body parts cast their votes on whether I kept going or went home.

It looked like two or three days of travel were ahead of me. The road to Aspen headed north out of Grand junction. That wasn't quite what I had in mind. South and east were my preferred directions but Aspen was northeast of Grand Junction so that's the way I headed. Getting out of town wasn't hard. Interstate 70 was still the route to follow. The road headed straight for a cliff that rises out of town. After running along its base for a while, the road found a notch and started running up a deep canyon.

That early in the morning the Sun wasn't high enough to get rid of the cool night air that hid in the shadows. The cold air making its way down the canyon meant I was headed uphill and into a cold wind. It was sunny and September and the wind chill was noticeable. I didn't mind too much because there were more places to rest and eat than I had seen since Salt Lake City.

I wasn't going to make it to Aspen in one day. I hadn't planned on it. Instead I was hoping to get about halfway and find a reasonable motel. With the comparative wealth of services along the road I was not worried as I went along. Canyon riding was a welcome change from the big open spaces. I couldn't take much of either for very long so it was nice to have a change.

They actually have bike paths along the road. At one particularly narrow point, bikes are directed off the Interstate onto their own path. The path looked to be the old road. A tunnel through a significant chunk of rock shortened the main road and left this other piece of concrete for me to enjoy all to myself. That stretch of ride along the river in the morning was peaceful and pretty. It didn't last long but it is one of the images that has stayed with me.

As I climbed up the canyon it got greener and wider. Eventually it turned into farm and ranch land. Two days off had helped my attitude a lot. I was able to enjoy the road despite the remnants of pain that were still with me. The weather even cooperated. I would get used to the winds changing direction in the afternoon from down the canyon to up the canyon. If it wasn't for the fact that I was riding uphill, the ride would have been nice and easy. At least that was the case until I found a too long stretch of rumble strips that were too wide. They covered the shoulder from the traffic all the way into the dirt. That was normally bad enough but it was even worse with my aching body. I tried swerving around the strips but that meant I had to continually turn my head to look over my shoulder for traffic. That went on for miles until I finally found an exit onto a good frontage road. I was so glad to get off the highway for a while.

The side road wasn't the best. It still had a considerable amount of traffic on it and no shoulders. It was, however, nice to be riding closer to the small businesses and such. I caught glimpses of the insides of garages and machine shops as I went by. There was something homey and relaxing about that. I wasn't separated from people's lives by miles like in the desert. Things were much more immediate. When garages and machine shops seem homey, it's probably a sign of having been out in the desert too long or having been brought up around folks with small businesses.

There was one tourist information rest stop that I dropped in on. It was being run by a couple who had just moved to the area. I guess that's one way to learn about the place: become its ambassadors. They were kind enough to assure me that there were plenty of places to stay as I headed up the valley. I got the impression that the husband thought I was nuts. He had seen quite a few people pedaling up the exit ramp in low gear so slowly that they were almost falling over. He couldn't imagine anyone having fun doing that. Downhill or flat made sense but that uphill stuff just didn't click for him. Considering my recent experience in Eastern Utah, I couldn't argue much.

A few miles later I started looking for a place to stay. Luckily there were a string of motels spread out every ten miles or so for the next bit of road. When I got to the town of Silt I figured it was far enough. I didn't want to push my somewhat healed body and damage it in the process. With the beginning of hunting season I had some competition for motel rooms. I hadn't expected that but didn't have any trouble either.

September 28   Silt to Aspen

The early morning downhill winds are there as usual. At least the days have been free of rain. Lots of fluids are the order of the day though.

I made it to the turn off for Aspen at Glenwood Springs earlier than I had expected. The valley has become much greener here and the town is much more urban again. This is the sort of town that has bike shops and coffeehouses. They also have an enticing hot spring swimming pool right down by the river. Maybe if I end up out this way again I can visit it. For now, on to Aspen.

The climb to Aspen should be steeper than the climb from Silt. Fortunately it is so well graded that there are no steep stretches and it is easy to maintain a pretty good pace. The morning winds died so that helped too.

Things are still a bit rural but there are a few more luxury homes, developments and golf courses showing up. It is a climb into money with some ranches thrown in. There is one funky convenience store that has been around since before 7-11 I bet, and they are selling an old soda fountain counter with freezer for $5,500. Anyone interested? I have their business card just in case.

Welcome to Aspen and the completion of a one day climb of about 2,500 feet. The concentration of luxury homes and amenities is definitely increased over the lowlands. There is a bus service here that evidently runs quite a way down the valley. It is my guess that it brings in all of the workers from where the housing is only slightly ridiculous. The stores in town include folks like Bulgari, Kenneth-Cole, Ralph Lauren, and bunches of high priced art galleries. The hotels are much more expensive and much more snooty. This is the first place that wouldn't let me keep the bike in the room. Maybe Aspen isn't a fine fit for me on this trip. The good news is that I feel good enough to try crossing the Continental Divide if the weather holds off.

The ride from Silt to Aspen gained altitude so gradually that the wind was more of a problem than the climb. I stayed on the side roads for the morning and got to pass through some nice, quiet, tree lined vignettes. Branches arching over the road made such a nice pocket of peace. The valley seemed to be much greener as I made my way along. Soon I was seeing a lot more trees. Mostly I was seeing a lot more trees bending in the headwind. There definitely wasn't any dust left on those leaves. They were pretty and the headwind didn't bother me as much as before. It still slowed me down a bit. I was fairly confident because I thought it would die down before lunch time.

The side road eventually ran out of room to run when the valley got narrow. All of the traffic, including me, got funneled down to the Interstate. All of the air got funneled as well. The headwinds became a real challenge. It even gave me the opportunity to do some road cleanup. My progress against the wind was so slow that I welcomed any excuse to take a break. Someone had lost a load of wire fencing in the on ramp. It was no big deal to stop and get it out of the way. I never realized how big the fencing industry must be until I went on this ride. It's everywhere.

It wasn't long before I noticed signs of a larger city coming up. There was a car dealership that was larger than some of the towns that I had been through. Not really, but it seemed that way. I was surprised and glad to come across a rest area bordered by shade trees. So many of the rest areas had been out there where there wasn't enough rain to grow much of anything. This area along the river was nice and green. I didn't spend much time there because I still thought I had a long way to go. Beside, the gardener was making enough noise to obliterate the "rest" part of the rest area. As I got back on the bike and came around the trees I saw the sign for Glenwood Springs. I was within a couple of miles of the turnoff for Aspen and hadn't known it. I was already on the outskirts of town.

I don't think that I had heard of this town before. That's a surprise considering how pretty it is. It looks to be well laid out for pedestrians and they have an amazingly tempting hot springs right by the river, which is right by a nice downtown. I don't know if most folks there think their main claim to fame is being the turnoff to Aspen, but to me it looked like a fine destination in its own right. Maybe if I had known it was so nice I would have pushed on from Silt.

Alas, I had to keep going. It was early in the day and I had a good chance of getting to Aspen. I had expected the side valley to be narrower and tougher. Instead the valley broadened. The colors in the rocks were wonderful and the Aspens had great color. The picture was one of red and brown set off by green and gold. The road did get steeper but it wasn't too bad. It's not like I could coast uphill or anything but I was able to set a nice pace and comfortably cover a lot of ground. I did take the opportunity to sit down and grab a burger and an enormous drink. It was good to feel well enough to take on the climb. The aches and pains were holding off. Maybe the better job of eating and drinking and taking more breaks was paying off. I was getting more of my confidence back.

It was obvious that there was a lot of money running around the area. The houses were nicer. The frequency of designer houses had definitely increased and there were more luxury cars running around. What I was more impressed with though was that the rest of the homes were nicer too. I'm not saying that there weren't any places that were rundown but there seemed to be a much smaller percentage than in some other places I had been. It looked like everyone was that much better off. Their yards were better tended and the houses looked like someone was caring for them. There weren't as many drab places being overgrown with uncut grass and weed trees. The neighborhoods looked like nice places to live.

The valley had straightened out and presented me with wonderful views up into the Rockies. I really felt that I was slipping past the foothills and making my way into the mountains. The snowy highlights on the ridgetops emphasized the point. They also emphasized that it was cold up there and was as likely to get more snow, as it was to have it all melt off. Considering the clouds that I was riding under, the snow looked like the more likely bet. Despite the weather I liked that kind of country. I could see why a lot of people have places up here. I wonder what the old time locals think. Do they feel the same way about the new folks as the old timers did in Grand Junction? Immigrants are rarely welcomed with open arms when they show up in great numbers. It doesn't seem to matter if they are poor and crossing the border to compete for jobs or rich and gentrifying their adopted hometown.

Just about the time I was getting cold and tired I happened upon a funky food store. I won't call it a mini-mart because it looked to have been around way before that notion developed. It didn't seem to have as much as a full grocery though it did have a lot of food. What really set it apart were all the knickknacks that were all over the place. Some were for sale. Some were part of the scenery. It was hard to tell the difference but after seeing the soda counter for sale I realized that I could probably make an offer on anything in the place and they would be willing to negotiate. One thing I had liked about getting to Colorado was that no one thought twice about a guy walking around their store in bike tights. It was good and comforting to feel somewhat mainstream again.

The road to Aspen was almost always a fine one for bicycles. Unfortunately, those places where it was not fine were downright hazardous. At times I was riding on nice wide shoulders beside a four lane highway. Every once in a while though the local geology would neck down into a pinch point that gave the road designers little or no option. The road would suddenly narrow to two lanes and no shoulder. There was the road and a ditch. The Colorado bike map had indicated that something was bad along that stretch. I was glad that I was on a mountain bike. Whenever I thought I heard something coming up from behind and could see traffic coming from the opposite direction I wouldn't even look back, I would just steer into the gravel and try to keep from sliding farther into the ditch.

Luckily the adrenaline didn't have to stay pumped for long. I soon found myself coming into the outskirts of Aspen. And what did I see but my frequent companion: road construction. These folks were busy getting ready for the ski season I guess. The place was a mess. I noticed that there was a police car sitting off on the side of the road. I hadn't found much good advice from the folks in bike shops along the ride so far so I decided to try the local constable. This guy was great. He was bored sitting there. All he had to do was slow down traffic and all that took was parking his car on the side of the road with him in it. Not only did he tell me how to get into town more safely; he even gave me a fairly detailed rundown on the road from Aspen to the Pass. He was even able to give me the mileposts for some of the things to look out for. That was probably the best data dump on road conditions of the whole trip.

Aspen is part of a whole other world. I've been in other such enclaves. They have an amazing array of amenities and an amazing cost of living. From what I could gather, a lot of folks who work there live down in the valley and have a long commute, or live up in Aspen but share a house with a lot of other workers. For all of its money, it wasn't making my life as relaxing as it could have been. This was also the city with the most signs saying don't do this, or don't do that. I probably wouldn't have noticed it if I hadn't just come from relaxed places like Grand Junction and Silt. It was a large culture shock. Of course if I was up there during ski season and didn't have to worry the cost, I might never notice the difference either. The lifts rise right out of town and I like that. Maybe I'll go back when things are whiter.

Finding a hotel was tougher and that was not a surprise. There were lots of them to choose from but they weren't going to be laid out like the ones along the Interstate. Some even had valets and doormen, which was something I wasn't used to. I decided to use the visitor center to make reservations. That was a first for me. The uptightness was evident in the hotels too. It wasn't a forgone conclusion that I could just take the bike into the room. When I finally got a reservation, it was in a place that offered a compromise for storing my bike. I tried their solution, which was a broom closet. I ended up parking it outside in the rain. It may have been the most expensive room I stayed in on the whole trip but it was far from being the most comfortable or having the best service. Being up there for ski season was probably quite a bit better.

While at the Visitor Center I was dealt a large unofficial informal cautionary note. The woman working behind the counter heard that I was planning to ride over Independence Pass. She figured that I should know that her husband had been killed on his bike while riding through the Pass just a few years ago. Then she told me that it would probably be alright and that I shouldn't worry. Imagine my relief.

That night I roamed around town and shopped for spare bike parts. I could find very high end components and fancy clothes but I couldn't find a good bike tire. My bike hat was being held together by radiator hose tape. I bought a new, and of course more expensive, one. Ironically the hat was made in Seattle.

My body was feeling just good enough and the weather was just acceptable enough that I went to bed thinking that I would try climbing the rest of the Rockies the next day.

September 29   Aspen to Buena Vista

Well this is the day for crossing the Continental Divide. A light rain and 44 degrees F sounds a lot like Seattle. Of course in Seattle I usually don't climb 4,000 feet on the bike in such weather. I figure that I might as well try it because the trip back into Aspen would all be a downhill steeper than anything I've seen for a few days.

The amount of traffic and the size of road drop dramatically past Aspen. This is one of those roads that they don't keep open in the Winter. Evidently the ground isn't quite stable either and there is talk in town about letting the road close itself for good. That's their debate. Once on the road it is obvious that it is a tough road to maintain. In some places it goes down to one lane and the rocks have left dents in the surface from when they have landed on it.

This area feels very familiar. Back in Glenwood Springs the rocks were still very red and looking like the Southwest. Up above Aspen it begins to look like Washington State's high country. The trees are tall conifers and the road is passing along a mountain stream that is cascading over big smooth boulders. The only changes necessary is to remember that this is at 10,000 feet in Colorado instead of 5,000 in Washington and that the Fall colors are from the Aspens and not the Larches.

Near the pass the altitude effects become much more important. This is essentially like bicycling over Mt Adams. It becomes much more necessary to stop and catch a breath. Out of Silt I would stop about every five miles. Up near the Pass the stops are about 5 times per mile.

The views are impressive. I could see the clouds playing with the mountaintops. Eventually there is some sleet but it luckily doesn't amount to much.

Lo and behold at the Pass I come across other cyclists. A group from Colorado Springs is bicycling up the Pass from the other side. They are having all of their stuff carried by a big rental truck from which they offer me free food. It is nice finding a surprise party going on at the Pass. That is a fine way to celebrate crossing the Divide. It is cold and windy though and there is a lot of miles to lodging so it is time to continue.

It is almost downhill all the way to Buena Vista. On almost all of the downhills there are a few bumps that have to be climbed. This ride is no different except that I am tired after climbing 4,000 at such an altitude. This side of the mountains is beautiful as well and again reminds me of Washington. I even find a deli that could be right at home in Roslyn.

I had to try crossing the Continental Divide. It didn't seem to make much sense to bicycle 1,400 miles and stop 20 miles away from one of the biggest milestones of the trip. My body was feeling just well enough and the weather was just barely warm enough for me to take a crack at the climb. Besides, the main reason for picking the route through Aspen had been the closeness of the Pass to the town. If I wanted to turn around before the Pass, I could coast back into a resort town within an hour. Turning around for home in Aspen would mean picking up the route there when I returned. As sore as I was, I was acclimated to the altitude and my muscles were in their best condition. Starting fresh from Aspen after the ski season would mean plopping myself down at 8,000 feet after a Winter of very little road work. I decided it would be easier to just go for it right then and there.

The closest place to stay on the other side of the Pass was booked solid for a wedding. I knew that I was going to have to travel 40 miles past the Pass to get to an open motel. It looked like it was going to be a long day so I got up early. With that much work ahead of me I wanted to fuel up with an omelet, some bacon and lots of fluids.

In addition to food I was delivered a lesson in cultural diversity for breakfast. The nicely attired and mannered waiter was from Mexico. I had talked to a lot of folks that worked in town and noticed that most of them were from other countries. I was fascinated by the difference between where they were from and what it was like to work in Aspen. I saw no reason not to ask him about what life in Aspen had been like for him as long as I was polite about it. His response showed a crack in his façade. He wanted to know if I spoke Spanish. I don't and he took a superior tone for his having learned English. He told me how Spanish will become the new second language so every one should learn it. I pointed out that I've had more reason to learn German, Russian and Japanese, though I am terrible at all of them. He said that the other languages were useless. Spanish was the only language that made sense for any American to learn. Frequently I have heard commentators chastise folks from the United States for a lack of cultural sensitivity. Evidently we are not alone. There are others out there for whom the only important culture is theirs. It is actually a little scary. It may not have made for a pleasant breakfast but it was memorable.

I had stayed on the side of town closest to the Pass. Anything I could do to shorten the trip up the Pass was a good thing. The Pass was twenty miles away and 4,000 feet up. I was starting at 8,000 feet and would be watching for the effects of altitude. Since I had left Silt, each time the road went through a town the road seemed to steepen. Aspen was no different. What was different was that I passed the gate that they use to close the road in the Winter. After that gate the road narrowed and steepened even more. There was hardly any traffic to speak of but then again I was headed out of town just after sunrise. Even though I was past the gate and above the town, there were still some large estates scattered around the valley. Are those folks stranded in the Winter, equipped with awesome Winter travel skills, or are the houses abandoned and only used after the thaw each year? Soon enough though they were left behind as well.

The valley floor was climbing up to the snow. I hadn't reached the snow yet, but it was on all of the hills around me. That was another one of those times when if I wasn't worried about hypothermia I probably would have enjoyed the view much more. As it was I enjoyed the view. It was that nice. The Aspens were near their golden peak. I like spending time up in the mountains as weather comes in as long as I am safe. Unfortunately progress, safety, and security were over forty miles away so I couldn't sit still and enjoy the view for very long.

I started to think about how tough living up there would be and soon had evidence of how tough a task that is. Independence Pass is named after the town of Independence that was founded below it on Independence Day back in the 1800's. That's what I recall from the historical marker. There's a wide spot in the shoulder there that looks down on what is effectively a ghost town. They had come to mine and did so for a while. But they are all gone now. The buildings are small and strewn around the valley in what is now a picturesque setting. The snow must have buried them every year. Maybe it was a seasonal settlement. In any case, I imagine that when the mines started having trouble it was easy to decide to live somewhere less picturesque and a little less life threatening.

One reason that traffic had been light might have been the sign back at the gate. Supposedly the road is limited to vehicles less than about 35 feet long. As I was getting ready to leave the ghost town, a very long trailer pulled off the road and onto the shoulder. There was plenty of room so that wasn't a problem but I hadn't expected to see something that big on that road. I figured the driver either didn't see the sign or figured that the road couldn't be that bad. He got out of his cab and came over to me hunting for help. He wasn't familiar with the road and realized that he may have gotten himself into something that he couldn't get back out of. He was a little disillusioned to hear that I was not a local. Evidently I knew enough to quell his fears. All I did was parrot back what I had heard from the police officer the previous day and from what Kaye had gleamed from the software when we were working out my route. We were only six miles from the Pass. That seemed a lot closer to him than it did to me but that wasn't a surprise. As long as he didn't get stuck in the couple of places where the road went down to one lane, he should be able to get through alright. I realized later why he was so worried. The truck wasn't his. He was supposed to be driving some equipment to a job site. He would have a lot of explaining to do, and maybe lose his job, if he got stuck in the Pass. I am glad that he didn't have a problem but if he had I might have been in a tight spot trying to get around him.

The country turned into the kind of high alpine that I am familiar with. The difference is that in Washington State, this kind of country is at 5,000 feet or 6,000 feet and there aren't any roads. Above Aspen the terrain was alpine at 10,000 feet and I still had 2,000 more feet to climb. Back home at 10,000 feet there is snow, rocks and ice and not much else. I guess that's the difference that a few degrees of latitude can make. It was pretty. The twisty streams with some stout conifers and every rock smoothed over made for a nice series of gardens.

It was in the midst of the alpine areas that the road had to make its way through some rocky terrain. The road did just what the officer said it would do; it went down to one lane with no shoulder with no way to see if anyone was coming. Sprinting uphill at 10,000 feet didn't really speed me up much. I wanted to get through that section as quickly as possible, but it was hard to gain much speed. I was so glad that the only car coming through was one of the more sane ones. They actually seemed to be watching where they were going. I appreciated that.

Once past the other choke point, the valley opened up again. The trees thinned out and the views expanded. I had gotten to the altitude where the weather wasn't good enough to let the trees grow. I was at 11,000 feet and I wasn't done climbing. The valley was broad and open enough that I could see the road creeping its way up the opposite side of the hill. It was getting colder and my heart and lungs felt the effects of the altitude. I'd spent enough time at these altitudes to know what was happening and how to counter it, but I hadn't spent so much time high up that it didn't affect me. I had to stop a few times every mile to give my heart a chance to get back inside my chest again. After pedaling a few hundred yards, my heart would start beating heavily and I would have to work a lot harder at getting a breath. I wasn't in a race though so all I had to do was nibble away at the hill. It wasn't going to get any taller and I wasn't going to lose ground while I took a break so I just kept alternating resting and riding.

As I turned into the last two miles of the climb the road lost its shoulder and replaced it with a steep drop. That meant taking rests where I could rather than when I wanted to. I made one exception. Coming down the hill was another bicyclist. I had to have this guy's story: how far he had ridden, what the road was like, etc. I thought that I would be cheating him out of his roller coaster ride, but he surprised me by being happy for an excuse to stop. As soon as we started talking he jammed his hands into his pockets. Evidently he didn't have the right gloves for riding in such cold weather and the wind chill heading downhill was freezing his fingers. I had more cold weather gear than he did and I was cold. He didn't have any place to store anything like more clothes so I just assumed that he had ridden up the hill before me and was headed back down to breakfast. Instead, he told me that he had come in from Colorado Springs. I felt like such a wuss to be relying on so much gear when he was getting by with just the clothes he had on. He started to warm up. I started to cool off. So we both wished each other good luck and got back on our bikes. After we went our separate ways I saw a few more riders. They didn't seem interested in stopping and talking so I guessed that they were his friends and might be having an informal race.

At the Pass I saw the rest of the group. In the midst of a barren windswept saddle in the ridge, there is a parking lot for folks who want to stop and take in the views from 12,000 feet. I had made the

Continental Divide at Independence Pass and found a party. It was a crowd from one of the colleges in Colorado. Every year they get thirty some odd people to ride for a few days from Eastern Colorado, over Independence Pass, and into Aspen. They were on the last day of their trip and it would be all downhill from there. They were a very happy, tired and cold crowd. One of them came over to me thinking that I was one of the crowd who had gotten turned around or something. When he found out what I was doing he led me right over to their food supply and started offering me cinnamon rolls, water, anything that I wanted. Free food at 12,000 feet after hours of bicycling was marvelous. All of my other milestones had been celebrated on my own. The biggest and highest was the one that I got to share with a bunch of generous and sympathetic souls.

They told me the story of how their ride is actually subsidized by the parents of a student who had died on the ride years ago. As much as they had mourned their child's death, they didn't want it to discourage others from getting out there. In memory of their child they subsidized the ride each year. I was so tired that I might not have the story completely right but it was so refreshing to hear that some folks out there still look to the bigger picture. They had acknowledged the tragedy and had encouraged others to continue on. I know that I feel that way. Everything involves risk and the only way to remove risk is to not live. Considering the option, I'll take the risks. The pragmatic side of me always chimes in at that point by telling me to not be stupid about it though.

It was hard to imagine that I had made it that far. So many times along the way I would cross a state border or a time zone, but it all seemed just another turn of the pedals along the way. The Continental Divide was hard to ignore. From there to either coast I wouldn't have to cross anything higher than this point. I hadn't made it before the snows, but I had made it before Winter. From there on in I would still have to worry about a lot of things but I wouldn't have to worry about the route being shut down in front of me for the season. I wouldn't have to worry about being stranded in the mountains. And I hoped that I would be making my way into the heart of the country where there were more people to talk to and maybe some easier roads ahead. I had crossed the Continental Divide and even water would eventually make it to the Mississippi from here. All it took was persistence.

I took a couple of pictures. As much as I would have liked to celebrate more, I had forty miles to go. I knew that even though I was going to get to play with a long downhill ride, I was still going to have to do some pedaling and some work somewhere along the line.

Instead of a nice long downhill grade for forty miles, I was treated to a road more like a bumpy bobsled run. A lot of that hard earned altitude zipped on by on the other side of the Pass. My brakes got more of a workout than I had expected. The road was as windy as mountain roads are supposed to be and it was far from smooth. I lost a lot of energy keeping the speed down so I could make the turns and not ruin a rim on the bumps. The sky was clearing on the east side of the mountains and I felt that I was leaving Winter behind me. At least the drop in altitude meant a nice bump in temperature. Kaye and I actually got a lesson in how much one can trust references at this point. We didn't believe it but we had found a reference that claimed that there was a place to stay at the Pass. Unless they meant the outhouse I feel they were sadly mistaken. I am glad we both had some healthy skepticism about that particular data point.

The area felt like it was in the midst of Fall. Which it was, but that was unique for the trip so far. Every other place had decided to be in either Summer or Winter. Only the trees and the hunters knew it was Autumn. There were a few times riding down that valley that I got engrossed enough with the views that I didn't see the bumps in the road. I should have been more vigilant but nothing broke and I had earned a bit of a celebration.

Finally I got down to where the valley broadened out enough to house a couple of lakes. There were lodgings there but a wedding party had booked the entire town. It was a beautiful sight down by the lake with the Aspens in gold and the mountains on the other side with snow along their crest. The lodgings weren't available but the restaurant was open for another hour or so. Even they were closing early for the wedding. I would have been happy with a burger and some fries but what I found was a gourmet meal. It was some kind of fancy sandwich with an artistic garnish on the plate. That made for a true celebration. Good food and a good view. I took the time to call my friends during their regular Friday lunch. I think I had the better lunch spot by far.

I made a few other phone calls as well. One was to my Dad and one was to Kaye. It was good to hear folks that I knew. They were prouder and more relieved than I had expected. Evidently there were a few folks worried about me.

I was right about having to climb a bit more. The road around the lake was not flat but soon enough I was headed down the other side and into the valley made by the Arkansas River.

Western Colorado had definitely been touristy. I had expected the east side of the Rockies to be more rural and productive. Well I got that one wrong. All along the river were signs for white water rafting and fly fishing trips. Evidently the tourism industry was as busy on both sides of the mountains. That was fine by me. The tourism business made it easier for me to find lodging. I was in a valley with fourteen thousand foot peaks edging it. That was awesome country. When I finally stopped for the night I was near some of the best food on the trip, had a chance to shop in an impressive outdoor gear store, and had beaten the weather. Looking back where I had come through, I could see the clouds in the mountains. They had built to thunderheads and I was glad to be out from under them. I was even warming up which was a nice treat. The only downside was a spillover of snootiness from Aspen. This was the only other place in America where I would find that I could not put my bike in my room. Luckily the competitor across the street saw no problem with it and wondered about how silly the other motel had been. This was a tourist town for outdoor recreation. They felt that a little dirt wasn't all that bad and my bike wasn't even dirty. The food was good too. I enjoyed the wild game medallions I had for dinner. They were pricey and fine. It was a nice way to end the day.

Already I was starting to wonder if I would finish by our wedding anniversary on October 24th. My progress had been slower than expected and I was having doubts about how far my bike, body, wallet and calendar would allow me to go. Thinking about it wouldn't change anything. All I could do was pedal, eat, sleep, and repeat until I ran out of time, money, or luck.

September 30   Buena Vista to Canon (pronounced Canyon) City

More downhill today. The climb up to the Pass gained so much altitude that it will be a few days before I lose it all. Starting at 8,000 feet is chilly but the tail wind is nice and the air is clear.

This is a pretty valley. Colorado has a large number of peaks that reach over 14,000 feet. They aren't as impressive as Mt. Rainier, but they are neat to look at and they line the road for the first few hours. River rafting is also big business around here, though probably not at this time of year. There are a few farms around but the prices for food and lodging are definitely those of a tourist area.

This is the sort of ride that I wish I had more often. Nice weather, good road, pretty views, and downhill. In the afternoon the valley narrows again and the road dives down into a canyon. Road construction rears its ugly head but with a bit of patience and allowing everyone else to go first, I make it through alright.

The day ends in Canon City. The valley broadens out and it is back to rural businesses and life style. The hotels are not to be known for comfort, but for convenience. The one I stayed in was convenient to the highway and the train tracks. There is even a sign in the room apologizing for the train whistles that one might hear in the middle of the night. Oh boy.

There actually is one tourist attraction in Canon City: the Colorado Prison Museum. Evidently this town has a number of correctional facilities around it and they are "celebrated" in a museum. I skip this one.

Buena Vista ends up being a surprise. I had expected a rural community and instead I find myself in a valley that caters to fly fishing and mountain climbing. Not bad.

It was another chilly morning but it was a pretty one. The mountains seemed to be passing in review. The tallest ones had signs on the road pointing off to them. Evidently peak bagging is a popular pastime around here. The goal is to get to the top of all the mountains that peak out at over 14,000 feet. Each time I passed one of the signs or a road that led up to the mountain I found myself guessing how hard it would be to climb it. At least these are not volcanoes waiting to blow up but the altitude problems would still be there. Maybe I'll be back some day.

It was only in fantasies that I could expect to spend every day rolling downhill. I started at sea level and intended to end at sea level so for every up there would be a down. With that in mind, I was going to cherish riding downhill for a few days. The first day would be the best. I would drop 3,000 feet in one day. I was so glad that the downhill happened while going through such appealing country with such nice weather. After all of my recent struggles, it was nice to sit back and watch the world roll by. Oddly enough, I started to see signs petitioning folks to vote against a dam of some sort. Maybe it was meant as a joke, but someone sounded worried that the valley would become someone's water project. It would be made into a big lake and dam. As a country we've done some stupider things than that. To me it looked like a place to visit, not flood.

By the end of the morning I was back on the original route that I had planned out before I left Seattle. I passed through the town of Salida. Salida struck me as the quintessential small Western town. A lot of that had to do with the kid's ball game I passed by in the morning. The kids were out on the field and the parents had backed their pickup trucks up to the field so they can sit in the back and watch the kids play. It looked to be a regular event because folks were comfortably settled in with lawn chairs and coolers. The town was undoubtedly larger than what I rode through so there may be a more modern downtown somewhere else. What I got to see were a few blocks of normal houses beside a downtown area of one or two story businesses. Everything looked to have been there for a few decades at least. It seemed to be a nice, comfortable, and quiet town with the mountains and river nearby.

The valley had been fairly broad but east of town it started to narrow. It was getting ready for the last run down a canyon that I would have on the ride. I was surprised that when the two valleys met, they formed a valley that was smaller rather than larger. That canyon was a lot like the others. The terrain seemed to be drying out for the occasion. There were still trees around but they were fewer, smaller, and more gnarly. Luckily the winds were heading down the canyon. They weren't enough to keep me from having to pedal but they did help. As usual there was road construction and it seemed like every highway crew was out there trying to get the road finished before Winter. I couldn't say that I blamed them, but it was getting old. Still, keeping a bit of patience was really all I needed to get past all of that: find a bottleneck, wait for traffic, sprint like mad, take a break, and ride to the next bottleneck. The one rest area I found supposedly had views of BigHorn Sheep. I didn't get to see any. At least it was a more comfortable rest stop than usual. There were picnic tables with shade, wind protection, views and a restroom. Usually my breaks were spent sitting on a guardrail.

Rivers passing through canyons are not always kind enough to leave enough room for a road. Frequently that meant that riding in the canyons would be interrupted by the need to follow the road up and over some outcropping that was too hard to build a road around. So much for riding downhill all day long. The land was pretty but I missed the mountains. I didn't expect to see any crags for the rest of the trip.

Coming out of the canyon the land opened up again. The last little bit was a fast downhill into town. In Cañon City the tourist trade seemed to have vanished. Except for the prisons and their museum, the primary occupations seemed to be farming and ranching. The rail yard and the truck traffic were both busy. The winds had picked up too. I considered riding on ahead. It looked to be another twenty mile an hour tailwind brewing up. Because it was late in the day, I talked to a bicyclist in town before continuing. He cautioned me that the road ahead was hilly enough that if the winds turned around I might have a rough time getting to the next motel. That was a good enough assessment for me. I decided to stay the night.

I was now committed to riding to Kansas. I didn't see any reason to stop. The next few days should be easier riding and would give my body a chance to heal. The thoughts of quitting subsided.

I wouldn't be on Interstates for a while. They were passing either north or south of my route between there and Wichita. I was heading into the land of the right angle road maps. I could go east or south, but not at the same time. In any case I needed a map of Kansas. I hadn't picked one up back in Ogden because I didn't want to carry something that I might not get around to using. Kansas was the next state over yet I couldn't find a map of it. Either no one needed a map to get there or no one went there. Maybe once I was past Pueblo I would find one.

Even though there was the warning of train whistles in the night, I was glad that I only had to listen to the highway traffic. Since having crossed the Cascades back in Washington, I got used to being serenaded by the sound of big dual axle diesel pickup trucks starting up in the morning. I didn't appreciate that type of wakeup call, but at least the trucks were there because someone needed them. These were folks who actually needed something that was big, powerful and useful. There are so many pickups that are nothing more than oversized toys. Waking up before dawn because of someone's need to impress themself with the amount of noise that they can make would have been much harder to tolerate.

The weather was cranking back up to record temperatures. It was supposed to make it into the 90's in Pueblo. My joints still ached. The weather was a trial. So much of the approaching terrain sounded like drudgery. Even the logistics were potentially a problem. The motels were just too spread out. I was past the Continental Divide but the trip ahead looked like it would have some old challenges and some new ones as well. I was finding that I wasn't drawn to Key West as much as I was drawn to Seattle and my friends. It just happened that my route back home took me through Florida. I think a lot of folks were surprised that I wasn't going through withdrawal from having been deprived of my daily Internet fix. It was refreshing to realize that people were still more appealing than electrons. I was tired of TV. A good book held much more appeal. Finding one was the hard part.

October 1   Canon City to La Junta

Well the road is still heading downhill though the slope is decreasing. The tail winds are still there though so by morning I am in Pueblo in one of the fastest segments so far. Rather than stop so soon I decide to continue on to La Junta. On the other side of Pueblo the land flattens out and the road straightens. This is rural flat land. Any trace of the city has been left behind. It is quieter and compared to Eastern Utah it is pleasantly populated. I can count on finding small shops and restaurants along the way. It is nice not having to carry an entire day's worth of food in the morning.

Getting into the lowlands has the price of getting back into the heat again. The heat was actually showing up in Canon City as well. It tends to make me stop just a bit earlier than I could. I'm just too acclimated to Seattle I guess.

The people have definitely changed as well. I get a much more reserved reaction from folks when I walk into the stores and such. The bike clothes don't help but I am sure that they would react this way even if I got out of a car. I am just not one of them and they know it.

La Junta is a large enough town to have a few motels but otherwise it is just another stop for me.

The previous afternoon I had considered continuing on into Pueblo. I am glad that I didn't. My euphoria from such a nice day's ride probably would have died after the second set of hills. I would have been a hurting unit come morning. Instead I had a good ride and a nice rest. My body and especially my joints seemed to be getting better too. It was good to feel that my body wasn't about to quit on me.

I was treated to an early morning ride past the prisons. Every correctional facility I had passed had warning signs posted about stopping for hitchhikers. Obviously they were worried about escaped prisoners. I kept wondering if an escaped prisoner would try to hijack my bicycle. I suspect a convict on a bicycle would stand out and have a very slow getaway. I wasn't worried about it but there wasn't a lot else to think about out there.

The road crossed rolling hills just like I had been told. The tailwind was wonderful. It wasn't possible to ride downhill every day but given enough patience, every day could be a tailwind day. I no longer felt the pressure to get over the Rockies, but I felt the pressure to finish before the holiday season. Originally the ride had been planned for the Spring so as I went farther the days would get longer and if it took more days it just meant having to compete with other tourists for motel rooms. Riding in the Fall meant I was losing daylight for every day I was on the road, and running out of time back home to prepare for the holidays. I wasn't sure what date I would consider too late to go on but I knew that picking one would make Kaye's life a lot easier. She didn't know when I would be home. Neither did I. I was on the downhill run to the Mississippi and if the weather cooperated I could eat up a lot of miles. Until I traveled a few days on the east side of the mountains though I wouldn't know if my daily mileage would change enough to make a difference. The only way to find out was to ride.

Pueblo came up on me faster than I had expected. The tailwind made small work out of the hills. I was pumped when I found myself on the outskirts of town. It wasn't even noon yet. My goal and desire had been to make my way through big cities on Sundays. I didn't want to have to navigate city streets or traffic during the workweek. Sometimes it was inevitable but in Pueblo the timing worked fine. I was able to make it through the city before lunch was over. It wasn't much of a visit. I saw a bit of the Interstate and was right back out of town again. East of town the road put one more hill in my way and after that the land flattened out and started a straight shot to Kansas.

I didn't think I would have much trouble getting to La Junta by nightfall so I stopped for a rare sit down lunch. It wasn't anything special: just a burger and fries and a lot of fluids. It was getting hot outside and I wanted enough fluids and fuel to make it to La Junta. The heat was rising and I didn't want to get dehydrated again. When I stepped inside the restaurant I watched a lot of folks make some quick judgements of me. I was too hungry to be concerned about it. It seemed that everyone in the place knew each other and a lot of them had just come from church. Either that or they dress for lunch. I had learned so far that even though most folks didn't know what to think of a guy in bike clothes, they also didn't know what to do either, so as usual they just left me alone. Whenever that happened I got to see how different people could be. The contrast between their side where they are sizing someone up and their side that was comfortable around their friends was easy for me to watch. By the time I had been there a while, they would have completely forgotten about me. I felt like an anthropologist studying a foreign culture. Well, I don't know any anthropologists, but I guess it was fair to say that I was interested in the other cultures within the United States. People frequently talk about cultural diversity as if it was something based on what country someone immigrated from. I think that there is an enormous cultural diversity within our own country that we frequently ignore or ridicule. All I cared about was getting some lunch and taking a break.

The rest of the day was hot again but the tailwind was sweet and the land was flat. What a wonderful way to travel. There wasn't much in the way of places to stay but the land was busier. More people were living there and there was vegetation about. The area felt much more comfortable. If something stopped me for the night I at least felt that I wouldn't have to go far to find some good soul who would let me sleep on their property.

The next day's hop looked like it would be through another area without many motels. According to the information I had, there was a short day to Lamar or a very long day into Kansas. I'd let the weather and my body decide how far I would go. If I stopped it would be to stay in a place called the Cow Palace. Now there's a place to stop in just for the name.

My simple estimate of the day's mileage put it at over 100 miles. No wonder I felt tired.

October 2   La Junta to Holly

I hadn't mentioned it before, but I am following the Arkansas River and the Santa Fe Trail for a while now. This route looks easier that the Oregon Trail was but I am not seeing it from a covered wagon either. The road is long low and rolling. I make good time and end up in my original destination of the "Cow Palace" in Lamar just in time for lunch. Since I got there so early I checked the Yellow pages and found another place to stay about 30 miles closer to Kansas. That is handy because otherwise the trip to Garden City would be a 100 mile day.

I go for it and find Holly, Colorado is a one motel, three churches, small town that looks like it came right out of some Hollywood movie. This feels like 1965. Just to get the feel for the place, the train station still looks good and aside from the churches and the bank is one of the best kept buildings in the town.

Dessert is a milk shake that they are happy to add any flavor to, but the only ice cream available is chocolate. I decide on a chocolate shake.

The best news is that I am four miles from the Kansas border and that feels like progress.

The road remained fairly flat though it started to get a bit more rolling as I got close to Kansas. Even though it was a workday, traffic was fairly light. It wasn't like things were deserted though. The area was definitely busy with farms and such. I was headed for the city of Lamar. It wasn't very far and seemed to have a lot of motels to pick from. After that would be the long haul to Garden City in Kansas.

I was still losing some of the altitude I had gained in the first half of the trip. As a matter of fact I was losing it faster than I had gained it. From La Junta to the Mississippi was a low gradual slope that very soon was going to be so shallow that it would not be much help. The rivers were slowing and spreading. With all of the farming going on it even looked like the irrigation systems might just drain the river before it got a chance to get anywhere.

Surprise! It's the Santa Fe Trail. I always pictured it as being much farther south than Colorado. Maybe I was just farther south than I realized. Pioneers that went through that stretch of trail may have had it easier than those on the bit of the Oregon Trail that I had seen. There wasn't as much terrain to avoid and there seemed to be more water. Of course, maybe that stretch would have been the early part of the trail where folks were still fresh. Despite that, I am sure it was tough enough. There weren't many landmarks around to give a sense of progress. Now there are cell phone towers, water tanks, and grain elevators.

There must be some ranching going on around this part of the country; otherwise, why call a motel the Cow Palace? The Cow Palace was much larger than a lot of the motels that I had come across. I would have been happy to stay there but first I decided to have lunch. I seemed to raise a few eyebrows in the restaurant again. At least the service was fine and so was the food. I could have done the buffet but the idea of sitting still while someone brought me a large iced tea and a club sandwich sounded great.

The various guide books, software and such may have a lot of stuff in them but it still was handy sometimes to pick up the phone book and see what's out there. Low tech still has a place in the world. Flipping through the book after lunch I was truly surprised to find a motel in Holly, Colorado that would be within four miles of the Kansas border. It would have been nice to have gotten into Kansas so I could claim another milestone. I was happy enough to make good progress through a nice afternoon. So I left Lamar and headed to Holly. That cut the next day's distance to Garden City down to 70 miles. Seventy miles sounded a lot better than the original plan of a hundred mile day. Every time I found such a motel in a small town I made sure that they were easy to find and that I could walk to dinner and breakfast. Having to get around at night on the bike would have been just too much and I didn't want to ride in the dark. Walking was a much better and safer idea. Everything sounded fine.

Getting into Holly was a pleasant enough ride through farmland on reasonably flat roads in reasonably good weather. I am glad that I got there with enough time to wander around for a while. Besides, it was a good opportunity to get some grocery shopping done. The town seemed dated and I suspect it was what stores used to be like. None of them were very large but each carried just what they thought you might need. Of course they were keeping the needs of their neighbors in mind, not the needs of a passing bicyclist. It was still a good excuse to go and poke around town. The store fronts didn't look like they'd changed recently. They were being kept up well enough and one was getting a new facade, but for the most part, each was unique if old. They didn't have the homogenized feel of so many of the strip malls that I have seen. Maybe it was homogenized in its time. Now they have character. The places that were kept up the best were the post office, bank, churches and of all things the train station. It looked just like the one I have for my model train set that we used to put up at Christmas. The town was alive. I wouldn't say that it was lively like a party going on all the time, but people were out and about getting things done or relaxing at the end of the day. So many places that I had gone through were too quiet. In some places, everyone seemed to be indoors. It was almost like they were afraid to go outside. There was no interaction. I would just pass through without leaving a trace or an impression. It could feel like a museum exhibit. In Holly, the people seemed to be more of a community. Just walking around I got a feel for what was happening. That was a welcome change from some sanitized towns that I'd breezed through.

What I couldn't get a feel for was whether the businesses were defending the old status quo, striving to change, or just doing just as well as need be. The national chain stores in small towns stood out like brand new plastic beside venerable old brick. They were new, slick, and sanitized. The chain stores didn't have the character of the old stores but they did have better selection, better service, and made it easier to find things. The character of the old stores was something to be proud of but I could see from a business point of view why the chains were winning while the Mom and Pop's were losing. Character is great but unless it means higher profits, it might not pay for itself.

While it was a big enough town, I found that I had misunderstood the restaurant situation. Instead of being about three or so blocks away the restaurants were more like ten blocks from the motel. That put me on the other side of town. It was a little disconcerting to go walking in search of dinner and realize that before you're at the restaurant you can already see past the last building on the opposite side of town. The one where they served sit down meals was closed for the night so I ended up with dinner at the burger place. Because I was about to finally make it past Colorado I decided to celebrate by having a butterscotch milk shake. After I ordered it, I noticed that it was taking a lot longer than I had expected so I went back to the counter and asked about it. They had run out of milk so one of them had run over to the local mini-mart to get more. They had also noticed that they only had chocolate ice cream. They'd be happy to add butterscotch to that. I appreciated their effort and satisfied myself with a chocolate milk shake. As I walked out I also found out that neither they nor their competition was open for breakfast. It looked like the next morning was going to start off with a mini-mart breakfast.

October 3   Holly to Garden City

Well it didn't take long to get into Kansas and also into a new time zone. The new time zone is going to make it tougher to keep in touch with Kaye. Bummer.

The road is along more rolling hills. They would be considered flat by most folks in a car but any rise is much more noticeable to a bicyclist; especially one loaded down for touring.

This is definitely a working community and area. The highway traffic and businesses are for farming and ranching. Evidently it is time to bring the cattle into the feed yards. Nowadays that is done by trailers running down to the feed yards. The smell isn't too bad.

There is also a lot of corn being harvested so every once in a while there is a very wide vehicle trying to make it's way down the highway.

Garden City is very proud of the number of motels and restaurants it has. Quantity is the key here. At the front desk they make a point of telling me that there is no such thing as a quiet room in Garden City. Oh joy.

Breakfast that morning had been whatever I could pull together in the mini-mart. Not exactly high cuisine but definitely enough to get me started. The best part of breakfast was the briefing I got of the road ahead from the road crew that was having coffee in the next booth. Of course these guys were from Colorado and weren't about to be working in Kansas, but they were familiar with the road. Their briefing was fair, accurate and free. Riding into Kansas meant leaving the shoulder behind and dealing with roads that were aching for some more budget. A state line is a poor reason to stereotype people but an excellent reason to stereotype infrastructure. Whether it was because of money or priorities, Kansas' roads weren't nearly as nice as Colorado's. For the first part of the day that wasn't a problem. If there is no traffic, there can't be much of a problem.

People had told me two conflicting views of Kansas. One crowd joked that Kansas was as flat as a pancake. The other crowd countered with the claim that there were hills in the western part of the state. As usual the truth is in the middle and also depends on how you look at it. I can see how someone driving along wouldn't even notice the warp of the terrain. I doubt that the car's transmission would even have to shift gears. On the other hand the area seemed hillier than the stretch between Pueblo and La Junta. I definitely noticed it. There was just enough relief to the land to make it a bit more interesting.

Some folks seemed to head to the ridgetop for their house site. Others seemed to be getting out of the wind and giving up a bit of the view. I guess that's the same as everywhere. In West Kansas the ridges aren't very tall but they are long. The view is the wide open sky instead of craggy peaks on the horizon. Some folks look forward to being able to sit and watch the weather pass through. A good storm has some great drama to it. Personally I like seeing storms passing in front of mountains on the horizon.

The traffic had lost almost all signs of tourism. There were hardly any RVs or tour buses. Most of the vehicles were dirty and diesels of some sort. Everything seemed to be farm and ranch related. Lucky for me I went to a cow college and got used to the aroma of neighboring farm life.

I wasn't sure about which way to go through Kansas. As usual I would have preferred the Interstate but they seemed to discourage that. The route I found on the Kansas web site was on nice quiet roads, but there weren't many places to stay along that route. Instead I was on a road that was busy enough to have food and lodging but not supported well enough to have much of a shoulder. The combination of no shoulder and lots of traffic was not calming. I took to treating the whole day as one long construction zone. I loved the shoulders when they were there, and waited for traffic to clear to hop through bottlenecks when the shoulders were gone. I had hopes that the shoulder would improve as I got to the busier sections between cities within Kansas. Until then I spent a lot of time looking over my shoulder.

There wasn't much to break up the day getting into Garden City. It was a long grind and I fought the wind a bit more as the day drew by. At least it wasn't as hot as it had been. There were more clouds around and they seemed to be building. I decided not to push it past Garden City. I had hoped that if the terrain, road and weather cooperated that I could make it to Dodge City. That didn't happen. It would have been a 126 mile day and the conditions weren't right. Instead I aimed for the far side of Garden City. While I am usually not a fan of billboards, I was glad to find the ones telling me where to stay. At least I had some choices.

My hoped-for flat ride across the plains turned out to be hillier than I expected though it was a far cry from climbing anything like a mountain pass. The temperature was falling and the wind was turning to face me. The next day's weather report looked cold and gloomy. At least I had made it to Kansas and the Central Time Zone. I was missing home, bookstores, and roads that pointed towards Key West.

October 4   Garden City to Dodge City

This is a major road between two good sized cities. Unfortunately the shoulder and the road are both narrower than usual. Lots of traffic, narrow roads, and weather coming in are a bad combination. Another storm system is coming in and ahead of it the temperature is dropping and the wind is picking up. A big cold cell is coming down from Canada and they are expecting snow here in a couple of days. Ugh. My hope is that by heading east I can make it to lower elevations and closer to the perceived warmth of the Southeast. The day is a struggle.

I make it to Dodge City and yes it is the one from the Westerns. There is a bit of a tourist area devoted to it but the hotels are all on the edge of town and I fall into the first one that has a laundry. Maybe I can get some laundry done while I wait for the weather to pass.

So much for that idea. After I check in, I find that they have a laundry but no soap. Also, as I watch the Weather Channel (my favorite), I notice that the weather will be bad for the next day but even worse for the two days following that. I decide to press on to Pratt in some tough conditions and wait out some of the weather there.

In Eastern Utah there had been a whole lot of lonely. In Western Kansas there was definitely more going on but in some ways was still empty. A lot of the traffic was local and in a hurry. It was time to get the cattle to market and the trucks didn't want to slow down for anything. The vast majority of the drivers were sane and reasonable folk, but there were a few who were pushing the limits. Once or twice I had to ride off the road to miss a head-on collision with an oncoming truck. A couple of horn blasts seemed directed my way but it can be hard to tell if it was coincidence or conscious intent. They were certainly timed for maximum eardrum damage though. In either case, they dispelled the notion of quiet farm country.

Despite all of that activity, there weren't many more places for me to stop or stay. This was all land in use. I was impressed with how much food they must be harvesting. It was obvious that a lot of it heads out of town to feed the rest of us. The land seemed full and fertile. It just didn't have a lot of rest stops or restaurants. Without tourism there was not much of a need.

The day was dark and dreary with wind in my face. I knew I had to make it to Dodge. Jumping past it to the next town looked to be a problem. That next hop looked too long and I was losing speed. I felt fine but ducking out of the way of traffic slowed me down. I was going slowly but I expected to still get to town with enough time left to do my chores. Before I got there I called around to find a motel with a laundry.

That was a lot harder than I had thought it would be. As it turned out, the only motel with a laundry and rooms available was one of the first ones on my way into town.

Well so much for doing the laundry. They had a washer and dryer but they expected guests to be packing their own soap. They were kind enough to point out that I could go buy some over at the local store about two miles on the other side of town. If I had known that I wasn't going to be able to do my laundry I might have put myself up in someplace a little nicer and closer to the center of town. Oh well, those things happened.

The weather was definitely coming in. I had been rained on a bit and the temperature was dropping. On days like that at home I like to sit down and read a book while I watch the weather go by. I thought that stopping in Dodge for a day while the bad weather went through would be a good idea. That was the thought I had until I started watching the weather forecasts for the area. It sounded like it would take more than a day for the storm to pass. In the meantime I could be sitting here in Dodge and running out of time. As bad as the weather could be, my optimistic side hoped that the road would improve and that I could at least make it to Pratt. I had hoped that on this side of the Rockies I would be able to pick up speed and make more than my usual seventy miles a day. Instead I was finding myself slowed by weather and the roads. Kansas was not turning out to be the experience that I had expected.

My mood sagged again. The weather wasn't helping and neither were the people. Maybe tourism had created better customer service through most of the ride. Whether that was the case or not, customer service in Kansas was a disappointment. Maybe it was the weather that was making everyone so dour. In any case, I had a tough time getting clerks and waitresses to smile. It felt very odd.

At least I got to learn more about the gunslingers and the Wild West. It is funny to me that I had been riding east for a month now and had finally gotten to the West. Is there something odd about this picture?

October 5 Dodge City to Pratt

Sure enough the weather is almost as bad as they had predicted. The crosswinds are a bit more than I had hoped for but at least the rain has held off. The road has widened again. I wonder if it will stay that way now that I am getting nearer to cities like Wichita and Tulsa.

Unfortunately a couple of the truckers driving the cattle to market are obnoxious. There are still more that wave and give a thumbs up but with the weather getting me down it is easier to put too much emphasis on the bozos.

I stop for lunch in Greensburg mostly to warm up. I am wearing most all of my cold weather gear and am quite chilled. When I stop I notice that my tire is blowing bubbles. That may be cute in a kid but not in a bike tire. A very nice couple running the Best Western in Greensburg let me change the tire in a dry wind-free spot beside their motel. The fix works, I get new and dry gloves from the local grocery and I head back out.

The winds are out of the North at about 20 mph while I am heading East. This is like steering to the left for 8 hours to keep on the shoulder. By the time I get to Pratt I am getting the onset of Carpal Tunnel in my right arm. The continual steering has not been without it's cost.

I drop into Pratt for a day off to let the weather figure out what it wants to do and for my body to heal up a bit. The weather is supposed to set new record lows tonight but the winds might be dying down. When I give it a chance, my body has done a good job of healing itself just enough to keep going.

Next major goal is the Mississippi with all of the usual caveats of weather, bike, and body.

Bike commuting in Seattle had put my bike and I through worse weather than what I saw in Kansas. But heading out for a whole day of riding into what was essentially Winter weather was a tougher task. A little misery for a long time was tougher than a lot of misery that's over fast. My bike commute was about an hour long. Riding to Pratt was going to take a lot longer.

I got out of Dodge early hoping to beat some of the traffic. It looked to be a big enough city that it could have a lot of car traffic in the morning. Let's just say that it was conservative of me and that there was no problem. Dodge City has at least visually kept some of the flavor of its Wild West image. The low buildings along the road looked very authentic. I couldn't spend too much time sightseeing because I was dodging what little traffic there was while trying to make sure I was on the right road. Maybe I didn't get such a good look at it after all.

Right out of town I was back in the rolling hills. At least the ride was a bit easier. A little bit of shoulder made a big difference. Considering the winds that I had to deal with, the shoulder was appreciated even more than normal. The winds were coming out of the north at about 20 knots. Maybe it was only 20 miles per hour. I wasn't carrying an anemometer with me so I couldn't know for sure. What I did know was that I had to steer into them to stay on the shoulder. That was tough enough with a steady wind but the winds were rarely steady. Between the gusts of wind and the buffeting by the trucks I needed that extra shoulder room to stay out of traffic. The weather stayed just on the dark side of gloomy so I always felt that it could start coming down at any time. At the start it was just a grunt. After a few hours though it started to get to me. The noise of the wind, wincing as I braced for another blast from a truck, and wondering when the rains would start wore me down. My morale was low and showed no signs of recovering.

Just before lunch I stopped at the side of the road to check my map and take a break. After riding for about a month the time between my breaks was increasing. At least I was getting in better shape to that extent.

Someone around there had a lot of time, energy, scrap metal and imagination. There were metal sculptures lining one side of the road for about a hundred yards. Some were funny. Some were definitely political. I'm a bad judge of art so I won't guess what they are worth, but they were definitely neat to look at. On a sunny day they probably are a fine way to spend an hour or so.

While I was getting something out of the panniers, I happened to look down at the back tire and saw it bubbling. I've seen that sort of thing before when I ride through something soapy and my tires were wet. It didn't look like I would be that lucky. In the mood I was in, I didn't want to have to deal with it. Instead I pumped up the tire and headed a few miles into the next town. At least in town if I had to change a tire I could do it somewhere dry and flat. The wet gravel on the side of the road was not appealing. Besides, the town had a motel and a restaurant. That sounded pretty good and civilized. It was a fine idea as long as the tire held up long enough to get there.

When I got to town the tire was obviously leaking and I was getting more than just cold. The weather wasn't as bad as it could have been but it was bad enough to chill me to the bone even though I was wearing all of my Winter gear. My safest option was to make sure I had a place to stay so I rolled on up to one of the motels to see if they had a room. The couple running the place were the nicest folks I had met that far in Kansas. Like a lot of folks though they didn't know what to make of someone coming through on a bike. When I told them about my flat tire, they had no problem with me turning a bit of the dry side of the building into a temporary bike shop. They were even kind enough to check ahead and see if the next town over had a room available in case I wanted to keep going after the fix was finished.

The bubbles were still coming out of the tire. I suppose that I should be grateful for those bubbles because otherwise I wouldn't have realized I had a flat until I was in the middle of nowhere in who knows what kind of weather. It was the tire I had bought in Grand Junction and it was no easier to get off the wheel than the earlier one had been. Of course handling a wet tire with numb fingers and a bit of carpal tunnel made it worse. By the time I got it fixed, it was on the far side of lunch and I had ripped up a pair of gloves. There was still enough time to get to Pratt, so I thanked the folks for their generosity and took off. Before I left town though I needed some new gloves. Instead of a good bike shop I found the local grocery and replaced my synthetic material gloves with some good cotton insulated gloves. Cotton is supposed to be bad in wet weather but my hands were warm and happy. I missed lunch but the tire was fixed and my hands were warm and dry.

The wind hadn't gone away while I was in town. It had just been diverted by the trees. There didn't seem to be many trees outside of town. As soon as I left town, I was steering into the winds again. It didn't take long before I had to take turns steering the bike with one arm and then the other. My right arm was getting shooting pains up to the shoulder. Isn't bike riding supposed to be fun? Better weather would have made an enormous difference.

The cruelest place to put a hill is at the end of the day. The smallest hill took on the feel of a mountain pass if it happened to be within the last few miles of the ride. Pratt was a pleasant town to get to because it was actually a city with lots of services around. I was very cold and my morale needed a boost by taking a day off. Cities the size of Pratt are good places to get lots of chores done. I guess the hills in town were a way of paying my dues for the privilege. After beating my way through the hills in town I found a motel that had food nearby and a laundry. I settled in to convalesce.

It was such a treat to find myself across the road from Chinese buffet. There hadn't been much diversity out there except when I was in the resort towns. I hadn't eaten Chinese food since I left Seattle. I didn't expect much but what I found was good food and some of the most pleasant Chinese music playing inside. Pratt seemed to have everything. I decided to spend a day in Pratt. There were chores to do. My body wanted a break and it would give the weather a chance to improve. That night I got the laundry done.

The next day started with a search for an Internet café. It had been some time since I had sent out any emails about my trip. Evidently I had ridden past my best bets back in town. I wasn't going to inflame my carpal tunnel by riding back so I headed out for a long brisk walk. That was a nice way to see what was really going on in town.

The library was usually a good bet so I went there first. They had computers but no Internet access. They did however know where a man had set up a combination Internet cafe and consultation business. The directions were hard to believe but he was operating in one of the upper floors of an old vacant department store. That sounded a bit odd. I didn't want to walk in on someone at the wrong address but I went into this somewhat old building, went up a couple of flights of stairs and started snooping around. There he was with a bank of machines and no waiting. That was nice. There were comfortable chairs, a nice environment, and time to sit and send.

After a few emails were out, the owner and I got to talking. He is a man with a vision of getting South Central Kansas hooked up in the cyber world. It was really neat talking to such an enthusiastic person. Most folks I had met on the trip were people who were just trying to get through the day. Either they were desk clerks or people traveling on business. Here was someone who was up and had ideas all over the place. I was glad to have a day off and I was glad to get the emails out, but talking to him was the high point of my visit to Pratt. I think he has a tough job ahead of him but if he succeeds the results should be gratifying in a lot of ways.

I was glad that I stopped for the day. The wind chill was enough that I was cold even though I was just walking along. On the bike the wind chill would have been even worse. The cold wind posed a dilemma. The faster I rode the colder I would get but I'd reach my destination sooner. There were a lot of days where a bit more speed would shorten the ordeal but would make the ride that much colder. My other choice was to go slow and keep the wind chill down. Unfortunately, that kept me out in the cold that much longer. I compromised by keeping my normal pace and stopping more often to thaw my fingers.

I felt like I was griping a lot but in retrospect the weather was the culprit. That many record lows and record highs were not what anyone should expect. Hot days and cold days made sense, but breaking records should be something for the cyclist to do, not the weather.

It was time for a new strategy. I quit focussing on the daily trials. Instead, I would focus on the next major milestone. That was the Mississippi. Between Cañon City and the Mississippi River there was a lot of ground and it led downhill. If it hadn't been for the weather the only major hurdle would have been the lack of a shoulder. Concentrating on the next milestone would hopefully help my motivation and help me see past the weather. I hoped it would work.

Nowhere to go but Home

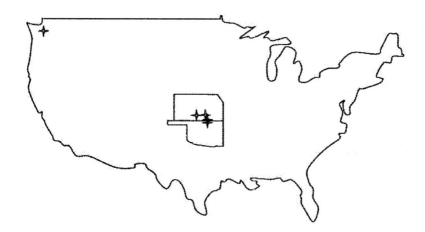

October 7 Pratt to Wichita

I wouldn't call Kansas flat. Not that it is hilly either. I call it rolling plains. If you are in a car you'd hardly notice. So much for that option.

The weather is still cold and blustery but better than the stretch into Pratt. The Sun is even shining even though Kansas is still setting record low temperatures. Throw in a bit of crosswind and my self generated headwind and the wind chill is definitely perceptible.

I pull into Kingman to get something to eat and to warm up. Thankfully there is a small convenience store with picnic benches inside where I can sit for a bit. A charmingly blunt young grandmother took one look at me and guessed that I was one of them cross country bicyclists. When I confirmed her guess, she proceeded to berate me for not dressing warmer in weather like this. This was all said with a bit of a scowl and fists on her hips. The younger women behind the counter were enjoying her act to no end. I thanked her for her concern and agreed that I wished it was a bit warmer. But even they had not expected weather so cold so early.

Stopping in such small stores is even more important for breaks now since hunting season is upon the land.

Wichita is thankfully a downhill ride from the West. I end up at a Holiday Inn across from the Learjet factory.

While Kansas wasn't as flat as most folks had told me, it also wasn't very varied. To my tourist's eye, each day's view was a slight variation on the norm. The locals probably see great differences. It could be called rolling hills or rolling plains. It's a lot like a rumpled bedspread; one good tug and it would all flatten out. Besides the open terrain there were the seemingly random scattering of feedlots, water towers, grain elevators, and cell phone towers. There were a few homes and the occasional view of a river. I wondered if some people felt that Kansas was flat as a pancake just because there wasn't much that stayed with them after they drove through. I rode in it for days and the land between the towns was slightly more than blur. I don't think Kansas is worried about that though. It is a working state. They are feeding a large chunk of the planet and that's impressive enough.

Either because of the view or because I had been on the road for over a month, I had become much more interested in the people that I met. Unfortunately for me, there were very few that had time to talk. Folks were concentrating on getting through their day and didn't seem to have a lot of time for pleasantries. There were those rare moments though that were precious.

The day off helped my poor wrists. The pains that had been shooting up my arms had abated. That was such a relief. Things like that can be so frustrating because there is nothing to point to as an obvious injury. Something visible like a blister can be easier to deal with because you can see it, point at it, and maybe even treat it or at least know where to put a bandage. Internal injuries are hidden and sometimes don't give a hint that they are getting worse until you try doing something with that joint or limb. Thankfully, things were better after Pratt. The winds cooperated too.

Kingman is a reasonably sized town on the way to Wichita. I kept it in mind as a stop just in case the weather got atrocious. I expected that I could get to Wichita that day but I always liked having a backup plan. Besides, I wasn't going to pass up the opportunity to drop into some place and get some food and some warmth. Mini-marts and me got along fine. I didn't have to wait for service and the dress code was a lot more relaxed than in the restaurants. This mini-mart had all the amenities that I looked for. A fancy restaurant critic might disagree but I was so glad to see that they had just the kind of simple food that I was after, something to drink, rest rooms and a place to sit indoors. I was cold. The record setting temperatures were still out there and the wind chill factor was not to be ignored. I was so glad to sit down and relax for a bit. The cuisine might not be fancy but shrink wrapped doughnuts and a bottle of milk can taste like high living when you're working hard enough.

That was one of the friendly places in Kansas. One of the customers looked to be a regular. He was retired and sitting at one of the other tables. I can't remember what he had on his cap but it got us to talking and he started asking me about my ride. It's not like my trip monopolized the conversation. I was glad to hear about what was going on in his life. He had the usual gripes about kids not growing up the way he had hoped but evidently turning out alright in the long run. There were two women working the counter and because they didn't have much to do, they joined us in a nice congenial conversation. After a while I was finally warmed up again. He had to get going and so did I.

About the time that we got up to go, another of the regulars came in to grab something quick. Well they all knew each other and we all got to talking. Even though I had gotten up to go I wasn't in that much of a hurry so I stood there and kept the conversation going. The woman who had just walked in turned to me, put both fists on her hips, made sure that I knew that she was a grandmother, and proceeded to chastise me thoroughly for not dressing warmer in weather like this. Didn't I know better than that? Did I know that I could catch something running around like that? What made me think I could do something like this? I knew that she was sincere and actually appreciated the sentiment. Better weather or better clothes sounded good to me too but I didn't have much of a choice. What made it an incredibly charming picture was the look on the face of the women behind her. They were having a hard time holding it in. They were grinning to bust their faces and hanging on to each other. Here was a grandmother, who was probably not much older than me, looking like a drill sergeant. The folks standing behind her were having such a grand time that I couldn't help but smile. I probably ended up with the wrong look on my face so who knows what she thought when I thanked her and said my good-byes. I thank her for one of my favorite memories from the trip.

The Sun was shining though the wind was unrelenting and the world was not warming up. At least I didn't have to worry about the rain though no one would have guessed that. I look like I was waiting for a thunderstorm. I was wearing all of my foul weather gear and was still chilled.

Wichita lived up to my expectations for being a big city. The main thing that meant for me was that it would take quite a while between me hitting the outskirts and getting to a motel. I had lucked out again. I would be passing through a big city on a Sunday. Amazingly the road into town was mostly downhill. One of the advantages of a small town is that it is easy to find the motel. Big cities can have them strewn all about except for the cluster that's always around the airport. The best bet for me was to head to the airport and hopefully not get lost in the labyrinth of on ramps that airports seem to generate. I ended up getting a room in a motel as close to one of the rivers as possible. That made it easier to find exactly where I was on the map.

Dinner that night was a treat. I can't say that I remember the food but I remember the restaurant and the people working there. In a past career I was in the airplane business. Without trying I was staying in a motel near the Lear Jet factory. After all of the restaurants with the Wild West themes, it was fun to sit in a place that had airplane posters plastered everywhere. Having worked at Boeing it was fun to see how some other company advertises their stuff. Lear does nice work.

My waiter for the evening represented the new high tech career. As far as a lot of folks are concerned, aerospace is out and computers are in. He really wanted to be a part of it but wasn't exactly sure what "it" is. Is the interesting work in hardware, software, services, networking, or is there something else? I had some background in the field just from what I had used at work and from what I had learned from our investments. His question sounded direct (i.e. "What is the best job?") but it also sounded like there was something else going on. The conversation was very disjointed. He had work to do so we just exchanged a few sentences as he delivered each dish. It turned out that his counselor really thought software was the only place to be and that he shouldn't consider anything else. Evidently the waiter decided to learn more about software by ripping apart a machine or two to find out how it ran. It sure sounded like he was more interested in hardware than software to me. The world definitely needs people who know how to do that. I don't like telling people what to do but I do hope he listened to my suggestion that he concentrate more on what he is interested in rather than on just what seems to be hot to someone else. You never know and I will wonder what he decided to do. It was fun to see his enthusiasm. He knew that the answer might not be in his hometown and he knew that the question was worth asking. Until he had made enough to move, he was going to learn all that he could by ripping apart machines and talking to as many people as possible.

I met a lot of people who limited their choices to what was available within a few miles of where they were born. That might be just the thing but there's nothing to say the answer isn't somewhere else. I think that partially explains the reaction some folks had to me. Lots of folks really understood life in their town and felt very comfortable with that and the way life worked there. That makes sense. I was the random unit that wasn't part of their normal life. Because they didn't experience much from outside of their town, they didn't always know what to do when something different happened along. Change is stressful and I was definitely not a part of a normal day. So I was a change for them. I have heard that we live a lot by habit. A lot of our lives are learned responses. Their learned response for me was the same as anything else that was out of the ordinary: be polite and wary. Not everyone was like that and I enjoyed talking with the ones who were more open, but the majority kept things safe and at a distance. I overheard a few of these folks talking about their lives when I was shopping or eating at the next booth and a number of them would be bemoaning their lot in life but couldn't imagine living anywhere else. That wasn't because they liked the town that much, but more because they were afraid to move somewhere with no friends, family or familiarity. It made me wonder what possibilities I was overlooking in my life. I might get out a lot but there is probably some comfort zone that I am stuck in that hems me in too. Will Rogers said something like, "We are all equally ignorant, just in different areas." I might know more about getting out and about but I wonder what those folks know about sitting still that I should take to heart.

The weather report was for even colder weather. Luckily if the wind held out of the north, what had been a crosswind would become a tailwind. Once through Wichita I would be headed south for a few days travel. The wind would be at my back and the wind chill could effectively vanish. At least that was my hope. My morale needed that hope. The break in Pratt had helped and the weather had warmed up somewhat, but I felt emotionally fragile. Where was the nice Fall weather that I had expected?

October 8   Wichita to Arkansas City

Record setting cold continues and lo and behold the wind shifts. Now that I am heading South the wind is no longer out of the North. That coupled with the frost on the cars is not a good sign.

Early in the morning I pass the Boeing Plant. It is a weekend so there isn't much activity.

Wichita and the environs are actually quite nice. There are a lot more trees and such and they seem to be growing naturally rather because of irrigation. While I like riding through relatively flat country, I still feel that the area would be too flat for my choice of places to live.

Outside of Wichita the land becomes much more bumpy. The road is back to the rolling plains.

The Sun comes out and helps to keep me warm as long as I am not moving. Once on the bike however, the wind chill drops dramatically. Part of the problem stems from building up a sweat on the uphills and getting chilled on the downhills. I understand layering and such but can not find a clothing combination and routine that compensates enough for the varying conditions. I end up stopping early as I feel the early signs of hypothermia. Nothing severe, but it is distracting and I need all of my attention for riding on these roads. If a state can be judged by it's roads, then Kansas is one of the poorest states I have come across. Most of the day's travel have been on four lane roads without shoulders. It is good that it is a weekend so traffic is lighter.

I am disappointed by my performance because I don't make it out of Kansas. I end up in Arkansas City (pronounced R-Kan-zass, NOT like that OTHER state). The towns are getting bigger the further east I go. That helps with the logistics each night though the hotel distribution is still thinner than I would prefer.

Before I got to Kansas I thought that they didn't allow bicycles on their Interstates. That's one reason for the route that I picked. To pick up the route on the other side of Wichita it looked like I had to use one of the Interstate bridges. There weren't any signs saying I couldn't ride there. Maybe I had missed a much easier way across Kansas. Maybe I had just missed a sign. Maybe they hadn't put it up. I decided to use the Interstate to get over the river and then return to my original plan. That meant meandering through Wichita until I popped out the other side. I didn't say it was a detailed plan. The route had a bit more structure than that but it ended up feeling the same.

Getting through Wichita itself went alright but I have to admit to being somewhat uncertain the entire time. Whenever I was wending my way through a big city, I appreciated the days on the open highway where I never had to worry about getting lost. Of course when I was on the open road I appreciated all of the readily available services that were in the cities. They all have their good and bad points. As usual getting through town was slowed down by stopping for traffic signals and the like. Yes, I am one of those boring cyclists that actually stop at stop signs and things like that. It is a slow way to bicycle. All of that momentum is lost every block or so. That can take a lot of effort when you have to do it dozens of times to get across town. It's also a lot safer and I like that a lot.

I rode through some areas where the houses were nice and obviously well maintained. They were good middle class houses and, at least on a Sunday morning, things were pretty and quiet. There was the occasional jogger or family heading off to church. I think a lot of folks were just staying snuggled up in bed and waiting for the Sun to get the frost off their windshields.

I knew that I had made it across town when I came across a big sprawling building with a large highway running past it. I stopped for a break and had to laugh. It was my old employer, Boeing. They have a plant in Wichita and I hadn't expected to come across it. They crank out a lot of work there so I was surprised to see how quiet it was. I figured they would be busy every day of the week. I snagged a photo and something to eat and got back on the road.

The nice highway soon lost its shoulder and then it lost a couple of lanes. Again I was back on two lane roads with no shoulder. If things went well I would be in Oklahoma later in the day. I was hoping that they had nicer roads. Until then I had to deal with hills again. One of the gratifying things about climbing a hill west of the Rockies was that I felt I was making my way up the mountain. There was a ratcheting going on. The rolling plains east of the Rockies were just extra work. They seemed to go on for a mindnumbing distance. Working to get up them was enough to break a sweat, which then chilled me when I coasted down the other side. At one point I even tried braking to slow myself going downhill. So much for that part of the roller coaster. I had a wide variety of layers to pick from but just zipping and unzipping them didn't make enough of a difference. I didn't want to have to change clothes at the top and bottom of each hill. My hope was that the Sun would warm me up during my breaks.

As least the terrain was a bit more varied. That was mostly because my route involved a few turns. There wasn't a straight shot headed to Florida so I had to stitch something together. In one direction I had to cross up and over the ridges. After a turn onto a new road I could be riding along a ridge's crest. The area had lots of deciduous trees and looked great. The trees were acting like Fall was just coming on despite the air making it feel like Winter. The colors were nice to see. There was a lot of green but the beginnings of the reds and yellows were starting to show through. They may not be as vibrant as in some corners of the country but I appreciated them.

My hope of making it to Oklahoma was a tough one to give up. It was barely even noon when my concentration started to wander. I was having a harder time keeping myself on the white line and was starting to drift a bit into the traffic lane. It hadn't gotten too bad but it started to get scary. Something wasn't normal and it didn't seem to be getting better. I wasn't getting warm and felt more tired than I should have. Maybe it was hypothermia but I did know that I had to do something about my symptoms. It wasn't supposed to get much warmer according to the forecast and I didn't want to be a traffic hazard or statistic. I did my normal check of motels with food nearby and had one of my shortest days of the trip. Only after checking in did I find out that the restaurant was only open for dinner. Breakfast would be in some mini-mart along the way again.

Arkansas City was a lot bigger than I had expected. There was even a choice of nice sit down restaurants. I skipped the one advertising a 44 ounce steak. That actually sounded painful. I was close to the border but not over it yet. Once I crossed that hurdle there were only two states between me and the Mississippi River. After that was only Mississippi, Alabama, and Florida. I was getting close but things hadn't been going my way. I figured my bad luck couldn't continue much longer.

October 9   Arkansas City to Ponca City

Hallelujah I made it out of Kansas! That didn't take much since I was less than 10 miles from the border. While it is still cold, the temperature is up a bit, and the winds while out of the south are not as bad as they could be. I even have a new clothing scheme to try out to keep the hypothermia at bay.

The road and shoulder in Oklahoma is not much better than in Kansas. Like there, the shoulder will sometime go from smooth to rough to dirt and rubble and back again within 100 yards. Somewhere in one of those stretches I get a nail through the tire. Not that I enjoy changing tires but I know how to do it and as I stop I realize that the day is warming up sooner and think that maybe things are turning around.

Adding one more element to a tragedy can make it a comedy. The weather and road conditions in Kansas had really been getting me down. So the onset of nicer weather buoyed my spirits. That's when I noticed the busted rim. As I was changing the tire I noticed a dark line in the rim. Sure enough, the rim on these 8 year old wheels had developed a crack along about 20% - 40% of the circumference. I can fix flat tubes and can manage some busted tires, but there is not road fix for a cracked rim.

That was the last straw but rather than getting down about it I had to laugh. It is almost as if someone was giving me one hint after another that I should give it up for a while. Here I was with the weather finally getting better and I end up with something like this. Well I decided to make it to the next town and see if there was a reasonable fix to be had there. Otherwise I would be checking out the transportation options for going home.

Luckily for me the tire held and the rim held into Ponca City; a fine small city in Oklahoma. Unfortunately, they only have one bike store in town and they are closed on Mondays. The next bike shop is 40 miles down the road. There isn't enough time left in the day to get there on the bike so I check into renting a car and driving on down there. Since this will cost about $70 I call the bike shop to evaluate whether they can help me. In the course of our discussion they inform me that I have to be more specific because a 26 X 1.5 inch wheel is not the same as a 26 X 1 1/2 inch wheel. Now, I don't know everything about bikes but that sounds fishy to me. While checking out options with REI and Nashbar I confirm that they think it is fishy as well. I decide to not spend $70 to go talk to such an odd duck. If the bike shop in town has a good rim, then I can work with that; otherwise, given the fact that I might have problems getting the other parts that I need like two new tires and a new chain and a few other parts, I might just give it up and go home. Mail order is an option but there is reluctance on both sides of the phone over choosing the right parts sight unseen.

Just for the heck of it I walk over to the bike shop to evaluate them by looking through their window. It looks like they might have what I need but I am not encouraged.

I settle in and find that next door to the hotel is a nice used bookstore with good tea and next to them is a place with truffles. This is a good way *to wait out the news. The evening is spent calling around for rental car, plane, and train information.*

It all just felt like one long punch line where I was the joke. It was ridiculous and hilarious. I had finally gotten Kansas behind me and was headed south for a change. There were still lots of hills but it looked like I had a chance of riding along without the foul weather gear for the first time in days. Even the winds had improved. Crossing the border happened within an hour after I left town. It was good to see the "Welcome to Oklahoma" sign. It was hard to keep from humming the song from the musical so I just gave into the temptation. That's one of the advantages of riding on my own. No one else has to listen to my singing. Things started to look up as I headed south.

It is still amazing to me how a nail and a tire can line themselves up so well that they not only hit each other but to do so in such a way that the nail goes straight in. Where do these nails come from? Broken glass I understand, but what's a nail doing out there in the asphalt? Are we nailing our roads together? At least it happened when the Sun was out and along a fairly dry patch of road. I was getting better at changing tires and this one seemed to go along fine. I don't think I noticed the rim going bad until I had the bike back together. Otherwise I might have inspected the inside of the rim. The rim was going bad from the brakes. Over eight years of riding the bike there had been enough usage that the rim walls had worn thin. That was what "The Dirt Dart" had noticed and mentioned back in Boise. The fatigue of bouncing along the road and hitting rumblestrips at 30 mph probably didn't help.

The rim hadn't failed yet but any number of things could happen when it was cracked so much. The rim is what the tire iron hinged on whenever I changed a flat. If I had to change a flat again, it might break off a piece of the rim. The cracks happen because of the thin metal where the brakes hit. It probably wouldn't wear through much more but if the rim started to separate, the brakes would stick and catch on the rim material ruining it for sure. If it was bad enough, hitting a good sized bump in the road could be enough to warp the rim or break off pieces that would catch on the brakes. A busted rim was very likely going to rip up the tire and tube and leave me stranded. I had hoped to make it to Stillwater that day but I was happy to make it to Ponca City without anything else breaking.

Rather than getting me down though, this whole thing had me chuckling. I had really hoped that the ride would have gone much smoother. I'd even been getting on my own case for being so gloomy. A busted rim on a sunny day was just too much. It was as if some bad luck like the tire had to show up to counter the good luck that I was having with the weather. It felt like the universe was saying, "We'll fix him. He's kept going through record heat, record cold, and early Winter storms. Now that the weather is better, we'll break his bike in a way he can't fix on his own and where there isn't a bike shop for tens of miles in any direction. That should be enough to convince him to stop this silly ride." Kansas had gotten me so low that there was nowhere to go but up. The bike broke and I had to just stand there and laugh at it.

I am so spoiled living in the midst of great bike shops in Seattle. In all fairness there must be similar bike shops somewhere near Ponca City and I tried to find them. The one in town was closed that day so that left me calling around through Northern Oklahoma for a bike shop that sounded like they would have the part and ideally could do the work. I would have to rent a car just to go shopping and that sounded expensive. Every day I spent working the problem was going to cost me more for food and lodging than the price of any part. Waiting for a mail order part had the same problem. That was ridiculous. I decided to give the guy in town a crack at it. If things went well and he could fix it in the morning, I would have only lost two half days. Otherwise, I would have to consider some fairly drastic options. As odd as it sounds, it didn't cost too much more to fly back to Seattle if need be. There were some flights out of Tulsa that didn't cost more than a few days lodging and food. Maybe the weather would improve in the meantime.

Waiting was very easy when I found the used bookstore next door that had good tea and chocolate. That was a rare treat. It felt so civilized to sit there with my book and tea. It was much better than the usual pop and chips in front of the TV while sitting on the motel bed.

I wished that I knew just a little bit more about the part type and numbers to order what I needed over the phone. The mail order places and I agreed that because my bike was so old, there was a fair chance that I would end up with the wrong part. If the wrong part came in I would have to wait even more days as I waited for the next part to make it to me. Originally I had planned on relying on the mail order places for parts on the road but it only made sense in practice if I ordered simple parts and could wait somewhere inexpensive. I had even considered buying a new bike on the road if things got bad enough, but I had underestimated how hard it was to find bikes that fit my long legs. It was frustrating to have to consider flying back to Seattle to get the bike fixed, but going home could serve a number of purposes. If for no other reason, it had been weeks since Kaye and I had seen each other. Besides, maybe listening to the progressively stronger hints that I should take a break wasn't such a bad idea. It would be good to get back home again.

October 10 Ponca City to Seattle

At 10 AM I have checked out of the hotel ready to either continue the ride on a fixed bike or to grab a rental car to catch a fly out of Tulsa.

The bike owner is a nice guy and he finds me sitting on his shop's doorstep waiting for him to open for the day. After explaining my situation he pulls out the one wheel that might work. It is a used one from the local police department. They gave it over to him because the spokes kept busting and it is no longer round. He thinks he can fix it but doesn't sound too certain. Knowing how empty some of the road ahead is I am very reluctant to use a wheel that may still have spokes ready to break.

After some commiserating I thank him for his time and trouble and declare an Intermission in the ride.

An Intermission was one of the options I kept in mind when I was planning out this trip. Anything that takes this long can be interrupted but any number of items that end up with a return home in the middle of the trip. I still plan on continuing though whether that is in a week a month or a year is what I can work on next. Since I made it more than halfway and quite a ways south, it becomes easier to complete the trip at my leisure. I no longer have to worry about winter mountain storms or hurricanes to the same extent. I also will be checking to see how much I've already spent. It also gives me the opportunity to do some detailed route planning. It was impractical to plan to any great detail when looking at the entire country, but focussing on the Southeast is doable. I might just put together a trip plan and have it ready to go for when the ticket prices and weather line up with my schedule. The remainder should take about three weeks depending on route, weather and how relaxing I want to make it.

As for the portion that I have completed,

> *I've gone more than halfway,*
> *covered about 2,000 miles (a more detailed accounting will follow),*
> *crossed the continental divide,*
> *passed through six states,*
> *found that I don't want to be on the road much more than a month or so,*
> *found that I can get by for 5 weeks on two panniers worth of clothes,*
> *found that computing is not ubiquitous (I might write a white paper on that),*
> *found that the Internet is not ubiquitous (I might write a white paper on that too),*
> *learned that there are more good than bad people out there,*
> *found that a lot of people don't get out much (but why should they, they have fine lives already thank you very much),*

and I didn't lose any weight or improve my body fat percentages (but I'll go back and check the scale again just to be sure).

Thanks for all of your support. Hope you've been entertained. Anyone interested in doing the rest with me? Oh yeah, and I am going shopping for something to carry along that I can crank out emails with. The effort required to generate these emails really surprised me. There has got to be a better way.

Stay tuned.

It was odd and pleasant seeing familiar faces again. The old routine was easy to put back on. When I got home I didn't know how long I would stay. I started to think that the bike repair would be tougher than I had expected. My eight year old bike was ancient when compared to what was in the bike stores. I lucked out. The bike shop that gets most of my business has a very active repair business. The bike mechanic that heard my situation jumped on the repair like nothing else. By that evening he had built up two new wheels by hand and fixed a handful of other curiosities on the bike. He was headed off to ride up to Alaska with a friend of his in a few months. Talk about someone who understood where I was coming from. What more could I ask for? His story will be awesome to hear about. They were planning on riding 1,600 miles carrying all of their stuff in a trailer. They would have to worry about repairs in the wilderness and fending off the bears while getting there in time for jobs in Alaska's tourist industry. I found that there is always someone out there who will do the same thing harder, tougher, longer, faster, or with more style. There are some amazing people out there and these are two more that are definitely impressive.

October 16 Bellevue

Intermission is over. It was good getting back to Bellevue. I got the bike fixed up with two new rims, spoke sets, tires, tubes and a new chain. It wasn't cheap but it all had to be done. I had talked about picking up the ride again once I had decided the best conditions under which to do so. It seemed that the longer I held off the second half, the harder it would be to get going again. If I went back soon, my muscles would still be in reasonable shape, and I would have the most time left before Thanksgiving. Besides, the sooner I started, the sooner I would be finished.

So it is back to Tulsa and Ponca City without nearly as much delay as I had originally anticipated. Luckily I was able to get a good flight and a rental car. It may take five weeks for me to ride to Ponca City, but it only takes about twelve hours using planes and cars. Amazing and easily overlooked on a day to day basis.

In the meantime, the weather in Oklahoma has improved and I've managed to get some rest. It was nice seeing Kaye and visiting friends as well.

I really didn't think it likely that I would be back on the road so soon. When I first got home I figured there was a good chance that I might not hit the road again for months. Putting off the second half just put a lot of life on hold though. Without a definite schedule, the possibility of a return ride would always be getting in the way of plans for the other things in our lives.

So, once the bike was fixed, it was time to return. Besides, if I delayed, I would get out of shape. Going back after a week off wasn't without its problems. I would be pushing it in other ways. It would mean riding with an even tighter schedule. The holidays were closer and I had just spent a week making no progress. I decided that I had to at least cross the Mississippi. That would give me a sense of completion. Finishing at Ponca City just didn't have the same feel. It was good that I had come back. The weather in Oklahoma had been terrible while I was in Seattle. The cold and wind had been replaced by heavy rain. I am so glad I missed that. At least I was getting better at boxing up the bike for travel.

Surprise, I'm on the Road Again

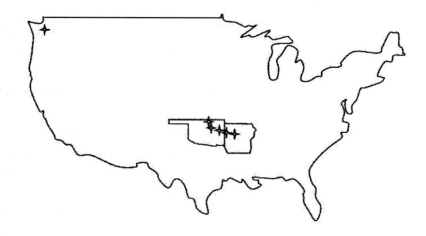

October 17   Ponca City to Stillwater to Cushing

Nice weather, hallelujah! There is even a nice enough shoulder most of the way today. This is what I wish the ride was like everyday. It is sunny and the winds aren't too strong. The land is still not flat but instead a series of ridges. Trees are much more common now which makes the ride much prettier to me.

The original plan for the day was to only do about 40 miles and end up in Stillwater. It was a conservative plan keeping in mind that I might have to return a rental car in the morning and do small repairs to the bike after it's journey in cargo. Well I was able to return the car yesterday and the bike came through mostly fine. One of the less obvious reflectors fell off.

With such good weather and roads I find myself in Stillwater just about lunch time. Unfortunately, I can't find the motel I was planning on staying in. Their directions didn't work well for me evidently. In trying to find the motel I came across a rarity: a cybercafe. Well plunk me down and log me on. Lo and behold I not only find directions to the motel via the web, but I also find that there is another motel about 30 miles closer to Tulsa. I grab a quick bite and continue on to Cushing.

The rest of the day passes well. The country doesn't change much though there may be more trees around here. The weather cooperates and except for a few relatively steep grades, I find myself in Cushing. The local restaurant is fairly authentic Chinese though I can't get steamed rice or chopsticks. Is that normal or a concession to the local culture? I don't know. In either case I end up 30 miles farther along than I had expected.

I was back on the road again and glad for the break. I didn't know how long the rest of the trip would take. The holidays were getting closer and getting to Key West was looking tougher. As much as I wanted to finish the whole trip I knew that I could only push things so hard. Logistics would still be the thing that really picked how far I went with the daylight I had each day. My main goals were: the Mississippi, Florida, the Gulf Coast, the Atlantic coast, the Eastern time zone, and Key West. If all I did was focus on Key West, I would bring myself down. The Mississippi was just two states away: a good close goal.

I had tried to do some detailed planning while I was back home but couldn't do much because weather, time and money were too hard to judge and might change my direction. If there wasn't any schedule pressure I would just find one route that eventually got me to Key West and stick to it. Because of the holidays, I had to get home sooner rather than later so I had to allow for a reroute to get to an airport or bus station. Trains didn't look like a good way to go from the Southeast to the Northwest. Because one route wouldn't work for all conditions, I ended up making a map and marking all of the towns that had motels that AAA knew about or were part of some chain. It didn't cover everything, but I did have something I could play connect the dots with. It was amazing that even down where it is warm and populated, there were still long gaps in the map where there wouldn't be a motel for forty, fifty, or sometimes a hundred miles.

Keeping first things first, I figured I would make my way to Little Rock and take another look at the calendar and my condition there. The Ozarks forced all of my routes through Little Rock. I hadn't decided on a specific route but there were lots of ones that were good enough. To start I flew back to Tulsa and drove a rental car back to where I had stopped cycling: Ponca City. After spending the night there, I planned on making a short trip to Stillwater the first day. With everything else going on, I also didn't want to find out that something on the bike would need tweaking or that my saddle sores had softened up. As each day went by, convenience and maybe some local advice would help me decide on which route to take.

About the middle of the morning I got to meet a tie-dyed, free spirited ex-Marine who was out getting his mail. He was near the top of a small climb so it was a fine time for me to take a break. It turned out he was very familiar with the Seattle area. I got to hear a fair chunk of his story about how he got from Seattle to Oklahoma. The more fascinating part of the conversation though was when he started talking about his dream of running a Frisbee golf course right along that road on his property. He figured that because he was halfway between the towns of Ponca City and Stillwater, he had a good chance of getting business from both. It was fun listening to him describe how he was going to phase it in, advertise it, and run it. The details weren't the entertainment, his attitude was. He was upbeat, positive, fun to talk to, and I hope it worked for him.

The bike and I must have been okay because I got to Stillwater a lot faster than I had expected.

That was one of the few towns that I got lost in. Most towns were small enough that getting lost wasn't an option. It wasn't that Stillwater was a lot bigger. It is just that it was big enough for the motels to be outside of town on a bypass. I had called ahead and the motel had informed me that they were on the main road. I am sure that some folks would consider the road going through downtown to be the main road and for some folks the bypass is the main route. I had ridden all the way through downtown and hadn't found a thing. I called for directions again, found the mistake and headed back through town. Before I got to the motel though, I found the cybercafe. I thought it would be a high tech way of confirming the directions. I had no desire to be lost all day long. Besides if the motel was close enough to the cybercafe, I could send out an email or two. Most of my friends still didn't know that I had jumped back onto the road. A lot of folks figured I would hold off until the Spring. I can't say that I blame them. I thought the same thing myself for a while. When I brought up the online business directory I also noticed some other motels that were another couple of hours farther along. Just for the fun of it I checked out whether they were nice and easy to find. Two of them were in a town called Cushing. That was south of the route that I had planned on taking but it meant I could accomplish about thirty miles more progress. The weather was nice, I was rested and I decided to go for it. I just hoped the road was a good one.

The never ending ridges that make up the terrain would have been fine if I could only have found a route that always was on the top or bottom of them. It seemed that I was continually riding up and down them. That's probably because when I was riding along their crest I took it for granted. Riding up and down them meant that the majority of the time I could only see what was in that particular valley. The broad vistas only showed up at the tops of the ridges. From there I was frequently looking out at a long series of ridges and valleys that I would be riding through. They weren't enormous like the ones in Oregon, but they were never ending.

At the intersection that would point me off to Cushing, I dropped into a mega-mini-mart. The concept of the mini-mart seems to have spawned a new beast with a lot of concrete, lots of gas pumps, and lots of shopping aisles. Is this whole thing going full circle? I plunked myself down in a booth to fuel up on their fast food. Chips and soda got me salt and sugar which I could use. After a while I noticed that the woman in the next booth over was working over some bookkeeping. It turned out that she was one of the owners. They had been open for a year and it looked like they were going to make it. Along the way I probably came across a half dozen of these mega-mini-marts that had just been opened. In most of them I got to meet the owners who of course were in there working their butts off and seemed to be happy, proud and tired all at once. I am simply astonished considering how much paperwork must be involved for someone who is selling gasoline, tobacco, alcohol, packaged food, and prepared food while also having to deal with the paperwork for employees, health care, taxes, environmental regulations, safety and health inspections, local ordinances, and who knows what else. I like this country because anyone can decide to try to open a business but we sure don't take what is a tough, risky proposition and make it easy.

Cushing was a fine place to stay for the night. The motel was much nicer than I had expected. It must have been the quiet season across the country. Except for a few places, especially college towns the night of a game, I was usually one of the few guests in the motels. Sometimes that could be downright spooky. In Cushing it meant that I got a nice quiet room back from the road. It also meant that I got to talk to the desk manager about his time in the Service. I liked having the time to talk to folks. A lot of places kept the desk manager busy enough that I didn't want to distract them from their work. It seemed like it would be such a culture shift to go from a military environment to retail desk work. He seemed to be handling it alright.

Finishing up thirty miles farther along was a good way to start the second part of the ride. I was farther south of Tulsa than I had expected but that didn't really change anything. The route around Tulsa had not been obvious so I just started concentrating on some of what had been backup routes. It looked like I should just assume that I would be in that type of terrain until I was past Little Rock. The frequent ups and downs were tiring. I had to keep that in mind when estimating how far I would get. From Cushing it looked like I wouldn't end up in Tulsa proper, but skirt it. The next hop was to Muskogee and I hoped the road and terrain would oblige.

October 18   Cushing to Glenpool to Muskogee

After talking things over with Kaye last night we decided it would be best to go around rather than through Tulsa. Big cities don't bother me too much but I do prefer to go through them on the weekend. By heading to Cushing I actually put myself far enough south that going into Tulsa would be somewhat out of my way.

These are the best of roads and the worst of roads. I am either riding on roads with nice wide shoulders or am trying to sprint from driveway to driveway where no shoulder exists. At one point I have to pull off the road, not go down into the culvert and lean out of the way of some passing trucks. Oh what fun. That slows one down. Luckily the other portions are well tended so I can make good progress there.

The Fall colors down here aren't the brightest, but they do make the place look nicer. East of Tulsa the road flattens out quite a bit. Though this area isn't known for being hilly, the cumulative elevation gain for the first half of the day is about 1,800 feet according to the software Kaye is running at home. No hill is very big but there are lots of them. I prefer the ones back west where there is one big hill each day followed buy one big downhill. It is easier to maintain a cadence and even pace. Here I am constantly shifting gears and essentially climbing never-ending false summits.

The local dogs aren't nearly as well behaved around here. I am starting to get chased much more often. That's another thing that doesn't happen on the Interstate. Oh well.

Muskogee is a small city that seems like it goes through booms and busts and is currently coming out of a bust. There are lots of vacant storefronts. I meet a waiter who has moved all the way from Paris, Texas. He is amazed by how different people are this far from home.

Some wildlife changes are happening. I no longer see magpies and coyotes and am starting to see bluejays and turtles. Most of these as usual are roadkill. Riding the roads is not the same as visiting a wildlife refuge.

The motel has an Internet kiosk in the lobby but it doesn't work though I try about six times at various times of the day. I almost got news out that day.

When I left Cushing I knew that I would be heading east but I wasn't sure for how long. Kaye was nice enough to run the route through the software the previous night so I knew that there would be lots of climbing in the morning. The data didn't lie. The total elevation gain was akin to a small mountain pass. The route went close enough to Tulsa to see it on the horizon but not so close to be tied up in its traffic. The city hung off in the distance like some mythical city. Considering that I had just flown into Tulsa's airport a couple of days earlier, the image was a little reminder of how much slower bikes are than cars.

Midway through the morning I stopped for a snack. It was a treat that I hadn't been able to count on out west of the Rockies. A couple of the regulars were hanging out in there on their way to the morning's chores. It was a nice group to sit and talk with for a bit. It was especially fun listening to them commiserate over which road I should be taking even though I didn't have much of a choice. I kept bringing them back by telling them that a road that was just twenty miles out of the way was more than just a trifle tough to get to. I didn't change my route but my confidence was firmed up. There wasn't any obviously better route.

I felt that getting Tulsa behind me would really make me feel like I had made progress and was on my way. Getting to Glenpool was really just backtracking through the general area that I had been through on the way to Tulsa's airport. Was that really the route? Not exactly, but feelings and emotions don't play by the rules of logic. Glenpool felt like backtracking and therefore it was.

At least getting past Glenpool left most of the ups and downs behind me. The road to Muskogee was much flatter and seemed to follow a river. I was surprised to see that the size of the farms was decreasing. The houses were closer to the road and so were their dogs. I don't think they were purebreds but I had no interest in their pedigree. I didn't get bit, but that didn't mean that a barking dog made me happy. I bark back. It usually would scare off most of them. Besides, sometimes they just got tired chasing me and stopped once I had left their neighborhood.

Riding without a shoulder was usually bad but it went past bad to ugly as I turned south. Narrow two lane roads at least sometimes have some dirt, grass or weeds to roll off into if the traffic got too cozy. This time a wide load came by during busy traffic in a spot where the road had been built up above the surrounding fields. Riding into the culvert wasn't the safe way to go and staying in the road wasn't looking too good either. I pulled off as far as I could and then leaned everything out of the way. I was hoping not to lean so far that I dropped myself sideways into the drainage. Long stretches of that morning were new road with clean shoulders, but there was a lot of riding into the dirt and waiting for the traffic to pass. That definitely upset any rhythm and momentum that I had.

Muskogee was a good sized city with lots of places to stay. It was big enough that I was able to get lost on the way to the motel. It was also big enough to have so many motels to pick from that I stumbled across an entire street of them while I was lost. There were lots of motels and restaurants strung out along a divided four lane road. All I had to do was ride along until I saw one that I liked. There were a lot of businesses that were closed and vacant. It looked like some boom time had built a lot and then a bust came along that cleared out a lot of hopes. Some places were being renovated though so maybe the next boom was just coming on.

Food started to be a bit different. I still hadn't seen much regional cooking going on but then again I was eating in motels and chain restaurants. Something was obviously different though when I asked for them to hold the gravy at dinner. The waiter got a funny expression as if he couldn't imagine such a thing. He was willing to do it but considered it such an important part of the meal that he offered me an additional side vegetable. Evidently gravy was important and would be for the rest of the ride.

The waiter was an interesting fellow. He made a point of mentioning that he wasn't from around Muskogee. He was from Paris, Texas. He had moved up to Muskogee to get away but wasn't sure that it had been such a good idea. People up in Muskogee just weren't the same as back home. Things were just too different and people didn't always act or talk the way he expected. I thought the move was just the thing for him. I don't think I'll invite him along on any long bike rides though. To me, people are people and there are differences all around but those are superficial. We all need food, drink, and shelter. We all just try to get through the day somehow and maybe make our lives better along the way. We've all had families whether we knew them or liked them. The rest is a dizzying array of details that can be overwhelming but worth diving into. That's where I find the really amazing stories. But if the difference between neighboring states was tough for him, then he might have trouble going from coast to coast.

The ride had gone well. The weather was much better. I had unintentionally missed the worst of it while getting the bike fixed back home. The Fall colors were doing their best to brighten up the place. Trees were turning from green to a dusty and rustier palette. Even the road looked like it might flatten out for a while. The bike and I were doing well enough and I had just gobbled up a lot of miles. Getting to Arkansas looked doable with one more day's ride.

October 19 Muskogee to Van Buren

Oklahoma continues to be a mix of the best of roads and the worst of roads. The land has flattened out but there are still ridges to climb. There aren't many hills. It is more like a big plateau with some serious drainages that I ride into and then back out of. The horizon is definitely flat. Almost every bit of untended land is sprouting trees so I suspect that the land is not too dry.

I manage to get back onto an Interstate. They are definitely the best way to travel. The weather is nice, the road is flatter and the land is pleasant. This is what makes a good ride. Yesterday's ride was 90 miles and today's will be over 80 miles so I am a bit tired and can't enjoy the ride nearly as much.

I make it out of Oklahoma. It has been one of the best states so far this ride. The good weather and having a nice break undoubtedly helped but I think it would be have been nice in any case.

Welcome to Arkansas: the home of President Bill Clinton. So says the sign at the border. I wonder if they will change it when he leaves office or much later than that. It seems to be more up lifting than the signs I saw in Kansas celebrating such ephemeral success as Heismann trophy winners and such. I don't get to see much of Arkansas since I am only steering for the first hotels outside of Fort Smith in Van Buren, Exit 5.

At first glance though the state looks to be prettier than Oklahoma though hillier. I am approaching, if not in, the Ozarks and their companion ranges.

Muskogee to Van Buren was a morning of riding to the Interstate and then an afternoon of heading east to the gap in the mountains along the Arkansas River. Once all of the highway construction is completed things will be a lot better but my day was spent on either new shoulders or balancing between dirt and traffic. The country was scenic with a nice mix of hills, trees, and open spaces. The best place for me to take in the view was on the new, wide shoulders of the completed portions of the road construction sites. Otherwise, I was on old pavement with no shoulder where my eyes were watching the traffic, not the countryside.

Muskogee is a good sized place but it didn't take me very long to leave it behind for rural country. Cities are amazingly dense and even with the sprawl out into the suburbs, it didn't take long to trade the manicured lawns for pastures and fields. Only in Seattle and Salt Lake City did it take me very long to get through a city. That was fine by me. I don't mind living in suburbia but riding in it for seven hours every day would be nothing but starts and stops and lots of random traffic. I suppose the ultimate would be riding on a well maintained bike path in good weather with good food and lodging in an area without a lot of hills. Did I just describe Holland? Probably not because the way I ride I wouldn't be able to stay in the country. It is too small. Maybe I'll have to get over there and find out for myself. Riding along the Danube in Austria came close to that ideal. The bike path along the Danube was enough to keep Kaye and me going for over a week. At least in Oklahoma the weather was fine, the terrain agreeable, the lodgings frequent enough and the foods were guiltily fattening and tasty.

It felt so good to get back out onto the Interstate. There was even a tailwind. The afternoon was warm and I enjoyed the view of the approaching mountains that I might have to climb through. I had heard that the Ozarks were tougher than the Rockies because even if they are shorter, they are more abrupt. I hoped to avoid that by following the Interstate which was following the Arkansas River. That afternoon reacquainted me with how well graded, maintained and supported the Interstates are. It felt like luxury after all of the farming roads from Colorado through Kansas and Oklahoma.

Oklahoma had been good to me. The biggest problems had been from my bike. Except for that and the roads, the ride through

Oklahoma would have been the model of how I had envisioned the ride: congenial people, moderate autumn weather, and days where I was able to chew up a lot of miles. A few more bike shops at my beck and call would have been too much to ask for.

At every state line I looked for signs telling bicyclists to do this or that. I was so glad to cross into Arkansas and not see anything telling me to get off the Interstate. Well, there were no signs saying that but there was road construction that left no room for a bike. I stopped at the Visitor Center just a few miles past the border to find out how many more miles of construction would be eating up the shoulder. As I came to the turnoff I noticed a couple of state patrol cars in the median looking like they were watching for speeders and keeping themselves company. I would have preferred asking them but riding across two lanes of traffic didn't sound very safe. The folks in the Visitor Center were friendly but distracted. Evidently there was a Chihuahua running loose and the three of them were wondering how to catch it before it wandered out into traffic. I stood there snagging brochures and asking them questions during the lulls in the doggie drama. They were happy to talk about the area but they didn't have much information for bicyclists. After Colorado I wouldn't find a bike map anywhere. They did point out that it was illegal for bicyclists to travel on the Interstate. I had heard that frequently before and almost always found out that folks were mistaken.

The troopers didn't seem to mind that I was there. They even waved back when I had passed them. The motel was only a couple of miles farther so I didn't have to deal with the Interstate and construction for long. It was also at a convenient intersection for rerouting the trip. I got myself there with not much energy left but a lot of miles behind me. I was past another state and just had to get to the far side of this one to reach the Mississippi. It was getting closer to when I was going to have to decide how I might cross the Mississippi River. There were only a few choices but none of them were obvious winners. Some didn't have many motels along the route. Some didn't quite go southeast. Once I got to Little Rock I would have to decide. In the meantime I settled in to checking out which roads I would have to take to get to Little Rock. That would get me past most of the mountains and put me into the flood plains of the Mississippi.

A short ride up the Interstate to the next exit got me to a motel. The desk clerk's disbelief in what I was attempting seemed to be flavored with scorn and contempt. That wasn't a very common reaction. Most folks saw it as odd, dangerous and impossible but they treated me with at least a sense of humor. Being different does not always make it easy to get respect or get treated with good manners when around certain people. Unfortunate but true.

October 20   Van Buren to Russellville

Well the first semi-surprise of the day is when I find out that I am not allowed on the Interstate. I start off with hopes that it is only true near cities, but find out later that it is true throughout the state. This is the first state that I have been in that doesn't allow bikes on the Interstate. Unfortunately I have found that the side roads tend to be narrower, steeper, with dogs and more bozos. Since I had looked forward to following the Interstate for nearly it's whole width I am now starting to think about replanning my route.

As for the side roads being steeper, sure enough within the first two miles I encounter a 12% grade. Luckily I am going down it and hoping that I will not have to come back up. Almost by pure luck I find myself on the old highway that parallels the Interstate. My previous experience on side roads seems to be amplified here. The roads are steeper, the drivers more likely to shout things at me and there are many more dogs to deal with. The dismaying aspect of the dogs is that the owners just watch them chase me and make no move to control their pets.

Arkansas is one of the nicest looking states so far on this trip but it is making a strong running for being the least bike friendly. It is a pity since

I think they could attract a lot of bicycle tours down here. The land is nice and there are wineries and antique shops scattered about.

I've been averaging 82 miles a day since I started back. The average for the first part of the trip was more like 65 miles. There is some weather coming in so I get a room for two nights just in case the weather turns unpleasant.

In the morning I look outside and find a Seattle type rain: mostly a heavy drizzle at about 60 degrees F. This is workable but I realize that I have symptoms of a cold. It is possible that I have pushed it just a bit too hard so I decide to take the day off. Otherwise I wouldn't have gotten these notes out. Handy thing, eh?

Kaye and I have revamped the route. I'll now go south earlier. It doesn't change the distances much and it gets me closer to the Gulf in case I decide to shoot for it rather than Key West.

Stay tuned

Evidently, most folks would better know this area for Fort Smith than for Van Buren. It was all new to me. The morning's downer for me was the unambiguous sign by the Interstate that said bicycles weren't allowed. I knew the other route took me closer to the river so I hoped it was reasonably level. Hunting for the new route I came to the crest of a 12% hill and realized just how steep the roads could be in Arkansas when you get off the Interstate. I didn't know that the correct route lay at the bottom of the hill but I sure didn't want to get down there and find that it was back up at the top. I could do the climb but it would take a lot of energy that I would rather expend making progress. There was no realistic alternative though. I couldn't find the route up top so I had to go down and hope for the best. It was mostly by luck that I found the right intersection at the bottom of the hill. Trusting to luck is not the best plan to stick by so I stopped someone who had just come out of a local breakfast place. He looked me up and down and told me that I was headed the right way all along. It felt like he was thinking I was the funniest looking thing around. At least I got good directions from him.

They can think what they want as long as they're helpful and not too ornery about it.

Ornery didn't happen much. There was never any physical abuse. But that day I started a string of days when the number of people honking at me, shouting things, flipping me sign language and such became much more frequent. I guess they don't get many bicyclists around there.

Their attitude was a pity because it was such a nice place to bicycle. The area was very pretty. Trees covered most of the slopes, and the water was like some quieting feature of a painting. With a few hills and ridges thrown in, there were scenic spots all over the place. Unfortunately, the terrain was a bit abrupt at times. I don't think I had to contend with any more 12% grades but the route wasn't flat by any means. The fall colors were still about. They lacked the power and brilliance of the reds of the Northeast and the depth of the Aspens' yellows and golds in Colorado, but the hues blended well. It was more of a welcome and subtle backdrop.

Once I got out of town, the switch wasn't to big sprawling farms but to smaller parcels and a mix of houses. The houses seemed to be closer together and didn't seem to clump into clusters of like-minded homes. Small farms were beside suburban yards which were beside homes with rusted cars in the front yard. I can't say that I saw any house with a car on blocks, but that is the image I was left with. Those were the houses that were more likely to have small yards and be closer to the road. Being closer to the road, the dogs didn't have far to run before they caught up to me. Some of the farm dogs and ones leaping off the porch from suburban two stories had to run a long way before they got anywhere near me. Some of the ones that chased me were big and right there defending every scrap of their territory with all their voice and power. What fun. The suburban dogs were wild cards. They could be as defensive as farm dogs or just wanting to play. It was hard to tell the difference usually. The worst was when I was climbing some small rise and passed a nearby house that had a pack of hounds lying around in front. Luckily for me the drainage ditches slowed them down and kept them from being able to come at me from all sides. I don't know if any of them would have bitten me. My bark and bike pump may have held them off. Maybe they just enjoyed the chase. I don't need to know how sincere they were. There was a definite lack of sincerity in any concern the owners displayed. Back home the owners are responsible for their dogs. They are supposed to maintain control of their animals even if it is only by voice. I can't recall any dog owners in Arkansas calling off their dogs.

Bozos, roads, and dogs were tipping the scales away from the side of impressive scenery. I even come across a few signs for breweries and vineyards. This could be such a nice area for package bike tours and such. The weather can be pleasant. Throw in a few wine tastings and it gets to look even more appealing. I didn't get to sample the wine so don't know how much of a draw that would be. This could be a little Napa Valley sort of thing. Oh well, that is the job of the local people and government. If they wanted that they would probably have done something about it. A sag wagon for some of these hills, or for those with too much wine, would be handy. For me it was Gatorade, grunting, and dodging dogs.

The weather was pleasant but the stories I heard were just amazing. In one store I mentioned how nice and quiet the area was. The clerk did an excellent job of dispelling that notion. She had been robbed and attacked at knifepoint a while back. Luckily she wasn't cut but she may have still been recovering from the emotional damage. She just kept going on about it for about 10 minutes. Maybe she needed someone to talk to who wasn't one of her neighbors. I got an uncomfortable earful. I hope she is okay.

For most of the day the weather was what I expected in the Fall: nice and moderate. It wasn't too hot or cold or windy. A few clouds hung around just to take the edge off. About mid afternoon, the morning dew clouds were joined by their cousins. The cloud family reunion looked to be fairly solid and well attended. By the time I was in Russellville I had gotten out my rain gear and was straining my eyes for the motels. Motels cluster at Interstate off ramps. I was not on the Interstate and had to get back over there somehow. Over there meant that I could see the Interstate across the big flat of water that I was beside. Sure enough there were the motels too. Despite what the map showed, I decided to abandon my course at the first opportunity to head over that way. There was a park that not only didn't have a shoulder, it had a curb. So much for stepping out of the way of traffic. Despite that, I wanted to get to shelter and I had no indication that any other route would be better. At least none of them could be shorter than this one. It looked like a nice place to sit and watch the water, but that was not the time. I leaned out of the way when the traffic would surge through and finally made my way to the exit.

There were more rooms in all of those motels than there were people in some towns that I had passed through. Getting into one was tougher than I had thought. This was a college town and this was a weekend in the Fall. Some reunion was slurping a lot of the rooms up. The football game wasn't helping either. Luckily I got in just early enough to get a room. I was tired and the weather seemed to be acting up. Just to be on the safe side I got the room for two nights. If everything was fine in the morning, then I could check out early. If not, I was in a good spot to spend an extra day. My progress had been better than expected. I was about a day ahead and pleased with how well I was doing.

It looked like I would shoot for the Gulf Coast once I got across the Mississippi. It wasn't the shortest way to Key West but it was flatter and gave me the opportunity to reach salt water sooner with the small price of possibly lengthening the total trip time. I was feeling the pressure of getting home before the holidays. It wasn't just the holidays but getting back home before the preparations really got started. Coming home on

Thanksgiving morning was definitely too late. I needed time ahead of that as well.

The following morning was wet, cold, and gray. That's the way I felt. It was also a good description of the weather. Evidently I had snagged a cold somewhere along the way. My average mileage had increased and that might have helped bring it on. Whatever the cause, part of the cure was to sit tight for a day.

Well, sitting tight is tough for me to do sometimes so instead I walked into town to find a place to shoot off some emails. So much for staying out of the rain. Before I got to town I found the college. Colleges have libraries. Libraries have computers. Viola, I had access. Well, I had access after standing in line and filling out paperwork. All of that was to provide rigorous computer security; a cause that I agree with. Humans are still the weak link. Despite the precautions, it was a while before I realized that the computer wasn't running under my new account. It was still logged on under someone else's name. All I was doing was sending some emails so I let it slide and kept on working. So much for computer security.

Aside from that walk I really did take it easy. There wasn't much else to do so when I got back, so I didn't miss the opportunity to sleep. The weather wasn't so bad that I couldn't have continued, but my body probably would have rebelled. A bicycle doesn't go very far when the engine is coughing.

At dinner I overheard an unsettling dinner conversation. I had a bit of good science fiction to read so I actually didn't want to overhear anyone. Unfortunately, some folks don't have much of a volume control over their voice so I didn't have much choice. I considered asking for a different table but then I heard that they were going to have dessert so I figured it wouldn't go on for much longer. On an upbeat note, the dessert was the father's way of celebrating his daughter's birthday. That was a nice thing to be sitting beside. The walls of the booth were high enough that I couldn't see either one of them but evidently father and daughter were there to celebrate something like her twelfth birthday. It started to get strange after the cake arrived. Instead of talking about her, he went on a long discourse about how her mother kicked him out. He claimed she was a thief because he couldn't take whatever he wanted when he left. I didn't want to remember the details so I can't recite them here. For that I am glad, but what stayed with me was how vehemently this man celebrated his daughter's birthday. I can't believe that he thought this was what she wanted to hear while she ate her birthday cake. Whatever had really happened between husband and wife is a big guess. What was so sad was to hear the silence from the daughter. Maybe she agreed with him. Maybe she didn't. Maybe she was really confused. In any case I have a hard time imagining her enjoying the evening. Timing is everything or at least counts for a lot. About the time things got so bad that I wanted to do something about it, they were gone. I wasn't from around there and didn't know everything about the situation. What would I say? "Hi, I am from someplace completely different and don't have kids and have a nice wife and I think you are a self centered donkey with the brains of a peanut." There's a good chance that listening to me say that to her father probably wasn't on her birthday wish list either. If she was sixteen and rebellious, then maybe. Who knows? It was just one of those moments that made me happy for knowing the people that I do.

I went back to the room for something a bit more upbeat and to prepare for riding out the next day. The weather wasn't supposed to be much better, but it would be a Sunday and that would be the best time to make my way through the city of Little Rock.

Am I Done?

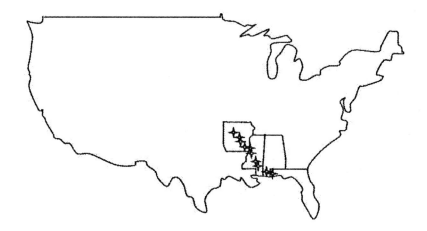

October 22   Russellville to Little Rock

Well a day off and the weather still looks like it wants to rain. It never got around to it though. It started out as a Seattle-ish gray mist and never amounted to much. By the end of it the skies had cleared off leaving me with only a light headwind. The road leveled out quite a bit as well and has a good shoulder. Not a bad day for a bike ride.

The area gets more urban slowly. There aren't as many dogs running out onto the road. There are more bozos driving by spouting what they consider to be witty commentary. By the way, I notice that it is always a car with at least two young guys in it. Solo drivers keep quiet. Well closer to a city there are more people so there are going to be more bozos.

The area is pretty. The Fall colors are nice to have going by as I ride. It is late enough now that the leaves are skittering across the street as the wind gusts. The houses look nicer as well. While the road keeps to the flats, the houses are built on small rises about 100 yards back from the road. Looks like a nice arrangement.

Arkansas shuts down on Sundays. Lots of the stores are closed which makes it harder for me to count on getting food, water, and rest stops. Traffic is lower as well.

Little Rock is a good proper city with confusing roads, one way streets, suburbs and an industrial district. Going through cities on Sundays is so much easier than negotiating them during workweek traffic. I find a hotel, not a motel, that is on the edge of town. This is the first time I've had to put the bike on an elevator since Mukilteo.

The weather didn't look the best but sitting another day in Russellville wasn't going to get me anywhere. As bad as the weather looked, my reaction was probably colored by how much it looked like the numbing conditions I had in Kansas. Luckily it just looked the same. The temperature was more agreeable as long as it didn't rain and the winds weren't too eager to get in my way.

It would be another day without the Interstate. Even though I had slept by it, I had to immediately steer away from it and seek out the old highway outside of town. That Sunday morning in Russellville was a quiet time. Saturday night hadn't been but that was because of the folks returning from the football game.

The first part of the route played tag with the water. I think that was the old highway. It did its best to stay flat which is easiest to do down by the shore. The hilly points of land were significant, short, steep hills that couldn't be ignored. Well, the important thing was to get a workout.

The area wasn't quite rural but it wasn't very urban either. There were lots of scattered homes. Some were small farms. Some were large yards. I had been hoping for this kind of density. It should be easy to find places to eat and rest in an area like that. Ah, but it was a Sunday.

Evidently, Arkansas' blue laws were still in effect. I don't know how much that had to do with it, but almost all of the places I passed by were closed. The first place that I dropped into was one of those mini-marts that was probably best known for its fine collection of pornography. Of course, calling those magazines as "a fine collection of pornography" wasn't my opinion but it must have had a good number of proponents. The store must have been doing a brisk business in them to have so many. I bought the bare minimum of fluids and fuel that I was after but couldn't use the rest room. One woman was running the store and the rest room was behind her counter. I can't blame her for not wanting to let a stranger in behind her back. Besides, from working in such a place, she might have an odd opinion of men. She seemed very nervous so I didn't want to cause her any extra anxiety. Fortunately for me I found a grocery with more useful things and a rest room just a little bit farther down the road.

Sometimes routes just worked out nicely. That time the twists and turns in the route took me to the far side of the Interstate for the afternoon. For me that meant crossing it about lunch time and finding a restaurant sitting right there on the other side of the interchange. A sit down lunch was one of those luxuries I got to enjoy only about once or twice a week. Diners could keep the same menu coast to coast from what I could tell. Breakfast and supper were more likely to change than lunch was. Early or late I could get a hint of regional cooking. Lunch everywhere seemed to be a choice between a bacon double cheeseburger or a club sandwich.

The afternoon was spent getting closer to the city of Little Rock. A city announced itself by distributing its commuters around its outskirts. About thirty miles out of town I would start to see houses that obviously had never had a farm attached to them, and whose lawns were probably treated with more care and chemicals than any farmer's field. The architecture would change and the house's layout would seem to be chosen for its looks and not its functionality. Nearer the city, image was more important. It may all be within an easy commute for a car but I still would have hours to go to get there. Closer in, the machine shops and stores would start to spring up. Closest in was the land of railroads and industrial buildings.

When I crossed back under the Interstate, it was obvious I was getting close. Besides seeing the skyline, I could see the difference in the litter on the side of the road and things like curbs replaced drainage ditches. Eventually I entered the rat's maze of surface streets that surround any city. Coming in through the Interstate was probably straightforward but the surface streets that I had to take had to wind around the on ramps and off ramps. Traffic was busier and the number of bozos reached the highest level of the entire trip. Why is it that young males that are probably homophobic whistle at bicyclists as if they were making a pass at them? That's a rhetorical question. The irony was so comical to me that I am glad they didn't stop. I would have probably laughed in their face and that was not the safest way through town. At least in town the bozos were kids in beat up compact cars rather than out on the road where some of the bozos were driving 80,000 pounds of truck within a few feet of my shoulder.

Finally I made it to one of the bridges over the Arkansas River. I was so glad to see the river doing well. In Colorado it had seemed big for its age, freshly thrown down a mountainside. In Kansas though it seemed to broaden, slow and then dissipate. I wondered if it was being sucked dry for irrigation and would just fade away. I like to see rivers flowing and alive. It had been doing fine since Oklahoma and was fun to meet it again in Little Rock.

I got to downtown later in the afternoon than I would have liked, but I was glad that I reached the city on a Sunday. There was a hotel right there on the waterfront but I decided to make it through the downtown so that Monday morning traffic and I wouldn't have to deal with each other. In a city as busy as Little Rock I had expected to find lots of hotels just by riding through. Well I rode through and found myself back amongst urban housing. Even calling on the cell phone didn't get me much better directions. Eventually I meandered along one way streets and sidewalks until I found the Interstate again and took a crack at the first hotel I found.

My goal was not to find interesting lodging. Most nights I wanted a simple bed in a clean and safe place. I suppose I did get that but life was odd in the hotel I found. Getting a bicycle through double doors was one rite of passage. Next came the disturbing step of listening to the woman in front of me getting a room while taking great precautions to make sure that her husband couldn't find her. I know that unfortunately happens too often, but knowing that didn't make it easier to listen to. When getting my room, the desk manager pointed out that they don't put people on the first few floors unless they have to. There was something about security and the condition of the rooms. At least I got a good view that way from the fifth floor.

Down in the restaurant was the most informal setting I have ever come across. The atmosphere was as casual as the family room of a household of teenagers and the food preparation and presentation wasn't much above that. The service was so casual that they didn't even bring me what I ordered. For that price I wasn't surprised. The food was food and I was hungry. The meal didn't sit well with some of the guests as one older man pointed out loudly to the man in charge. The place met my needs but I don't think I would recommend it as a vacation spot. Maybe stopping early at the nicer place at the cost of having to deal with Monday morning traffic wouldn't have been such a bad idea.

Little Rock was a decision point for the route. Whether I was taking the short route to Key West or the longer flatter route via the Gulf Coast, it made most sense to go through Little Rock. Once there I could no longer just debate which way to go. A decision had to be made by the morning. I had to point myself towards one of two bridges over the Mississippi. North, and I would be near Memphis heading towards the Key West route through the middle of Mississippi and Alabama. That was a hilly route but it could shave some miles off the total distance to Southern Florida. It looked like I was running out of time and money though. I had kept to my budget. There wasn't any slack left in it and the stock market was doing terrible things. I had to keep in mind closer destinations just in case things didn't work out for getting to Key West. There were two other goals that I could aim at: the Atlantic Coast and the Gulf Coast. The northern route would keep me inland longer so quick trips to either coast would be tough. South, and I would be down near Louisiana and crossing in a more empty part of the country. It would bring me closer to the Gulf Coast; but if I decided to continue on to Key West it could add a lot of miles. Neither way was obviously quicker. The shorter, hillier routes could be slower than the longer but flatter routes. The season was wearing on and I would rather have made it to one of the coasts if I couldn't reach Key West. Besides, I didn't know if bicycles were allowed on either of those bridges. While I had been pretty scrupulous about following traffic laws, if I had to cross the Mississippi illegally, it would be easier to do it off the beaten path. The more traveled road might have signs clearly denying me the use of the road. The less traveled road might have less stress and no sign. I couldn't find a reliable source of information. It was odd having to go that far to find out whether I would be allowed to cross. In the Rockies, the road could be closed to me for physical reasons like snow. Over the Mississippi it could be because of someone's whim. Considering what I had experienced since Kansas, I didn't expect to find a nice arrangement like what I had when I crossed the Columbia.

At least past Little Rock I would have the Ozarks behind me. The rest of the terrain shouldn't get any hillier than that. The weather was cooperating and I was halfway across the state.

October 23 Little Rock to Pine Bluff

It is apparent that this road is getting closer to the Mississippi. It is the flattest road of the trip so far. So this is what the flood plain looks like. I start to see signs for bayous and sure enough there are some big wet places around here. One has picnic tables in the water. How inviting.

The farms are getting bigger so the people and dogs are more spread out. Some of the yards as far enough from the road that the dogs are tired by the time they get out to me.

As I approach Pine Bluff I come across their Army Arsenal. It doesn't blow up. I am glad.

The weather is heating up again and the headwinds are picking up too. Stopping for lunch I notice that I am feeling very tired and am not looking forward to riding 40 miles to the next hotel. After much agonizing I decide to stay in Pine Bluff. As I am checking into the motel, I notice that I am falling asleep at the counter. Maybe that bug I had back in Russellville is still with me. Oh well, at least I can get some laundry done here. They give me a brand new room that was only finished a few days ago. I am honored.

Now, that is truly flat land. It was such a nice thing to find. I don't know for sure if that area is considered flood plain. Maybe it isn't now, but it felt like it was at one time. It is mostly unruffled land where the main thing that kept me from seeing very far was a turn in the road and some trees. When the world gets that flat there isn't much reason not to spread out. The farms started to grow. Maybe they weren't as big as the ones in Kansas or the ranches in Utah, but the houses were way off the road. It was nice to get to the point where I could watch the bigger dogs run after me without worrying about having them catch me. They got in a good run and a lot of barking and never got close. I had a minor distraction. They had an excuse to feel like they did something deserving of their next nap.

The bayous showed up before I thought they would. I hoped the next surprise wasn't an alligator lying on the side of the road. Southern Florida still seemed the best place for that to happen but the image came to mind. As long as I stayed near the bayous I knew the road won't go up or down much. At one point I passed a bayou and realized that it was also a city park. The sign said so but I figured it was just a small nature preserve. I noticed that not only was the sign in the water, but the picnic tables were too. Maybe this was a sign of poor drainage rather than any attempt at providing habitat for wet critters.

There is balance in life and just as I started to enjoy the flat land, I also started to encounter headwinds. Otherwise riding along there with a tailwind in fine weather would be a real joy and a chance to cover lots of mileage.

That corner of Arkansas was busy but not exactly brimming with motels. They were still usually about forty miles apart. I hoped to make about seventy miles a day but the days were getting noticeably shorter. I always wanted to get into town with at least an hour to spare so I had time to run errands before the Sun went down. I would also allow another hour just in case I had to fix a flat or wanted to talk to someone for a while. That accounted for a couple of hours a day. Whenever I came across a motel I would have to figure out if there was enough time to get to the next motel and leave myself that extra hour or two. I made it to Pine Bluff in fine time right around lunch, but it was getting tough with the wind. The motel I found looked new. They were still pouring the driveway sealant. They had a desk manager who was nice enough to call up ahead to see if there were rooms in the next town up the road. That was very nice of her. They didn't seem to be getting much business with all of the asphalt activity. It sounded like there was a place to stay in the next town, but about the time she got off the phone I realized that I was having a hard time staying awake. Without noticing it, I leaned forward and had rested my head on the counter. I don't think I had ever been that tired after my hundred mile days. Either the wind was worse than I thought or I needed more rest than I had given myself back in Russellville. Looking out the front window I notice that the flags are full up and flapping. That was not a light wind. I took a room there for the night. It looked like another good day to do laundry.

Walking over to my room I met a businessman. I was in my bike clothes so we fell into talking bike trips. Evidently he had lived near

Seattle at one time and had done a lot of riding. Seattle has rain, wind, and hills and for some reason still has a lot more cyclists than a lot of places. Why aren't there a lot of them down where it was warm and flat? In any case it turned out that he is off to pursue his dream of inventing a bit of medical hardware and software. Kaye works at a company that does that sort of thing so we get to talking about how the industry works. At the start of the conversation we were as superficial as any two strangers: pleasantries and such. After talking about some shared interests and common experiences he left me with the good advice to take a break and be nice to myself. I was not in a race and shouldn't stress out over the ride. Talking to a fellow cyclist always helped.

My room was brand new. No one had ever stayed there. If so, they would have noticed that the couch blocked the control panel for the air conditioner. No one may have stayed there, but someone had used the bathroom. So much for getting a brand new place. I didn't complain. It was a nice large room and gave me a comfortable place to read and lie around for a day. Once I had a chance to relax I realized that I probably still had a bit of cold. I hadn't lost weight but I was evidently in good enough shape to ride 45 miles in a day even when I had a cold. That must account for something.

By stopping halfway through the day I possibly delayed my crossing of the Mississippi. I looked forward to that crossing and dreaded it at the same time. If the next morning I woke up amazingly refreshed, then it was possible for me to cross. I would hesitate from doing that though because there was a long dearth of lodging on the west side of the river. Getting to the river late in the afternoon and then having to turn back would be bad. I wanted to cross in the early afternoon. In any case I still had a lot of riding to do but I was getting there.

October 24 Pine Bluff to McGehee

Hmmm, this headwind is not letting up and the Weather Channel is talking about the unseasonably warm weather this region is having. I believe it. The flood plain continues so at least I am not fighting hills and such. This road is leading to one of the two bridges in Arkansas that crosses the Mississippi so the traffic is picking up. Luckily it also has a nice shoulder.

I get to see my first fields of cotton. It is cotton harvesting time and the sides of the road have all of these furry balls of dirty white cotton. It looks like someone should comb the shoulder and make some money. The farms have gotten big enough that dogs are no longer much of a problem. This stretch still has fewer bozos than the rest of my time Arkansas but still more than the average for the trip overall.

This is a long day. Partially it is to make up for the short day yesterday but it is also nice flat roads. If only I had a tail wind instead of the headwind.

Outside of McGehee I find one of the few roadside parks of the trip. Most breaks are taken inside a convenience store or just standing by the side of the road. It is nice to sit in the shade for a while. As I roll on in to McGehee I find that by taking the break I missed out on the last room in the Best Western. Luckily the place next door has rooms and they are about half the price. You get what you pay for but I won't complain since it is far better than riding another 20 miles to the next town or trying to find a campground. There aren't many of those around in some of these rural areas. Dinner and breakfast are a fine repast of food made at the local convenience store.

The biggest hill of the day was an overpass built to jump over the railroad. It was right beside a picturesque abandoned cotton mill that was beside fields of freshly picked cotton. It was almost like I was being given as many hints as possible that I was definitely in a different part of the country. The old building may have looked quaint but I wondered about what drove it out of business. It obviously wasn't because it was too far from the road, rail, or cotton.

The day was nice and clear so it was a nice place to stop for a bit and get a look around the countryside. I couldn't expect any grand vistas but there was a series of vignettes of trees, towns and fields. I didn't expect to see a big change until I was over the Mississippi and maybe not even then. I wondered if the area gets flooded. If it does, then I had stopped on one of the few high points. It must be awesome and terrible to be stuck there and surrounded by water without any other land in sight. In the early nineties I got to fly over the floods up by St. Louis, but seeing it from the air, while impressive, can't have the same impact as standing on a island of highway.

Each day I was constantly aware of how far I was from the next motel and was always thinking of contingencies and alternatives. If I was riding with someone I might not have worried so much. Instead there were some days where my brain hurt from concerning itself with what was effectively something that I needn't worry about. I was aware that I was thinking too much. That was why I tried to make more time for breaks and such. Outside McGehee I noticed a convenient, and more importantly, shaded rest stop. It was a local one without rest facilities and was not much more than a gravel lot with some picnic tables under some shade trees. It still looked wonderful and cool to me. That was one of the few times that I actually laid down and closed my eyes for about ten minutes. Most of my breaks were spent leaning on the bike while I downed a sport bar and some water. Laying down in the shade was such a treat.

About the time that I was ready to go I decided to call ahead for reservations. Hopefully having reservations set up I could relax more and coast into town. Instead I found out that the town was almost completely booked up and that I would have to hope for cancellations when I got there. That was not relaxing. If I couldn't get a room there, I would have to ride another twenty miles to the next town. That was not a comforting thought. When I got to town there were only two motels. I pulled into the first one and found out that there had been a cancellation but that they had just given it to a couple of businessmen ten minutes earlier. I was tired. It was hot. I wasn't happy. The desk manager was nice enough to call next door though. The two motels were neighbors. They had plenty of room. Hallelujah.

Within a few minutes I had gone from preparing myself to ride for a couple more hours to thankfully collapsing in a heap. The folks next door were quite friendly. They explained that the local industry, which eludes me now, was retooling their facility. Most of the people doing the work were from out of town and had been living in those two motels for the last few weeks. I was lucky to come by just when the work was almost done, which had allowed some folks to go home and free up a room for me. Those motel owners may be the most generous I met. My habit was to mail a postcard from each place that I stayed. Unfortunately there weren't any postcards nearby. When I asked about where I could find some, the proprietor offered me the keys to his car so I could drive to the local mega-store to pick some up. That was incredibly gracious but I couldn't accept. I couldn't see risking someone's car that was worth thousands of dollars for a twenty five cent postcard. The offer was most impressive.

It was only after I got settled that I thought about food. I hadn't seen a restaurant nearby but I was sure that some one would deliver pizza if nothing else. That was silly of me. Just because the town was good sized does not mean that every strip mall will have food or that people would deliver pizzas. I was lucky enough that the local gas station had added a mini-mart like so many others have. This one was unique. It was not part of some chain and didn't have a fast food franchise stuck on its side. Instead it was a local outfit and they had a regular old grill in back. Dinner would be no problem but I had better like it fried. In my normal life I have fallen out of the habit of eating fried food. I still have a craving for it though and was amazed to see the variety of foods that had been fried up. Considering how healthy my diet is at home, that dinner was a very guilty fried chicken treat. They even had fried sweet potatoes.

While I was paying for dinner, I got to talking about the town with the woman behind the cash register. There was the usual chitchat about how things were fine but according to her they weren't as fine as they used to be. What was chilling was the tidbit she threw in about how many people were dying around there. I had heard that a lot of small towns were getting aged populations because all of the young folks were moving out. If so, then an older population would naturally see a lot of funerals. Nope, she assured me that these were folks in their forties and fifties. This thought sunk in as I realized that my dinner was definitely not low fat and that the wall behind the counter was stacked with cigarette cartons. Maybe she exaggerated or maybe it was a fluke string of unfortunate deaths, but I didn't come away from that with a nice comfortable feeling. Asking about how many people had died recently was not a common topic of conversation when I would roll into town. I wondered how many other towns possibly had such low life expectancies. Thinking back I realized that there were a lot of people with walkers and oxygen bottles. The actual numbers may not be high, but there were enough images that it was a disquieting thought. I wasn't losing as much weight as I had hoped for on the ride but at least my cardiovascular system was probably doing well.

That night I was a little anxious. The next day was when I would try to cross the Mississippi. If for some reason I couldn't get across, then I might have to do a radical route change and head south into Louisiana. Maybe the end of the ride would be New Orleans. At least they know how to celebrate down there.

October 25 McGehee to Indianola

I cross the Mississippi! The day started out with headwinds as I headed south towards Lake Village. There are some big nice homes and estates along the lakes down here. There are also some run down homes as well. Arkansas is like that; the neighborhoods are a mixed bag of big houses on big yards beside houses that look like the next hurricane will put them into Nebraska.

As I turn east to cross the Mississippi, the winds turn and become tail winds. Oh what a feeling!

The bridge is as tall and as long as I had expected. This is the Mississippi after all. The bridge has to be tall enough for the ship traffic and the long enough to span the levees on either side of the river. All along the ride I have been aware that they might not allow bicycles on the bridge. One thing I have found on this trip is that most people, including police and tourism officials, are not aware of the actual conditions a cyclist will face on a ride like this. Because of that I realized that I could not find a credible source of information about whether I would be allowed to use the bridge. This potentially could end the trip right here and had been on my mind for days. As I approach the bridge I notice that there are no signs saying I can't proceed. I also notice that the shoulder is disappearing and that there are only two lanes of traffic. Sure enough, after waiting for a BIG gap in traffic, I start over the bridge and find that there are two lanes, no curb and a somewhat bent steel "sidewalk" that is separated from the road bed by about a half a foot of air. It has a railing on the waterside but not on the roadside and may not be wide enough for me and my panniers. This now becomes a sprint. I try to cross as quickly as I can to get out of the way of traffic. On a bridge this long it is inevitable that the trucks will catch up with me. My sprint got me past the high point of the bridge first so the trucks can see past me and are able to pass once they see it is clear ahead. Before I am across though there will be two times where I slowed traffic down to my speed. I didn't like doing it but decided that it was time to assert myself. Once across I am delighted. I have biked from Washington all the way to Mississippi and I am exhausted. There is no air left for me to cheer with.

On this side of the Mississippi there are still cotton fields but rising out of them are billboards for the casinos on this side of the river. The Mississippi Visitor Center leading to the casinos is a renovated sternwheeler in it's own artificial pond by the side of the road. The women working behind the desk are so naturally relaxed and comfortable while *getting me information that they create an atmosphere where I just want to sit a spell. But enough of that. I decide to celebrate the tail wind by going on to Indianola. A bit more riding today made it easier for the logistics line up through the rest of Mississippi.*

The unseasonably warm weather is enough to make this the hottest place in the nation today. How do I find this kind of weather?

Riding that last little bit of Arkansas was pleasant. I came across the first big estates that I had seen since Colorado. They were big houses down by what is probably an old bit of the river that had been cut off and was now a lake. Calling all of that grass a yard just doesn't seem to capture the view. It was grass but it was manicured and measured in acreage. What do people do with that much green carpet? Most places with that much land are using it for crops, livestock, or for really big pets. Some of the land looked like it was only touched by the wheels of a riding lawn mower.

Right beside it, or more likely on the other side of the road, were all types of houses. Some could be plunked down in any patch of suburbia and fit right in. Some looked like they could be picked up by those little gusts of wind called hurricanes and tornadoes and blown away as debris. At least folks weren't living in little enclaves where everyone makes the same money, drives the same cars, wears the same clothes and thinks the same things. If these folks get together for parties there could be fascinating conversations that pop you right out of your comfort zone.

I had expected there to be more services on either side of the bridge. I guess that was kind of silly considering that locating a business right beside a flood prone river might not be the best idea. As I approached the bridge I was very aware of whether traffic was coming in waves or a continuous stream, whether it was predominantly trucks or cars, and whether it looked like I would have a place to ride. The ride to the bridge had been reasonable but the river was a significant hurdle for me to cross and I wasn't going to approach it lightly.

The last little bit of shoulder died out on the approach to the bridge. I stopped at the end of it and tried to see as far ahead as possible. I checked out the bridge's height, length and surface. It didn't look good and it wasn't. In my decades of riding that was the scariest bridge I have ever crossed and it looked that way even before I set out on it. I waited until I couldn't see any traffic coming. Being somewhat up on the ramp to the bridge I got a good long look back down the road, but couldn't see past a small forest so I didn't know how much of a break I had to deal with. Bridges over rivers like this are surprisingly tall. Climbing one is not much different than climbing any other hill. It is just that they are man made and surrounded by air. Did I mention that I have a fear of heights? My greatest dread would be that the bridge would have an open metal deck instead of something solid like asphalt or concrete. At least I had something solid below me. Beside me however, there was a raised sidewalk. Instead of a gutter between the roadbed and the sidewalk there was gap big enough to drop my foot down into. It wasn't really a normal sidewalk and might not even be there for that purpose. It was above the road surface by about a foot and a half and was constructed of metal. It looked like it had a hard life. There were lots of dents and warps to the surface. It might have been wide enough for my bike but I would have had to ride near the edge by the road. My choice was to jockey with traffic and sprint my way across or to prop myself up on what might not be a sidewalk after all and hope I didn't get dumped back into the road. The prospect of falling from that sidewalk into traffic without losing anything down that air gap while cars and trucks might be bearing down on me was too much. Out there in the lane I sprinted for the other side of the river.

I actually made it quite a way before any traffic came up from behind. It didn't seem to be a main road. I suspected as much. One reason I picked it was to minimize the traffic hassle. That didn't mean the road was empty. Once I was past the midpoint, the trucks coming up from behind were able to see past me and use the other lane to get around me. The two times when there was oncoming traffic were incredibly tense. I really appreciate the patience or at least the lack of horn honking by the truckers. When they had a gap they took it and got out of my vicinity. The Mississippi is big enough to make the bridge length feel like it was over a mile, and the levees make it even longer. By the time I got to the opposite levee, I was wasted. I said a weak yippee more as a joke commentary on my energy than in any celebration.

The bridge might not be all that bad if I was to go back and look at it again. Maybe it was worse. I wasn't about to sit down and measure things out or stop in the middle and take pictures. All I got to see of the Mississippi River was a glimpse at a barge making its way upstream. All the other images are a blur of pictures of the road surface with glimpses of the traffic that I saw over my shoulder. The bridge is probably an engineering marvel but for this bicyclist it was a terror.

I was in Mississippi and back in cotton fields. My fear over the bridge slowly faded away. What would come to the fore were the horror stories about Mississippi that I had heard from folks who had moved from there. They were confident that I had a good chance of being hung off the back of a pickup truck and dragged to death. Now isn't that just the sort of imagery I needed as encouragement? The first step was to make it past the casinos. Their billboards had been announcing them for a long time.

There was a Visitor Center a few miles in from the border. It seemed to cater mostly to the casino crowd. They had water, facilities, and some of the nicest people. Seeing an old paddleboat in its own little pond was definitely a unique part of the trip. Inside the paddleboat was the Visitor Center. The folks working there were all women wearing nice blue and white dresses. Sorry for not being sure of what to call them. I don't shop for dresses. These ones though were kind of bloused out. They weren't the big bell type things but they were relaxed and very Old South. I am sure that was the atmosphere they were trying to create and they succeeded. No matter how many people were in there asking questions, they were always answering everyone with marvelous manners and grace. One in particular was sitting in a wing back chair reading the newspaper and would just conversationally answer people's questions without seeming to upset her reading while leaving the visitor relaxed and informed. That didn't mean that they could produce a bike map for me but they made me feel good about that. They were wonderful people.

There were plenty of places to stay near the casinos but getting a few miles farther to Indianola would line me up nicely for the rest of the state. It made for a long day. The casinos would have had great amenities, but I was happy enough to enjoy a tailwind. Everyone has their own luxuries and, when riding a bike, a good tailwind is hard to beat.

The next main milestone would be the Gulf Coast. From there quite a few things were possible, but at least if I made it there I could feel like I had gone coast to coast. It wasn't my initial idea of a coast, but it was a welcome new idea. Getting to the Atlantic coast would still be possible. I would let the weather help decide. If I got to the Gulf Coast and the wind was out of the west, then I would shoot for the Atlantic. A head wind would be a different story. My luck with weather had been lousy. Especially since I came across Kansas, often enough the winds had not been my friend and all along the trip the temperatures had usually been unseasonably hot or cold. Moderation didn't seem to happen often. The prospect of riding through Florida into a headwind just seemed ugly. A tailwind on the other hand would be marvelous. There was nothing to do about it until I got there.

October 26 Indianola to Yazoo City

The choice of stops today is either Yazoo City at about 50 miles or Jackson at about 100 miles. As I head out the door I hope that yesterday's tailwind out of the west will become a tailwind out of the north as I am now headed south again. Jackson is possible with a good tail wind and a good level road. Of course Yazoo City is a fine place to stop just because of the name.

I actually end up staying in Yazoo City because the wind returns to being a headwind, and the heat continues. The road is still flat in the morning. The Mississippi flood plain is enormous and makes for some potentially fast riding if not for the winds. I end up geared down as if I was climbing some hill.

This area is definitely rural. The farms are still large and the houses spread out. It takes me a while to realize that the ponds that I am passing are man made for raising catfish. They are growing a lot of catfish down here. Well, that is a guess. Seeing cotton in the fields is much easier that noticing catfish in a pond. There are lots of artificial ponds and lots of businesses selling catfish farming equipment. There are not many stores though. This is a working area to the extent that it seems to be easier to find farm equipment than food and drink. Maybe people don't like to build gas stations in flood plains.

The lack of a shoulder slows me down. I pull over whenever I can to get out of the way of traffic. The traffic really doesn't slow down for me but I figure that whenever I can make it easier for them I will do so. I definitely watch for oversize loads. There are lots of manufactured homes on the roads around here.

Things go slowly enough that I decide to stay in Yazoo City. Lo and behold it is on the edge of the flood plain and a good sized city. I find myself having to climb some fairly steep hills through town as the hotels are on the other side of town. I'll miss the flood plain.

Riding on the flood plain was nice. If I could only have done something about the other people trying to use the road. So many of them insisted on using cars and trucks. Oh well, a shoulder would have made a big difference, but there was nothing to do about it but get out of the way. I could've asserted myself and plunked myself out into the road. In some states that is actually what a bicyclist is supposed to do. Realistically that seems a questionable way to ride for a few thousands of miles. I gave up a lot of momentum pulling over and taking short breaks to let clumps of traffic pass. One of the few times that there was a wide spot to pull over into I found myself in the way of farm equipment. The wide spot was where they drove the equipment out onto the field. Sometimes it was hard to win.

Catfish ponds were such a surprise. I wouldn't have imagined people having to do so much building to raise a bottom feeder like catfish. Lots of the ponds were contained in berms of earth so they were actually above me on occasion. There was equipment for aeration and I guess some of it was for harvesting. The water table didn't seem to be too far away and it seemed easier to just dig a hole in the ground and throw in some fish. Evidently it wasn't as easy as I thought.

The heat and headwinds kept the air nice and clear but they were not making my life better. The flat lands and the views were appreciated but the wind and lack of a shoulder slowed me down a lot. Yazoo City was not far from Indianola, but I was tired enough when I got there.

Usually the motels were the first thing I'd find coming into a town. That was especially true if an Interstate was nearby. Other times they had erected really tall signs. In Yazoo City, it looked like I had come in via the back door. Instead of motels, I found industrial buildings. That was one of the things the cell phone was for. I called around and finally found someone who would answer the phone and give me directions to his motel. I pointed out to him that I was on a bicycle. It was amazing how many people would hear me say bicycle and figure that I had really meant motorcycle. There were two routes to the motel. One went through town and up and over a couple of steep hills. It became very apparent that I was on the edge of the flood plain and leaving it behind. The other route was flat and along a bypass. Unfortunately, I didn't know about that one until later.

Riding through Yazoo was an odd and sometimes unfriendly experience. The four guys hanging out the window of a gold BMW shouting and hollering as I climbed a hill didn't help. One of those hills was probably one of the steepest sections of the whole ride. Luckily it wasn't too tall. I wasn't sure that I was headed the right way but eventually I got myself to a cluster of strip malls and motels. They were on the north side of town. I had come in from the west and would be heading out to the south. In other words I got more of a tour of Yazoo City than I had of most towns.

I hadn't made it to Jackson but by that point in the ride I knew that persistence would win through. At least Kaye was off the hook for a lot of the work now. Since Colorado she hadn't had to worry about mapping out terrain and such. We still talked a lot about where I could stop and what route to take but the planning for the Southeast didn't eat into her time the way the mountains had. She deserved the break. The next day would be on a busier road. I hoped that it would have a shoulder. I felt that I deserved a break too. The bigger the road the better the chance that there would be a bit of concrete on the side. I would find out in the morning.

October 27 Yazoo City to Jackson to Magee

The heat continues but the wind dies. I think the wind gave up because it saw that I was back in hilly country again.

As the road gets closer to Jackson it develops a shoulder. I am so glad. Climbing some of these hills without a shoulder has been uncomfortable. Luckily the road is now a four lane so the traffic is spread out over more lanes.

Approaching Jackson the area becomes much more cosmopolitan. The dogs are smaller and kept behind fences more often. There are more services and the condition of the poorest homes is closer to some comfort level. They don't look like a strong wind will blow them over as easily. The kudzu is showing up now though.

Luckily for me Mississippi is like most states by letting cyclists on the Interstate. I don't get the advantage for long but it does help me get around Jackson much quicker than if I had to travel through it. I end up on the south side of Jackson early enough that I decide to push south. There is a lot of traffic around Jackson and evidently there is even more as the Gulf Coast gets closer. There are lots of trucks taking products to market and they are heading the same way I am. At least this seems to me that the roads are getting more attention and that gives me a shoulder to ride on.

On the other side of Jackson the hills die down. This definitely helps me along on a hot afternoon. I am also getting some relief from the heat from the trees along the highway. The trees are big enough and are close enough to shade my side of the highway during the afternoon. It is things like this that make Mississippi look that much nicer to me.

There is not much to say about Magee except that I like its location. It helped me make some good mileage today. I am getting close enough to Florida now that Kaye and I are talking about what day I'll get back. We've had this conversation all along but now it has become much less abstract.

Breakfast in Yazoo City was at a fast food franchise that had a play area and a lot of elderly people in walkers. Things looked a bit mismatched there. How different would the play area be if it was designed for elderly folks instead of kids?

The day started with a few hills along the road. The shoulder that I had seen as I came into town the previous night only lasted about a mile. After that I climbed hills by riding up the white line and not stopping until I got to the top. Traffic just felt that much more insistent when it was that close. Starting in the morning helped though. That kept some of the traffic down for a while. So much for the ride being a vacation where I slept late everyday and leisurely meandered along idyllic roads.

The whole area was nice and green. That was such a contrast after such large chunks of the West where there wasn't a tree for miles. I was glad that I hadn't gotten caught in any of the rainstorms that water the area. There was more wildlife too but a lot of it slithered away in the grass as I rode along. I knew it was there and didn't get to see any of it.

Jackson came up soon enough. Riding through the city on a workday did not sound like a good idea. Luckily there were no posted bicycle restrictions on the Interstate that bypassed the city. That was a much better way of getting around town. The first part was easy because I just followed the shoulder of the state highway right onto the shoulder of the Interstate. After a few miles of that nice set up came the interchanges. The on ramps and off ramps weren't what I had expected. There was a lot more traffic and very few gaps for me to slide through. There was a lot of trash on the shoulder as well. Every city had that problem. Even if there wasn't any litter, there was usually a lot of wind blown dirt and gravel that took away some of my traction. I don't think there were any close encounters but I felt the stress by the time I got to the south side of Jackson. I also knew that going through town would have been much more harrowing. After Jackson I expected the next city to be Mobile and that was half a state away.

I celebrated getting through Jackson with a white bread, bologna and American cheese sandwich. That was all they had for lunch in the mini-mart. That's better than nothing. A regular sit-down lunch would have been nice but it was looking like a 90 mile day and because it was near the end of October, the Sun was setting early.

South of Jackson I had hoped that the increased traffic would have inspired someone to install a shoulder. Where there are lots of cars there are that many more chances that one of them will have to pull over to get out of the way. I guess they just expect everyone's cars to run well or they expect folks to park in the grass and not get stuck. The shoulder went away and the traffic got worse. At least the trees had all their leaves and provided some shade just when I needed it. In the morning, the Sun had been on the opposite side of the road. As the day wore on and I headed south, the Sun came around and the shade was on my side. I still had to take breaks to let traffic by but at least that was a cool and not a broiling thing to do.

I wasn't sure how big Magee was but I was glad that it was as nicely located as it was. Getting there was much more gratifying than stopping in Jackson. I made a lot of progress that day and was nicely set up for the next day into Hattiesburg. Dinner that night was a classic for me: well done steak and a baked potato. That day's ride was one of the nicest ones of the trip as long as there was a shoulder. The people helped too. While none of them really stood out, they came across as one of the nicest set of folks that I had met.

I had set out for Key West but it looked like I might just stop in Pensacola. I was almost out of October. Key West was a long way away and I hadn't had a break in quite a while. This trip was being funded by some of my lucky investments and the market was not just sick but down right critical. It seemed like I was running out of time and money. The holidays were coming up and the bank account was running dry. The stock market was doing so poorly that it didn't look like I could go back to that well for more. Despite all of that, if the weather provided some obvious opportunity I would find some way to continue on. It wasn't looking good though.

October 28 Magee to Hattiesburg

The wind is nice enough to turn around for me today but the hills are back and the shoulders have vanished. While the shoulders may be gone, the traffic is not. This is a Saturday so the RVs are added to the mix. I worry more about RV drivers more than the truckers. The truckers are professionals. They have a much better idea of how much room they need and they are more definite in their actions. Most of the RVs are alright but some even forget to pull up their stairs before hitting the highway. To me they look like they have a bit of that Ben-Hur chariot race thing going on. The stairs would catch me right at the pedal or bottom of the pannier if they didn't get the wheel.

The hills in this area are short and choppy. Looking back into traffic doesn't give me the long clear view of what is approaching 3 miles back like I've had in most places. I end up pulling over to the side more often than usual and this slows me down a lot. Still, getting there safely is way more important than getting there quickly.

This ends up being a short day. I end up in Hattiesburg about Noon instead of my usual 2PM. The next town past Hattiesburg is about 60 miles away. That is a big jump to do in an afternoon and the traffic is getting to me. I think the area was pretty but I was too busy to notice.

Hattiesburg is about 200 miles from Pensacola. With good weather, roads, and support I've done that sort of distance a number of times on my road bike for the Seattle-to-Portland bike ride. Cool. Of course that was also with a younger body and with about 16 hours of daylight to play with. This would be a bit much for a mountain bike loaded down like I've done.

I'd prefer big cities like Mobile on Saturdays or Sundays so I might push for there if the roads and weather cooperate.

I hadn't even thought about the potential for tourist traffic on the weekends. Shouldn't there be a lull in late October? Maybe it was a lull and I would have been astonished to see it at its busiest. Evidently a lot of folks head down to the Gulf Coast on that road. The only reliably quiet days were Sundays. The road was a four lane so there were two lanes headed my way. When traffic is light, having that extra lane can greatly help ease the stress of not having a shoulder. Anyone wanting to pass me has an extra lane to play with. Unfortunately, traffic wasn't light by any means. It looked like rush hour traffic but with a much heavier mix of RVs and trucks. Sometimes I would sprint from one bit of dirt to the next. Other times I would ride to the top of the hill and wait for the next break in traffic. Neither seemed the better choice. In either case I was burning myself up in the sprints and stops and starts while wearing myself down from worrying about the traffic. I really missed the Interstate and those long open roads where I could see back for miles. Luckily no one was moving a wide load while I was out there. The day was such a blur that I don't remember much else from the ride.

I made it to Hattiesburg by lunchtime. Without any clue that the traffic might abate, I decided to sit out the rest of the day there. The next hop was much too long to do if I had to keep pulling off the road for traffic. I didn't want to get that close to the coast and get squished by traffic because I had pushed too hard. If it took an extra day or two then that was better than not getting there at all.

Hattiesburg is a college town. I don't know if that is its biggest claim to fame but it was the main thing I kept in mind as I went shopping for a room. Getting a room in a college town on a Saturday in the Fall can be hard if the football team is playing at home. Luckily for me it was an away game. There were lots of rooms to pick from. It was also another good day for doing laundry. One clue about how far south I was came from the location of the washer and dryer. They were outside under a stairwell. I can't imagine such a thing in Colorado. In Winter the clothes would freeze if you forgot and left them in the washer. What a potential mess. In Hattiesburg it made a lot of sense. All that heat and humidity from the machines could get vented straight to the atmosphere.

Because I had some spare time I roamed around looking for the postcard of the day. I had only missed three or fours days so far. All the other days I had managed to find something to send, even if it was only a note on motel stationery. Amazingly I was in a college town and couldn't even find a card about the local school. In the meantime I got to visit lots of stores and chat with more than my normal number of folks. They were all full of polite conversation and without any of the horror stories I had heard in Arkansas.

The high point was a Cajun Jambalaya dinner that had me pulling down two beers to make it through. Sign me up for more. That was good. Any hotter and I couldn't have had any. I am not one of those fellows that sucks down Jalapeno peppers just for the fun of it though I do like some heat. I don't want to know how much hotter it could have been. For most of the trip I had steered clear of alcohol. It seemed time to relax a little.

Like I'd said before, I like getting through big cities on Sundays. Mobile is a big city and it was 100 miles away. Getting through it meant riding more than ninety miles first, hopefully recovering enough to make it through the downtown area, then having enough left over to find a place to stay. That would be a tough day especially if the road and traffic didn't improve. I didn't expect a change in the weather either. It was still too hot for someone who had gotten used to Seattle's numbingly mild climate. There was an early stop in about sixty or seventy miles. If it came to staying there, I would try to get through Mobile on Monday when it wasn't rush or lunch hour. The gap between motels was one of the longest in the trip. It was such a surprise to have such a large gap in such nice country. I had expected gaps like that in the desert but not in the South. Nothing to it but to do it.

October 29 Hattiesburg to Mobile

To get to Mobile in one day requires going about 100 miles. At my normal 10 miles an hour that can take 10 hours and there are only 11 hours of light this time of year. The only breakfast near the motel is the doughnuts and fruit that they have in the lobby. Oh well at least I won't burn a lot of daylight waiting for the check.

Daylight Savings time changed the clocks last night so everyone is sleeping in today. It is also a Sunday so there shouldn't as many cars on the road and the RVs should be going the other direction. Sure enough the first few hours on the road have such little traffic that the lack of a shoulder doesn't make any difference. The hills are more spaced out as well and I can see long stretches of highway that I have all to myself. How special. There isn't even much truck traffic.

The highway is much wider now with larger medians and such so the trees aren't right beside the road anymore. There also aren't many people out this way. Instead of farms there is lumber so the number of houses and dogs is way down. Such a nice quiet peaceful Sunday morning bike ride. The only real pressure comes from my choice of making this a 100 mile day. Of course there would be pressure in any case since the first hotel is 60 or 70 miles down the road.

A few hours into the morning I think I find why the road is so empty of truck traffic. There is a 3 to 5 mile long detour around a bridge project. The detour leads off through some small towns with small roads and small bridges. *Unfortunately for me they never say how long the detour is or where it is going. I don't have any choice and luckily it doesn't take too long to get back out on the highway.*

About 4 hours into the ride I end up riding past the motel that I thought was 60 miles down the road. It was probably closer than I had thought but the sign for Mobile shows about the expected mileage. I must have been cruising. It's nice not having to dodge traffic. As I leave Mississippi I realize how nice the people were. They tended to be quite friendly and there weren't nearly as many bozos as back in Arkansas. I don't like generalizing like that but crossing the Mississippi did seem to change things.

Welcome to Alabama. Now where is a motel? I wanted to get through Mobile on a Sunday because it has some tough route finding challenges. Mobile sits on a bay on the Gulf Coast which can make it pretty and give it a nice shipping industry. Getting past Mobile Bay though can be quite tough for a bicycle. The two shortest routes go through tunnels that don't allow bicyclists. The most scenic route heads south to some islands off the coast and is a quaint way of adding 40 miles or so. There is a land based route which goes on the Interstate but it too adds lots of miles. Kaye jumped into the task of tracking down one of the local bike experts via email and found a route that only added about 10 miles and took me through the industrial and shipping parts of town. It seemed like the best way to get through Mobile and I sure didn't want to attempt it on a Monday morning.

Mobile has some nice tree lined streets running through town. There isn't much room for a bike to ride on but at least it was pleasant scenery. I think I'll skip all the parts about getting lost in the seedier parts of urban Mobile. The fun part of taking this particular route is that it ends up at a motel adjacent to a military museum park that includes the battleship U.S.S. Alabama. I was not sure I was on the right roads until I noticed that I was headed for a warship. Now that is a distinctive landmark. After over 100 miles I end up in a reasonably nice motel where the guy behind the desk is a bicyclist himself. I end up with a room with an awesome view of the ship, about a dozen pieces of armored vehicles, and a bunch of planes. There is a B-52, an SR-71, an old Sikorsky and about a dozen other airplanes. Really neat.

I hadn't expected such a setting for when I made the coast but I'll take it. After I check into the room and shower I walk down to the water and as the Sun is setting I touch the Gulf of Mexico. It may not be the Atlantic Ocean but I have made it coast to coast. It has been a long day and a long trip that is not yet over. When I set out on the trip I had a number of milestones in mind and this was one of them. It feels good to have accomplished it. Tomorrow I make for Florida which will be another milestone.

The traffic the day before had been nasty and I didn't look forward to another day of it. With the time change and my light breakfast I was on the road much earlier than usual. That was what I attributed the empty streets to. As the Sun finally made it past the treetops, I warmed up and concentrated on making mileage before the traffic woke up and caught me. After about two hours of that I was way out of town and the roads were still mostly deserted. After the traffic of the previous day, the silence seemed downright spooky. I still don't know if the cars and trucks vanished because of the road construction, because there was a better road to the coast elsewhere, or because folks were only trying to get as far as Hattiesburg. I didn't exactly survey the folks to find out what happened to all of them. I was just pleased to have the road to myself. There still wasn't any shoulder, but that didn't matter when there was only one vehicle every five or ten minutes.

There were trees everywhere along that stretch. The land had turned into longer rolling hills and maybe folks didn't want to farm that. There was definitely lumbering going on though. I could see where the trucks came onto the highway from the dirt and debris scattered about. At one point in the midst of nothing, I just stopped to enjoy the silence. The timberland and the army base ate up much of the land. No one seemed to have a reason to fit any food places into the gaps. That small breakfast was it, though considering how far I made it that day I should probably give a lot of credit to the Jambalaya.

When I came across the detour for road construction I felt my heart drop. It could explain why the traffic had vanished. If the detour was that bad I might be riding off into who knows where and adding a ton of miles with no clue that I would be headed back onto the original road anytime soon. All kinds of fears popped up. What if the detour made me miss the next motel and I would have to backtrack to find it? What if the detour led through some nasty roads that were gravel and not much else? I knew the greatest likelihood was that it would lead right back to the main drag, but I had to at least consider the other possibilities and be somewhat prepared for them. Blithely trusting the highway department to keep a touring bicyclist in mind was not very reasonable. I didn't have much choice though. Hopefully things would be okay so I took the detour. I actually considered ignoring the road closed sign but knew that all it would take to botch that idea was to find out that the road was closed because the bridge was out. I had no desire to cross a major ravine and river with the bike on my back while swimming against the current.

The detour wasn't as bad as I had feared though it wasn't very good either. It went on for miles on roads that were falling apart and over bridges that probably weren't wide enough for two trucks to pass each other. As it worked out I was in the middle of one of the longer bridges when a truck came up from behind. He was able to pass me without any problem, but he might not have been able to pass a car at that spot. I was so relieved to get back onto the main road after that detour.

The hills were benign enough that I was able to crank out some good cadence and momentum so that when I came across that motel at sixty miles I was caught by surprise. The surprise actually came before I saw the motel. I had expected the town to be small, but it was spread out over miles. It might not have many people in it but it took up a lot of room. At least the signs were spread out over miles. I found the first one much sooner than I had expected, so I expected the motel to be nearby. It ended up being miles down the road. Before I found it there was another brand new mini-mart. It was so new it looked like they hadn't even turned on the hot deli food section. Maybe they just didn't have it stocked when I got there. I celebrated my progress with some cold salty lunch type food. The woman behind the cash register was another one of those who felt that what I was doing was nearly impossible for anyone like herself to try. As much as American culture rewards people to succeed, it also seems to have an amazing element out there that is discouraging people from trying anything different.

It was time to get back on the road and commit myself to making it to Mobile. At the top of each hill I kept in mind that Mobile was at sea level so the end of the day might be a blessed downhill roll. All the intervening hills made that point academic. It was effectively downhill but I did a fair bit of climbing too.

I crossed the border into Alabama and immediately began eagerly looking for the signs for Mobile. They couldn't show up soon enough for me. Getting to the edge of town wasn't the key. I was trying to get to the other side despite having gone over eighty miles already. Getting to the far side of town was not trivial. Kaye had sleuthed out a route but I wasn't sure that I could find and follow it. As with most cities I got introduced to the city slowly. From the outskirts, through suburbia, into the city proper and then into downtown. In each of those areas the road changed for me. Sometimes I had a shoulder but then curbs would show up limiting whether I could get out of the way of traffic. Finally the sidewalks showed up along narrow streets so that sometimes I was in the road making good time but nervous, while other times I was on the sidewalk maneuvering around mailboxes and trash. In between were the rain gutters where I could not only get a flat but maybe even bend a rim in the storm grates.

The bike environment was bad but the city was much nicer. The section of town with the tree lined streets was very inviting when the traffic had abated. It was a very pleasant place. All along though I was focussed on getting to and through downtown.

As I got deeper into town, the road signs got more confusing. Out in the rural sections I could find the right road just by looking for the highway number. In town there were roads with more than one name. For folks living there it probably isn't a problem. As a tourist I was having a tough time figuring out which way my route had gone. There was one intersection in particular where the road I was following split into two. I circled around that intersection for about five minutes before just guessing at which way to go. At the time my guess seemed to be the wrong one. Within a few blocks I was out of the residential area and riding behind businesses. The road was rougher and most of the buildings looked abandoned. A little bit farther and the number of vacant and boarded up buildings grew. That didn't feel like the part of town that I wanted to break down in. I trusted to the fact that as long as I kept heading east I would find the water. Coming into one intersection I finally saw container ships a few hundred yards away. I got myself out onto that road and felt better even though I still didn't know where I was.

Getting lost in downtown late on a Sunday meant there weren't many people available to help me. I also knew that I could head south and run into water. If I did that then I would have two landmarks to help me find my place on the map. Instead, within two blocks I found a fancy downtown hotel. They were so kind to me considering that I was probably not the type of ornamentation they wanted in their lobby. They had rooms and they had advice about my bike route. They knew the route I was trying to follow and I was actually right on it. But they suggested that I try the tunnels. They didn't remember seeing any sign saying that a bicycle couldn't go that way but then they also couldn't remember if it had a sidewalk either. I took a break out on their sidewalk while I consulted the map. Why not try the tunnel? I knew it might not work but if it knocked ten miles off the trip it would be worth it. Sure enough I found the entrance and read the signs. No bicycles are allowed in the tunnels. I wasn't surprised and I wouldn't break the law so I had to head back to Kaye's route again.

All of that route finding took time. I didn't want to backtrack into downtown in the dark. Kaye's route headed north along the dock area, over a bridge, and back down the other side of the dock area. That sounded simple but it wasn't. There were lots of roads and rail lines and abandoned buildings down by the docks. It made for a confusing jumble of signs and roads. Some of them were closed for construction, which didn't give me good feelings of confidence. Two or three times I got turned around and unsure about which way to go. Eventually I picked the right path, not because it was obvious, but because that road looked like it headed back out to the Interstate and if nothing else I would be on the edge of town where there might be motels. I was so surprised to find that I was headed the right way. The main clue wasn't a road sign but my first view of the bridge. It is enormous and marvelously tall. I just kept that in sight and kept pedaling along. As I got closer to it I realized how much of a climb I was going to have to handle after 100 miles of riding. At least the shoulders were broad and the traffic was light. Getting around the expansion joints was a recurring problem but that was all doable. From the high point on the bridge I saw my destination. The battleship Alabama was hard to miss from up there.

Before I got off the bridge though I had to take a picture of it. My fear of heights is enough that every once in a while I snap a shot of a place that I am amazed to have crossed. Besides, it is a nice looking bridge. So much for documentation. The camera's batteries had died. At least I was close to the motel and the coast. Getting there was more important.

There was still a bit of confusion at the last intersection but finally I rolled up to the motel. I could see the Gulf of Mexico and would make sure I touched it before dark. I had gotten there late enough that there wasn't any place open to get postcards or batteries. Of all of the places that I documented this was one that I wanted to document the most. That doesn't mean that the universe wanted me to do so.

I made it to the Gulf Coast. It was good to see wide open water again. Getting there on my own made the celebration an fairly quiet event. I walked out around the museum pieces and went down and touched the water. Originally I had expected to not get to water until I was in the Keys. This wasn't as showy but it worked fine for me. I was on the coast now and waiting for that twenty mile an hour tailwind that would convince me to keep going.

Whether the winds showed up or not I would head for Pensacola the next day. That would get me into Florida at a point where I could conveniently fly out. There were a couple of routes to pick from and they could wait until the morning.

I called Kaye and told her when I might come back very soon. We had been having that conversation for quite a few days and the details were solidifying. Pensacola shouldn't be a problem and it looked extremely unlikely that I would be continuing on to Key West. Florida was reputed as being unfriendly to bicycles. An extra week of heat and headwinds through unfriendly environs didn't sound appealing. I kept in mind that I could always come back later.

October 30 Mobile to Pensacola

I'm on the coast and looking forward to a nice flat ride into Pensacola. Where do I get these ideas? Sure enough on the other side of the bay the road goes right up a hill and stays hilly for hours. Isn't it supposed to be flat down here?

Surprisingly I find one of the first bike route signs in a long time. Evidently it is "bike route to Florida" and is along the route that I have chosen. I like this. Then I notice it heads right up a hill with no shoulder. Argh. Soon enough the route diverges from my plan. I don't know where it is going in Florida so I keep to my old plan. I end up on a flatter road with a nice shoulder and plenty of places to eat. I think this is another one of those bike routes that governments establish that puts the cyclists on scenic roads that don't have traffic. The fact that the road is hilly, without shoulders, and has no place to get food has no bearing on the matter. Pardon the editorial commentary.

Eventually the road I follow puts itself onto a plateau that has nice houses on big lots and has a few small farms sprinkled about. I even see someone actually riding a horse. A couple of girls who look like they should be in high school are out for a leisurely ride. I've seen lots of horses cross country and now I realize that very few of them seemed to be doing anything. How rare to see one in use even if it is just for fun.

It is still hot. Evidently the last few days have tied records yet again. I'm still not used to it.

Finally I cross the Florida state line. I do so while climbing a hill. This is not my image of Florida. A trip like this is good for shattering images of places I haven't been. It is still rural where I cross so there is still a bit of riding to do before I am done. At least I have completed another milestone: I have ridden from Washington to Florida. Somewhere along the line today I should have also crossed the 3,000 mile mark. Not bad.

The end is somewhat anti-climactic. Kaye and I looked around in various ways and realized that the fun beaches in Pensacola are off the coast on a long causeway. Originally I had expected to finish on some coast and hang out on a beach for a while. The way it is here, I would still then have a long bike ride back to the airport. I decide to go straight to the airport, find a hotel there and call it good enough. After all of the heat and sunshine that I have ridden through, the prospect of lying in the Sun has almost no appeal. I'd rather back home where I can see Kaye, sleep in my own bed, and eat some healthier food.

The morning started out on a causeway that crosses Mobile Bay. I probably saw more wildlife along that stretch of road than anywhere else. There were all varieties of birds out there. The birds and the people on the side of the road were all there for the fishing. The fish probably didn't appreciate the attention. It was supposed to be yet another record setting high temperature so I was on the road early. Luckily for me the shoulder was nice and wide. I was so glad that Kaye got in touch with that bike club in Mobile. They are the ones that talked about this route and I really appreciate that bit of help. The surprise for me was finding that the route dumped out at the base of a hill on the other side of the water. All along I had grand visions of getting across the Mississippi and finding it flat all the way to the Keys. The hills weren't enormous but they looked higher because I had expected to find flat land.

The route wasn't going to be a straight one but it seemed like I couldn't get too lost. I found the bike route to Florida sign just after I crossed the road carrying the rush hour traffic. It was a fine sign and one of the few bike signs I had seen since Colorado. It felt like some one was trying to give me encouragement at the same time that they were playing a joke on me. The sign helped my confidence that I was headed the right way. It was just funny to me that it was right back onto a two lane road that went up a hill with no shoulder for a bike to ride on. Even six inches of asphalt on the side of the road can make a big difference. Instead I was grinding up a hill riding the white line. Why would this bit of road be any different?

I wished I had calibrated my altimeter back at sea level. It would have been useless but nice to know if I had really climbed much or if it just seemed that way. At least I was in a busy section of town where there were plenty of places to eat. The motel in Mobile didn't have a mini-mart nearby for me to stock up at so it wasn't too long before I was low on supplies. Somewhere in the morning I saw another of the bike route signs. It was at an intersection and pointed off in a direction that didn't agree with me. The sign didn't say that it was headed to Florida so I didn't know if it was the main route or just another recreational bike path. In either case I had no reason to believe that it was headed to Pensacola. A bike map would have been so helpful. The land flattened out and eventually left the land of strip malls and parking lots. Just past all of that I came across yet another bike sign. This one was an actual bike path that was totally separate from the roads. It crossed the road I was on and headed off into the trees. I still didn't know where these paths were going. It would have been so sweet to end the ride on a quiet bike path through the trees.

Back in rural country, there were a few suburban style homes thrown in but for the most part the land was pastures or fields. The day started to heat up as all other days had since I crossed the Mississippi. This time was different though. The humidity was thick enough to see. The haze hung there and kept me from seeing the horizon. The forecast was for head winds. Could the air be that thick and windy too?

After a long grade down to some sort of lake or bayou, I started to climb up through land that wasn't even rural. I wondered if it was some sort of park or refuge. As I climbed up from the other side of the water I found the sign welcoming me to Florida. I never would have guessed that I would be climbing a hill as I crossed into what I thought was the flattest state in the nation. I was not going to complain. I had made it to Florida from Washington State. I got off the bike and relaxed. It was a pity that I still didn't have new batteries for the camera.

The next destination was Pensacola. Unless the weather improved radically I was going to call a halt there and fly back home. I had made it to Florida but as with many goals, once they are attained there are still things to do to truly be finished. Getting to Florida wouldn't be much of an accomplishment if I didn't make it to the airport.

It didn't take long to get to the outskirts of town but it felt like it took forever. My patience waned as I got closer. The route got more confusing. Right after I passed the entrance to the military bases I started to get confused by the road signs. It was just another case of a tourist hunting for a numbered highway while the street signs were using the name the locals were more familiar with. I knew I was close enough that getting to a motel by dark would not be a problem so I stopped for a burger. Just for the odd chance that the person behind the cash register could help I asked for directions to the airport. Within a few minutes I was getting advice from about a third of the people waiting in line and they got to talking to each other about the best way to get there. I was a little sorry that I had asked. At least I did find out that I was on the right route and that the path that I had chosen would work well enough. All I really needed was the translation of the street names on the sign for the street names on my map.

In Wichita the airport and its motels were off on their own on big wide streets. In Pensacola, the route to the airport was right past a shopping mall that was surrounded by strip malls. There were cars going every direction and I couldn't make any sense out of the signs. After a while the best thing to do was follow the airplanes. They tend to hang out at the airport. I hadn't been very lost so it wasn't long before I was at the airport. It would have been so much nicer to finish at the Gulf. I wasn't so lucky. They didn't build the Pensacola airport that way. The beaches weren't that far away but they weren't that close either. I didn't want to ride for another hour or two and then find that the next day's flight out would be so early that I would have to ride to the airport in the dark. Pragmatism won out over style. As it turned out, I found a nice hotel right by the entrance to the airport. They had rooms on the first floor so I could roll the bike right into the room. They even had a computer terminal in the lobby. Finally I found Internet access that didn't entail a scavenger hunt. I tried sending out an email and found that someone had fiddled with the settings so nothing worked. I'd be home soon enough and decided to send out the news from my own machine.

I intended to have a marvelous meal. A well done steak, a good beer, followed by some apple pie or a chocolate sundae and maybe even a stiff drink sounded just right. I walked back over to the restaurants I had seen on my way in. Alas all they had were fast food chains. My visions of steak, beer, pie and a stiff drink became a burger, fries and a soft drink. So little had gone the way I had hoped but I had made it.

Key West is still out there and I intend to get there, but at that point I was glad enough to have ridden 3,000 miles through eleven states and hit sea water at both ends. Other people would undoubtedly do it faster, better, with more style or whatever, but I didn't ride in some competition against them. I rode for myself and I was glad that I did it.

I checked the forecast one last time but it looked like the weather wasn't going to change so I booked a flight and got ready to head home.

November 1 Bellevue

I'm back home now. It is so much easier writing emails on a real machine. I'm planning on compiling all of these notes and adding them to a web page that I have in mind. The page will also have stuff in it like data, some summary stuff and acknowledgements. I hope to make it another data source for other cyclists who might want to do some thing similar.

I definitely learned alot, and I expect I will only understand some of what I learned as I get back into a "normal" life. I've seen a lot of how other people live and act and I've seen what keeps me going or stops me in my tracks.

The trip was not what I had expected. It was harder in ways that I hadn't expected, like motivation and logistics. There is a lot of empty out there. It was also easier in some ways that were hard to notice at the time. Despite a few bozos and the horror stories people were telling me ahead of time, there are lots, let me emphasize lots of nice people out there. They far outweigh the bozos and I am so glad they are out there. They may not know what to do when a bicyclist walks in the door but I don't blame them. If it isn't part of your everyday life you haven't built up the habits to handle it. We all have that going on to some extent. I would have like to have seen more of what was going on in the towns and such but the roads don't line themselves up that way anymore. One thing is for sure, the buzz about the Internet and computers means almost nothing to almost everyone I met. Their reaction to the Internet and PCs is right up there with their reaction to a cyclists from Seattle: It isn't a part of their life so at best it is a curiosity to add to the small talk over lunch someday, maybe.

I'd like to do the rest of Florida someday but I'll probably wait a good long time and only do it when the weather is nice, the crowds are low and I have someone else to do it with. Don't expect it any time soon.

I hope you've enjoyed these notes. I think they got to be a bit long myself and they contain way too much about rumble strips and headwinds but hey, that was my life for the last two months. Right now I think I'll go pour myself a nice cup of tea and enjoy the fact that today I'm back home.

MENTAL SOUVENIRS

I can't say that it was fun but I am definitely glad that I did it. For the most part of two months I pushed myself every day through weather that had a habit of setting records. Most of the time it was either too cold or too hot. Goldilocks would have a rough time on a trip like that. Part of that problem was probably only my perception and memory. I remember so many days where the winds were out there to slow me down. I realize though that there were lots of days where the wind wasn't a problem. Undoubtedly some of those were tailwinds that I didn't give any credit to. I got used to being in the saddle for hours each day but my butt disagrees with me. It was sore every day. It took about two weeks for the sore spots to soften up again.

Getting home was a relief as much as a joy. I would miss the road. It was nice to not have to worry about the yard and cleaning up the house for a couple of months. For two months I set my own agenda, traveled at my own pace and only had to argue with myself over the details of the day. Some of those arguments went on for longer than I would have suspected. It is such a relief though to be back in familiar surroundings where I can wake up in the same bed each morning and not have to worry about itineraries or weather. It is nice to be back with my wife and amongst our friends again. It is also nice to be able to wear something a little less obvious than bike shorts. Nice roomy sweatpants never felt so good. Not having to worry about traffic for hours a day is nice too. Though some days I feel that I was safer on my bike than I am in my car.

There are very few points on the trip that I can point to and say "That was fun". That would sound like there was no reason to do such a trip.

The overwhelming balance though is that there are even fewer days that I can point to where I didn't learn something. Most of what I learned I didn't even realize until I was back home. Days of fighting weather made me realize what life must have been like when people spent much more of their time outdoors. Seeing the various wagon trails made me realize how far those folks had to go, how tough it was, and amazed me with what they accomplished. It doesn't seem that very many people would be willing to take on such a task in today's society. People may never get such a chance again considering that today's frontiers all seem to require amazing technologies and expense.

I learned that the Internet isn't everywhere no matter how much hype it gets. Maybe it is better put that it is everywhere but that doesn't mean everyone can get at it. It is like this huge underground river that has enormous potential but can't be tapped by the people above it unless they dig some incredibly deep wells. Cell phones are something else though. They are almost everywhere, and their towers are a new part of the rural landscape. The infrastructure of this country wasn't as much of a surprise. I have always been impressed with the distribution of roads and power. What surprised me were the fences. Where did all these fences come from? It was a rare stretch of road that didn't have some fencing along it.

People were the best teachers I had even though most of them didn't really say anything to me. I knew that life for most of them was far removed from what is in the media. Most lives are just not as extreme as what is shown to us. When I set out I knew that intellectually. When I came back I also knew it on an emotional level. I can't fault the media though. I fall prey to it as well. It is far easier to talk about the folks out there acting as angels or devils. It is hard to stress how many people are leading lives that they can be proud of even though their stories aren't so clear, concise, and compelling as the lives as some unique individuals. The hundreds of truckers I would see each day were carrying around all of our stuff from food to trinkets. It was hard to focus on all of the good ones when one or two of them blasting their air horn in my ear caused me to recoil in pain. Two bad ones out of a few hundred is not a bad percentage. All of the farmers and ranchers out there are feeding us and are easy to not think about when flying over or driving through.

The sad part that I learned is how many people are just dragging through the day and see no way that things can improve. I definitely feel that way sometimes too. That doesn't make it easier to witness someone's downfallen attitude about their day and their life. It can be particularly difficult when I would realize how great their life already was in someone else's eyes or how easily they could change their life. A lot of people feel powerless to change themselves. A lot of people would instead spend a lot of time and money on things that vanish so easily.

One woman who wanted to get out of her hometown was convinced that there was no way she could actually leave. She was unmarried, didn't have kids and only had to take care of herself. Nothing obvious was keeping her there. Instead of saving her money to pursue some other life she was saving her money to buy a used Honda and trick it out as a show car. That is a far better use of funds than spending it on drugs or illegal activities. But it was sad that she wouldn't even consider using that money instead for classes at the local college or as a nest egg to start life in a some other town. She was energetic enough. She was working two jobs to get the money for the car. She seemed to be intelligent enough in our conversation. Somehow, somewhere along the way she learned that even if she didn't like life in her town, the odds were that she wouldn't like life anywhere else either. Maybe in her mind, it did no good to dream of a better life, but a fancy car was a wiser goal and worth working a second job. It is almost as if some people feel that others have more power over their lives than they do. In fact they still have the power and just have to realize it and use it. I am still struggling with that myself. Maybe that was one thing I got out of the ride was seeing all of these aspects of my life played out in so many other faces and places.

I am glad the saints are out there to balance the sinners. It might be better to have the saints without the sinners but if we got rid of the sinners we would probably just redefine sin and end up with a whole new batch. The balance between whether folks as a group are good or bad is probably not defined by the folks out on the extremes, but more by where the mass of the average folks sit. The unique individuals are easier to spot and talk about but the true balance is swung by the rest of the people and how they live. There are those out there who will go out of their way to help and those who will go out of their way to hurt. To my eyes, the rest are out there to live their own lives and not to get in the way of other people's lives. What more could we want out of a free society? The fact that almost everyone is not getting in other people's way is a very positive sign to me. As long as things are going well, people tend to concern themselves with their own life. That is very appropriate. That is personal responsibility. That doesn't mean that they approve of the way some one else may be living. They don't have to. Freedom is just letting other people live.

Luckily in a crisis people come out of their lives to help others. It is a wonderful aspect of this country in particular. And of course there are definitely conflicts when someone is responding to a crisis and trying to help someone who doesn't think one exists. If we all agree that there is a crisis, things work well. If we all agree that there isn't a crisis, we all get along. There are those issues where those who think there is a crisis are trying to convince those who feel that there isn't one. At least that is the way I read some of the conflicts like: gun control, abortion, and the environment. The abortion signs I saw in Kansas were the most prominent example of the trip. Of course I wish we would just talk about those things rather than screaming about them. My point though is that I learned that for most people out there maintaining their life and maybe making it better is their main task in life. All of the horror stories folks had told me about truckers running bicyclists off the road or punks beating up bicyclists are the extreme and unlikely cases. Most folks were polite even when they didn't know what to make of a bearded guy standing there in tight bike shorts. There were far more people who offered to help me in some way. People are good and imperfect and I am glad to see that. It is the simplest, most powerful lesson that I learned. The main flavor that I hadn't come across before was how that showed up, not in the way they rose to crises, but in how they were conscientiously living their lives for themselves, their family and their community.

At one point I likened the bike ride to being just another rut. It is easy to fall into a rut. Living life by a series of habits is how most of us get by if I believe the experts. The bike ride was nothing but another rut. Being in another rut was not a bad thing though. It made me look at my old rut with brand new eyes when I got back to it. I appreciate so much of so much more now. I also can see parts of my life that just don't make sense and I have to do something about those. It is almost as if the ride itself was nothing more than a way to look at the life I had been living all along. Maybe I could have done anything for two months and learned some of the same lessons. You just have to step back from the canvas every once in a while to see how your painting is coming out. Don't step back too far though or you fall off the scaffolding.

Where did all of this philosophical commiserating come from? I was just going on a bike ride to get rid of some fat. My waist size kept expanding and all I wanted to do was reverse the tide. I don't know if it was ironic or just depressing but when I got back, I hadn't lost any weight and my pants were tighter than ever. I had to just give in and go buy new clothes. My percentage body fat hadn't changed either. Three thousand miles on a bicycle and I was no leaner than I had been when I started out. So much for "exercise more". I hadn't even been eating three meals a day. I certainly felt like I was eating less. I have yet to hear a logical explanation for what happened or failed to happen. Basic physics states that it takes energy to do work and I felt like I did enough work. If the calories didn't come from the food and the calories didn't come from stored fat or depleted muscles, then where did it come from? By the standard exercise tables I was working out at over a 5,000 if not 7,000 calorie a day effort. One day I will figure that one out. Unfortunately it meant I wasn't be able to give my wife the skinny husband for Christmas as I had hoped.

This is the sort of ride that lots of people can do. I had the advantage of living in a region where enough people are doing amazing things that something like this is fairly acceptable. I also had the good fortune to be somewhat prudent with money and also quite lucky with investing. I can't ignore how fortunate I am to have a wife who is just as independent as I am and who understands that I would have to do things like this every so often. Who knows, maybe she liked having the house to herself for a while. As for the ride, I didn't have the fanciest equipment and was able to get by on very few things. I wasn't and am not an incredible physical specimen. I do have a tendency for persistence and perseverance that served me well, even though I did find its limits. I don't think everyone should get out there and ride solo across the United States. Of course, if they did we might end up with some safer bike routes that way. I do know now that every once in a while I have to get myself out of whatever rut I am in just to get a better look at that rut.

I started out on a journey to lose weight and ended up working on my mental fitness instead. It may have even unearthed a skill that lay dormant within me. I hadn't intended to write a book about the journey. That idea came from my friends and my family. Setting out on a journey like this is worthwhile and you have to have some goal in mind. Just don't get discouraged if you don't seem to be reaching your goal. You might be heading somewhere even better that you had not expected and you might not notice it until you're back home.

I'd still like to lose a few of these pounds though.

EPILOGUE

FLORIDA

I had to go back and finish the ride. When I made it to Pensacola I felt that I had done something significant but that I wasn't done. It was like baking a cake but leaving off the icing. All year long as I wrote the book I kept going back in my mind to how much I wished I had made it to Key West. Nobody downplayed my accomplishment but coming up short had stuck with me. The only way to get past that was to save up the money and get back down there. The previous year's ride had been financed with money from the stock market. That wasn't going to happen in 2001. So many people were hurting from watching their retirement plans get delayed or cancelled. We were no different except that we had a bigger cushion to start with. After months of saving I finally had what I hoped would be enough. I had a good handle on the costs but Florida could be a lot different. It is a tourist state so the prices could be all over the map. As many problems as the Fall has, I had to do it then. The days may be shorter but the book had kept me busy and saving the money had taken time. About the beginning of September I made up my mind and roughed out a schedule.

That made it time to start the route research. For some folks Florida has a bad reputation for being bicycle unfriendly. I knew that I had seen some bad cycling conditions in other places but wasn't sure about Florida. Some of the stories were unsettling because they were first hand reports of violence and some of the stories were actually data on bicycle related injuries. Evidently at one time Florida had some of the highest bicycle accident rates in the country. Kaye had read some stories years ago that bemoaned the treatment that cyclists got in the Sunshine

205

State. I met a person who worked for a bicycle tour company who had lived there and wouldn't go back because of the treatment she received. This didn't sound good. I noticed one thread through the stories though. Most of them reached back about ten years or more. Being an optimist I decided to give the state the benefit of the doubt and back that up with a bit of research. A few web searches, a few guide books, some browsing of the Internet discussion groups and a call to Florida's Director of Bicycle and Pedestrian Transportation left me with the feeling that there had at least been improvement. Measuring improvement was going to be a personal thing based on riding there. Road conditions and attitudes had improved but that didn't mean Florida was better than anywhere else; it only meant that it was better than it had been. What I was gladdest to hear was that Florida was building lots of bike trails. There is even a plan to put one all of the way along the highway in the Keys.

That was the other stumbling block that fell away. My earliest researches back before I even left Roche Harbor suggested that riding through the Florida Keys was something the police would not approve of. From what I could tell, as of a couple of years ago south of Miami one-third of the way to the Keys had bike paths and all of the bridges had shoulders that were at least four feet wide. After my ride across the Mississippi a four foot shoulder sounded like a luxury. It was apparent though that my route had to be down the middle of the state. The areas that were worst for cyclists were all along the coasts. Unfortunately that meant that yet again I would be out there where lodgings were hard to find. If I followed the safest route, from the time I left Pensacola I wouldn't see salt water again until I was south of Miami. My first guess of the distance was about 700 miles. I knew they weren't completely flat ones but I could pack lighter since I wouldn't be worrying about snow storms. I'd leave most of the winter storm gear at home.

September 11 came along and I hadn't purchased my tickets yet. The prospect of flying to Florida, or anywhere, sounded risky in its own right. There was anthrax in Boca Raton and other places and we didn't know what was going to happen. To stay home may have been prudent. Lots of folks stopped travelling. But I didn't want the terrorists to run my life. Besides, like I learned earlier, there are risks everywhere and sitting still does not mean you are absolutely safe. I booked the flight. One thing I did different was to book the return flight as well. Committing to flying from Key West seemed reasonable because if I had to abandon the ride somewhere else, I could rent a car and drive to the airport in a day. This time though the ride would be different. I had no expectation that I would lose weight. The ride would be through the Sunshine state so maybe with some nice weather I could enjoy the ride and finish this whole thing. I picked a return date that would give me four days off along the way. It seemed so nice to consider getting to Key West early and sitting on the beach for a while. When folks knew that I was headed out on the trip I received advice on what drinks to imbibe once I got there. It was a long list and I had a lot of drinking ahead of me.

Like I said, the planned route went right down the middle of the state. That would reduce the amount of traffic I had to jockey with. Unfortunately it reduced the frequency of motels too. I had hoped for motels strung out every twenty miles or so. According to the software we bought and AAA, there were fifty miles gaps between some of the motels. Riding through the Everglades was even worse. From the bottom of Lake Okeechobee to Miami looked like a 65 mile hop. Eventually I convinced myself that I could line everything up right. Then came the revelation that the route wasn't 700 miles but more like 830 miles. Instead of having a cushion of four days off along the way I was down by two. Groan. I decided to leave the airplane tickets as they were. My progress through Florida might be better than usual. It isn't perfectly flat but it isn't the Rockies either. Maybe my daily progress would be better than it had been through the rest of the country. It was a pity that I had only done a couple of training rides though. I had no idea what kind of shape I was in. In a worst case I could always change the ticket from the road once I had a better idea of my progress.

The tickets were bought. The bags were packed. The manuscript was off to the publishers. It was time to start.

October 21, 2001 Pensacola

I had heard all of the stories about how empty the airplanes were. That was true for the flight to Atlanta but the plane to Pensacola was packed. With all of the increased security, packing the bike and its tools was more of a challenge. Anything sharp had to go in the checked baggage.

My flight arrived just before dusk. Down in baggage claim I somehow ripped through the tape on the bike box. Because all of my sharp tools were inside it, getting into the box wasn't very elegant. Once out of the box, everything went together well.

I rode the bike back over to the same hotel I had finished at almost a year earlier. As usual getting a room on a Sunday night was not a problem. Of course this time I already had a reservation. They obviously weren't busy. Just by chance I got the same room that I had before. One of the problems with the hotel was that they didn't have a restaurant. Some pizza delivered to the room looked like a good way to give me time to repack the panniers and go over everything one last time. Unfortunately the desk manager informed me that they do not allow food deliveries to the room on the Sabbath. That was one I had never heard before. As sensitive as people were after the terrorist attacks I decided to not get into a philosophical discussion about whether they should maintain that policy for every religion's Sabbath. That would cut a few days out of the week. Fortunately they allowed and even suggested that the hotel shuttle's driver take me to one of the local restaurants. Evidently that was okay. He was a real and nice guy. Unfortunately for him, business was down so much that his workweek had been reduced to one day. That was his last night there because he was quitting to take a steadier job. He was astonished at what I had done and at what I was about to try. I'd rather take on my challenge than his.

After getting back from dinner and shopping for the ever-needed Gatorade and Powerbars, I settled in to repack everything. My body was on Seattle time so staying up wasn't a problem. Some of the repacking was necessary. The sharp tools got put back where they were accessible. My jacket that I needed in Seattle was stuffed into the bottom of the panniers. I didn't expect to wear it before the flight back. For the most part though I went through everything to reassure myself that I hadn't left anything behind. If I had, Pensacola was the place to buy it. There didn't look to be much chance of finding bike stuff before Tallahassee. I was a little nervous and anxious and knew that I would have a bit of that until I was a day or two down the road. I hadn't trained my butt for sitting on the saddle for hours on end and I didn't know how much that would crimp my performance.

I had gone from rain, wind and cold in Seattle and was looking at forecasts of hot and dry with the chance of a tailwind. I called Kaye, told her everything was fine and settled in to try and get some sleep. Jet lag wasn't going to help me get up the next morning but I knew that I had managed hundred mile days on little sleep and very small breakfasts. If I made it to De Funiak Springs the next day I would be glad. Last year's goal was to lose weight. This year I hoped to relax, have some fun and get to Key West. Either way I had a lot of pedaling to do.

October 22, 2001 Pensacola to De Funiak Springs

Back on the bike again. The weather felt like it hadn't changed since I'd left. It was in the eighties and I had a headwind. Fortunately taking twelve months off does help. When I started out, nothing was sore and I could concentrate on riding. Another thing that hadn't changed was not getting a full night's sleep and having to make a breakfast out of some bagels and some fruit.

The first thing I had to concentrate on was how to get out of town. Meandering through unfamiliar city and suburban streets can be tedious. Besides watching out for traffic and trash I had to keep looking for street signs. Luckily Pensacola has some bike lanes so I had more elbow room than I had expected. After navigating around road crews and strip malls I finally got back down to sea level and US-90. The simplified version of my route was to follow US-90 to US-27 to US-1. The details muddy that a bit while passing through towns but once I found US-90 I didn't have to look for major changes until Tallahassee.

Heading out of town the road makes its way along the bay. It was nice looking out across the water. There was a mix of open water and marsh grass. It looked good for birds and fish so it is probably good for hunting and fishing too. The sky was clear and the traffic wasn't nearly as heavy as it could have been. Within a few miles I was back up in rolling terrain amidst trees. I was really pleased to see that there were good shoulders along the road. The panhandle of Florida doesn't seem to get the attention that the rest of the state does so I had braced myself for roads that lacked attention as well. As the Sun came around to the south there was even some patchy shade. The shade was a blessing and appreciated because the temperature was not wasting any time on its climb into the eighties.

Looking at the map ahead of time I noticed a large area to the south of the road marked off as "Eglin Air Force Base". It seemed to be about fifty miles long and the maps didn't show any evidence of a motel the whole way. I imagined a long, empty road with lots of low flying planes. Instead I found an area that was rural without being desolate. There were lots of pine trees and a lot of them were being harvested. They were small compared to what I am used to hiking around but I got the impression that they were being grown for paper mills. The drivers were fine and I didn't come across a bozo all day. The odd part was the contrast between the main road and the side roads. I was riding on a well paved road with a broad shoulder. The roads heading off into the woods and even the roads heading to homes, businesses and churches tended to be unpaved, red and dusty. On a previous trip to Florida I had wondered why anyone would need an SUV. Those roads made it obvious. One nice thing was that the roads existed. Like I said the area wasn't desolate. There was a nice distribution of people all along the road. I didn't feel that I was out in the middle of nowhere. A lonely horse I chanced upon may have felt differently. It perked up when I came along and kept pace with me for the length of its pasture. I hope that its days aren't so boring that a passing cyclist is its high point.

Despite the lack of loneliness, there was a lack of lodging. The first day out on a ride it feels good to make some progress. So after fifty or so miles when I finally came across some places to stay, I only took a break and got myself ready for the motels that were a little less than thirty miles farther in De Funiak Springs. The extra thirty miles were as tough as any long day of bicycling. It was hot out and I was pushing myself as usual. I kept seeing vultures circling but I hoped they were concentrating on the road-kill armadillo and fox that I had seen.

Relaxing is a tough challenge for me. Of course, only having a two day buffer in my schedule helped encourage me to continue. I was glad to roll into town. The cluster of motels over by the Interstate seemed the most reliable bet. Unfortunately that meant a detour of a couple of miles and a couple of hills. At least the rooms were good and reasonable and the family restaurant had a fine buffet that I jumped into much earlier than the clock or my jet lag would have suggested. I was hungry and there was no line for the food.

My body wasn't too sore at the end of the day. It was tired but the only things that were sore were just the initial hints of a sore butt, quads, and some slight carpal tunnel. I knew that any real soreness would let me know about itself emphatically in a day or two. Whatever condition I was in didn't matter; I was on the road again and remembering the old routines and habits that defined their own rut. It was good to be back.

October 23, 2001 De Funiak Springs to Marianna

Riding in 2000 was spent setting record high temperatures in the South. Riding in 2001 beat those records. It was hot. The shoulder vanished and with it the opportunity to take breaks whenever I found a patch of shade. When a road loses its shoulder I commence to what I call "driveway hopping". There were a couple of problems with that. One was that the sideroads and driveways weren't paved and sometimes were just grass. The road kill started to look mean and I didn't want to visit its cousins that evidently lived right by the road. The snapping turtle and big fat snakes were not inviting sights. The other problem was that when I did find a bit of pavement or at least smooth dirt to pull off onto, it was most likely out in the sunshine. Stopping in the sunshine in that heat defeated the purpose of the breaks that I took. Standing still only gave my butt and back a short rest. It was actually cooler riding along because I at least generated my own breeze.

It was timber country again but there was also some cattle traffic as well. The cattle trucks and the rolling terrain reminded me of Kansas. The truckers were friendlier though. I also started seeing cotton again. There were fields of plants that looked awfully dry but crowned with puffs of white.

Parts of me felt sore but that was no surprise. In particular my butt was complaining but I recalled that it always does that after a few miles. To keep from hurting myself and to respect the climate I decided to make it a shorter day. It was over fifty miles but I like to think that I can do seventy miles a day and anything less feels like a copout. Intellectually I know that isn't true, but emotions don't pay much attention to intellect. Besides any performance issues, the hop after Marianna was another forty miles. If I had continued on, it would have resulted in a ninety mile day with temperatures in the high eighties. Marianna looked like the right place to stop.

And it was. It was a much bigger town than I had expected. With it came the lack of a shoulder and the growth of a curb. So much for maneuvering room. There were even some pretty rose bushes decorating the side of the street. Unfortunately they hadn't been trimmed so they forced me out into traffic. That took some of the sweetness out of their beauty. I found a motel with a restaurant attached and located across from a Wal-Mart. There were some supplies that I wanted and I was hungry too. The motel looked like it had a prime location.

Books are a better way for me to relax than television and I had been surprised at how hard they are to find. Fortunately, Wal-Marts are fairly reliable sources of at least the best sellers. Nothing fancy but I wasn't picky. I was surprised that no one had postcards. I send one out each day just so Kaye can keep track in case I don't call. Actually I just do it for the fun of it. Luckily this time I had stocked up with some generic ones for just such an event.

Dinner was more of an issue than I expected. After going shopping I plunked myself down in the restaurant with my new book and waited for the waiter. It was early so I wasn't surprised to find that I was alone in the place. Twenty minutes later I hear the phone ring. The folks at the motel front desk saw me sitting in the booth waiting. They called over to the kitchen to tell them that a customer was sitting out there waiting for them. This was service. I'm not sure what kind, but it was service. Out sauntered a waitress to tell me that the restaurant was open but they didn't have a chef. He was over at the fair so they couldn't cook anything for me. I am not sure why they had their doors open. So much for a sit down dinner. I went across the street to the fast food joint and upped my cholesterol.

Overall it had been a good day. Near the end of it thunderclouds formed up, but I stayed dry. I got food, lodging and supplies so I couldn't complain too much. The next day looked to be about the same number of miles but it would end in city traffic. I was headed into Tallahassee. I hoped the weather would hold.

October 24, 2001 Marianna to Tallahassee

That chef must have been really busy. The restaurant wasn't open for breakfast either. I started the day with a banana. Even if it was a short day to Quincy, a banana was not going to be enough. I started out despite that. There is always hope for finding some small place along the way. That hope was usually based on faith rather than knowledge but that's the way it was.

I had to be somewhat strategic about each day's destination. A shorter day that ended in Quincy would help my body recover but that meant the following day would either be much shorter and end in Tallahassee or much longer and end in Perry. There didn't seem to be much in between. One thing that could change my mind was the chance of thunderstorms in the afternoon. I didn't want to ride through lightning.

The rolling hills kept right on rolling with me rolling over them. The tree farms and cotton fields kept passing by. The area was a nice mix of treed wilderness, working farms and old houses. Some of the houses were grand plantation style buildings. Other smaller places were best described as fragile. It must be tough keeping any building in shape where there is so much heat, humidity, moss, and insect life. The day was clouding up too so it all had wonderfully subdued lighting.

Off to the side of the road on the side of a moss covered stone sign was the only hint that I might be near the high point of Florida. I was over 300 feet above sea level. I was also as close to leaving Florida as I would get. The road passes very close to Georgia. From that point on the road would start heading south. But first the road had to pass through Tallahassee.

Finally I crossed into the Eastern Time Zone. That was one of the major milestones that I missed out on when I stopped in Pensacola. I had to explain that shortfall a few times when I got back home. Most folks think that Pensacola can't be on Central time because it is in Florida. The Florida Panhandle sticks out to the west a lot more than I had realized too. Maybe it should be part of Georgia or Alabama.

The afternoon was dragging on and I was so happy to hit a KFC for lunch. Despite the frequent lack of a shoulder I had made good progress so there was plenty of time for food. It was hard to relax though because the weather started to concern me. It was getting darker from thickening clouds. My sunglasses didn't help. They made things look dreary even when it wasn't that bad out. The sound of thunder while I was still miles from town made me wonder. Within a mile though I was educated as to the source of the noise. I had been passing the Police academy's shooting range. Of course which is worse, an errant bullet or a stroke of lightning?

Finally I made into Tallahassee. There were two things to look for: a motel for the night and US-27 South. Looking for both while navigating city traffic was a chore I did not look forward to. It takes a lot more time to travel a mile in town than it does out in the country. That was especially true for me because I had to alternate between riding on the street with riding on the sidewalk. There was also an occasional detour into a parking lot to get my breath back and check the map.

I didn't take very long breaks though. The clouds were thickening and darkening. They looked like they were set for a good downpour and I didn't want to deal with that. When I thought that I was within about three miles of the brewing storm I called an end to the day's ride. There was a collection of motels and restaurants and there was even a used bookstore. That looked pretty good to me.

Looks can be deceiving. The motel was nearly empty so getting a room wasn't a problem and the rate was fine. There were reasons why it was empty and cheap. The motel was across the street from a college. The room looked like it had been partied in more than often enough and it looked like the management didn't see any reason to undo all the damage. Who knows what would happen after the next weekend's visit? Nothing was grossly wrong but the room didn't have wear and tear, it was worn and torn. The only thing I decided to ask the front desk to fix was the always running toilet. Maybe the next guest might appreciate a tub that drained a bit quicker too. The fairly large motel only had one person on site and she had been instructed to stay behind the counter. Costs were being kept down by moving guests to other rooms rather than fixing the problems. So all she could do was reassign people. I had already spread out my stuff so I decided to just put up with it for a night.

After a quick trip back to the room I decided to head back out and grab some food and a book. That's when the cloudburst hit. I love to watch torrential rains from under a good roof but I don't like shopping in them. Rather than brave the streets I decided to try the motel's vending machines. I could stay mostly dry by walking along the walls and timing my progress from doorway to doorway with the gusts of wind. After all of that effort I was treated to the vision of a vending machine that had one bag of chips left. It was a couple of slots back from the front. So I had one choice and it would cost me two or three times as much as it should have. I decided to create another choice by telling my stomach to shut up for a while.

The rain abated after a while and I hit the Krispy Kreme doughnut shop on the way to the bookstore. It wasn't hot and fresh but I didn't care. I should have realized that the bookstore might not have been what I had expected either. In retrospect it was obvious. Used bookstores beside college campuses sell used textbooks. Well sometimes you just have to work with what you got. Once I was inside the situation looked far better than what I dreaded. I couldn't find today's bestsellers but I could find books that had been selling well for decades: used English literature. Some of them were in pristine condition. They had never been read. After a bit of thought I wasn't too surprised. The person that was surprised was the dude who was working there. He got a strange look on his face when I told him I would just browse the shelves. He looked like he couldn't imagine anyone buying a book for the fun of it; people only do that because they have a class. I picked up a work by Mark Twain that didn't even have anyone's name or notes in it.

I thought the day had gone weird enough and decided that dinner should be something nice and simple like Denny's. That was a silly expectation. Without going into all of the nuances of the event suffice it to say that the waiter, who was incredibly casual about his work, only knew of some of the pantry's deficiencies. The cook, who wasn't exhibiting a calm demeanor, would eventually inform the waiter that "we don't have that tonight either" while also questioning the waiter's intellect. This would send the waiter back to me. He would act as if I couldn't have heard the full volume argument that just had happened twelve feet from me and would politely inform me that I should decide on something else. I can't remember what I ate but I do know that I needed a plate full of patience and developed a strong desire to never have to work there.

I was more tired than on the previous two nights. My legs, butt and right arm were tired. There had been a bit of a crosswind and that usually wears down my downwind arm. The next day into Perry would be a short one. I wasn't in shape to do the big jump past it to the outskirts of Gainesville. I was getting ahead of schedule and buying back some time so I was starting to think about when and where I would take a day off. Luckily it looked like some tailwinds were forecast and that would ease my load.

October 25, 2001 Tallahassee to Perry

I had forgotten that I was going to be in Florida's capital. In the morning I passed by some of the state offices. It was tempting to drop in and give them a critique of their roads from a bicyclist's perspective. It was hard for me to imagine that getting from Tallahassee from Pensacola via the backroads was safer than doing so on the Interstate. The traffic wasn't much slower on the backroads and the shoulder just disappeared for miles at a time. Give me the Interstate anyday.

The ride to Perry would be the shortest one so far. That was good because my body was sore and I could use the rest. There were a few things that would keep the day from being easy: temperatures in the upper eighties, more hills and the getting up at what seemed to be too late in the day. I hadn't adjusted my mental clock to the new time zone. When I hit the road an hour after sunrise as usual it was already an hour farther into the morning. I felt slow because of a couple of clock hands.

It didn't take long for me to start feeling slow despite the change in time zones. The heat and the hills weren't my friends. I felt very weak at the breaks and they were happening more often. At the top of a hill I came across a boiled peanut stand that was set up in an old gas station. Boiled peanuts looked like a big local business. I was more interested in the sweet tea and water that they sold. I may have carried Gatorade everyday but one of the great attractions of riding in the South is sweetened iced tea. Iced tea may be available from coast to coast but sweet tea is something marvelous east of the Mississippi. It must be something as simple as iced tea with a truckload of sugar in it, but to a bicyclist who is sweating buckets and burning calories, it tasted like the highest form of gourmet consumption. True fitness fanatics may decry its value but I didn't care. It tasted wonderful and I couldn't get enough of it.

Sitting on their curb revitalizing myself was such a relief. I was drenched in sweat. That happened whenever I stopped. Once I lost my self induced breeze, my pores would open up and drench my shirt. That's why I decided to sit out on the curb rather than inside with the rest of the folks. One of the regulars came out to visit. He was from Georgia and wanted to hear my story. I was more interested in his. Evidently he was in his mid twenties and helped run a logging operation in the area. Back when he graduated from high school he decided to get out there and see the country. He had a pickup truck and $3,000 and figured that would get him around to a lot of our country. He had no plan; just drive each day anywhere he felt looked interesting and eventually meander on home. His description of his family's reaction was very familiar to me. They couldn't imagine how he could do such a thing. He might get lost and might run into bad things. He figured that he'd keep his eyes open and wouldn't have too much trouble finding home again. Eventually he made it as far west as Beaumont, Texas and as far north as Chicago. It sounds like he had a good time and might try it again sometime. Sounds good to me. Because he knew about the logging and the roads in the area he gave me some hints on what to expect and then he had to get back on the road himself. He is a fine fellow.

The shoulders were fairly good for the rest of the day and after a couple more hills the land flattened out and the road got straighter than any that I had seen in a long time. When the hills disappeared I was surprised. The road headed inland so it seemed that things would get hillier, but they didn't. I didn't complain. The temperature climbed just like they said it would and I was glad that I didn't have to grunt up some hill. At one point I unsuccessfully chased the shadow of a cloud trying to get some shade.

It looked like the road headed off into a lot of nothing, and it did. Luckily there was the occasional convenience store. One in particular was at a crossroads and was memorable for a few reasons. It was a bit past the correction facility, which had kept me from taking my break earlier. It was also across the street from a motel that wasn't in any of my research. Looking at it quickly suggested that it wasn't a motel, but while sitting outside the store I realized that the cracked pavement and three foot tall weeds surrounded a building that had customers. Perry looked better to me and I hadn't seen it yet. One more thing that intrigued me was a small, simple and ingenious item. The store had a restroom out back that folks could use once they got a key from the store. That's common enough. The neat part was the way the keys were stored. When someone picked up the key from its peg on the wall, a spring would lift a switch that turned on the lights in the restroom. That was cool.

It was a short enough day that getting to Perry wasn't a problem. The temperature was an issue but not an obstacle. So when I found one of the nicest rest stops that I had ever seen, I stopped because I wanted to, not because I had to. There was pavement, restrooms, picnic tables and little shelters. It doesn't sound like much, but it is amazing how infrequently such simple pleasures can be found. I laid down for a while and watching some really big bugs go by.

I knew I was getting close to Perry when the fast food litter started showing up. Despite our great improvement in Keeping America Beautiful, each city and town ends up with a ring of trash around it. The ring is a few miles out of town. It is probably just long enough for most litterbugs to finish their meal that they picked up at the drive-through window. Those that toss such things out the window all seem to do it in about the same place. It is sort of a roadside advertisement for the restaurant. I wonder if the big chains consider that part of their advertising strategy. What other purpose does the name on the package perform? The person who bought it already knows about the place. If it was just for them it would seem redundant.

Perry was a decision point. Since Tallahassee I had followed US-27 but in Perry, US-27 decides to go two directions at once. The one branch is labeled "US-27" and heads towards Gainesville in the middle of the state. The other branch is "US-27 Alternate" and heads south along the coast. The winds were better lined up along US-27 Alt. The supposedly safer route was along US-27. By accident as I got into town I ended up on the Alternate. That was auspicious and unplanned. That route had a nice collection of motels. Once I checked in I found out that my timing was also auspicious. There weren't any rooms available for the next day. Even though it wasn't the weekend, there was going to be a big parade. Folks from all over were coming in and had booked the place solid. If I had gone slowly enough to arrive a day late, I would have been in trouble. Taking a day off in Perry was not an option. That night I reviewed the maps, the Weather Channel, and my tired body to see which route to take in the morning.

October 26, 2001 Perry to Alachua

I decided to head to the interior and miss the opportunity for a day of tailwinds. If the wind kept blowing I'd be able to enjoy them the next day. Alternate US-27 looked okay but I guessed that it would have more traffic and didn't want to encounter that if the shoulder disappeared.

As it turned out, the cross wind was just enough behind me to act as a bit of a tailwind. It wasn't anything major but I welcomed it anyway. Not fighting it was good enough for me. The weather changed too. The temperature was forecast to drop and even have lows in the thirties. What a change.

My main goal for the day was High Springs. Getting to it meant riding through one of the longest stretches of no motels than I had seen across the country. This was in Florida; a busy populated state with tourism. Where were all of the motels? Despite the research, which I was starting to have doubts about, there were motels out there. For some reason they were hard to find out about until I passed their sign. Maybe they don't need to advertise or meet AAA's standards. The lack of data made it hard to plan, but I was glad to see them.

The land wasn't perfectly flat but it was flat enough. My quads and butt were as sore as ever and welcomed anything that made the ride easier. It was my fifth day of riding and my body wanted a break. I wanted to give it one but hated the prospect of ignoring another tailwind opportunity. Midway through the day I got a very good sign that my psyche was in need of a break as well. I hadn't been feeling overly pressured. There was always the focus on whether I was making good enough progress to catch my flight, but I wasn't as nervous as I had been west of Pensacola. Despite that feeling, some rumblestrips, a guardrail and a narrow bridge provided the conditions for me to vent a lot more energy than I thought I had bottled up.

Rumblestrips are necessary evils of road construction but sometimes they are overdone. I particularly didn't like the ones in useless places like after a bridge. Before a bridge it makes sense to warn drivers that are straying from the lane, but after they crossed the bridge they should be okay. For whatever reason there was a bridge that had rumblestrips right up to the guardrail. These strips were a series of reflectors that had been glued to the asphalt. I had to swerve around them or risk bending a rim. I swerved and my pannier caught another reflector that stuck out from the guardrail. The pannier jumped off the rack and plowed itself right into the rear wheel's spokes. My skull flooded with images of bent and busted spokes miles from the nearest motel and probably counties from the nearest bike shop. I had spares but that didn't mean I wanted to use them. For a good few minutes I could only stand there and vent my frustrations at the Department of Transportation. Luckily the wheel and its spokes looked fine. I put everything back in place again and watched that wheel waiting for some nicked spoke to pop.

The odd thing about the event was that the stretch of road I was on was one of those being improved for bicycles. Supposedly somewhere along that stretch of road was a bike path but I hadn't found it.

A few miles later was a surprise. There was a small tourist community with a motel, some shops and food. I hadn't expected it and jumped at the chance to regain my blood sugar level and my composure. My performance back at the bridge probably entertained some driver passing by, but I didn't like it.

I knew High Springs was going to be a long ride but I felt much better after my break. If things got bad I knew that I could turn around and have a place to stay. That helped a lot. During my break I realized that the bike path went right through the area but didn't find it until I was a mile or two down the road. Even then I couldn't figure out how to get over to it. It was on the other side of a ditch. At least I hoped it was the bike trail. It was narrower than a road, had no traffic, but didn't have any signs on it. Eventually there was a flat strip of grass covering a drain pipe where I cut over to the path. It was like jumping into cool water on a hot day. The shoulder was a mess and the traffic was full of dump trucks trying to get past each other on a two lane road. The bike path only lasted three more miles but it was in the shade and a welcome relief. When I got to the end of it I was happy to see that they were in the process of extending it. One member of the crew told me that eventually it would make it to High Springs. The road was a bit hazardous and they were going to do something about it. I was starting to think that advice I had received from the Florida Department of Transportation was based on how things would be in the years to come rather than how things were for my ride. This was supposed to be the safe road and there I was being told that it was the hazardous one for now but they would make it safe in the long run. The future looked great but I had to get back on the shoulderless road an jostle with the trucks. At least they told me that after I crossed a small bridge up ahead a few miles I would get back to a good shoulder.

They were right about that shoulder and they were also right about that hazardous road. I was driveway hopping where there were no driveways. When I heard the traffic coming I would look for any patch of dirt or pavement to pull off onto. Six extra inches was all I got to use sometimes. Sure enough, thirty feet to my right I could see the early phases of the bike path construction. Eventually that stretch looks like it will be a fine ride but it wasn't that day. When I crossed the bridge I took a nice long break and once again was glad for a four foot strip of asphalt.

Road construction was always a cause for concern. Usually it came in the form of a big orange sign and I would have to guess what lay ahead. This time I was surprised to see that it actually specified a detour for bicycles. I groaned. It was nice that they were keeping bicyclists in mind but the day was already long and a detour rarely makes the trip shorter. After a few miles I hadn't come across any arrows pointing me off the road or even any construction. I figured that the sign was either up too early or too long. The answer came from a couple of cyclists that caught up with me. I was on their detour. A bridge was out on another route and they had been detoured over to the road I was on. What a relief.

It was also nice to come across other cyclists. They were the first ones going my way in over 3,000 miles of riding. They were a couple out of Vancouver, British Columbia and were finishing their coast-to-coast ride too. Without intending to, they made the strongest case I had seen for the efficiency of a road bike. Fully loaded down with tents and camping gear they were breezing by while I was grunting along. They also unknowingly showed me how much easier it is to ride when someone else is there. My energy level picked up amazingly. Talking to someone else, even when it is shouted over a shoulder, got my mind off its aches. Suddenly riding was a much easier thing to do. I wasn't going their pace but after a short break we realized that we were heading the same way. I think they slowed down so I could stay with them. Their coast-to-coast ride was also being done in stages. They had started in San Diego but had only done a portion of the ride each year. The final destination was somewhere due east on the Atlantic coast.

We pulled into High Springs together and stopped to figure out the road signs. They were hunting for the local campground. I was looking for the motels. It was late in the day for me but we decided to spend some time visited a local coffee shop before we split up and looked for lodgings in earnest. Talking on the road is possible but talking across a table is much easier. It turned out that they were doing about forty miles a day following a trail guide published by a bike touring firm. It kept them on the backroads and in campgrounds and they loved it. They were surprised when they found out I was touring in a much more independent fashion. They were amazed at my logistical challenge. I was amazed at their physical challenge. Their bikes were much heavier than mine and yet they were making much better progress. Granted, when they passed me I was at mile sixty and they were on their thirtieth mile but I was impressed anyway. They had two days of bike travel to get to the coast and tickets that were for flights two weeks later. They were ahead of schedule and thought they might go to Orlando for some fun. I was heading much farther and had a flight out two days prior to theirs. I started to feel some pressure build. They were nice enough to pay for my tea. Well, they are Canadian and always polite. I gave them my email address and went back out to get started finding lodging. It was later than I liked and I didn't know where I would sleep that night.

High Springs looked like it was trying to make itself into a more tourist friendly place. The coffee shop was more cute than utilitarian and the local stores were more likely to be arts and crafts instead of hardware and groceries. It was a pity that the motels weren't anywhere near the nice stuff. When I found them I was uninspired. I wanted better food than what I saw so I grunted and turned the bike to the next set of motels about eight miles away in Alachua. It meant deviating from US-27 but I looked ahead and liked the support and facilities that US-441 might offer. It would take me right through Gainesville but that would be on a Saturday so traffic might not be too bad.

Turning onto US-441 I saw two familiar bikes up ahead. To pay back their generosity I tried setting a draft for them but couldn't keep up enough speed. They appreciated the effort but I had to just find my own pace and watch them disappear ahead of me.

When I found the motels I was somewhat disappointed. They were from some of the major chains so they were in good shape but none of them had restaurants. Fast food was the only dinner and breakfast I would get within walking distance. At least it was easy to get a good quiet room and pick up supplies without any great hassle. The next day was supposed to start off in the thirties so I would be digging out some of that cold weather gear after all. It also looked like I would get to play with a tailwind and get to ride through much less desolate terrain.

October 27, 2001 Alachua to Ocala

A day off sounded good to my body but spending it at a bunch of fast food restaurants while a tailwind blew by wasn't appealing. It was a beautiful Fall day right down to the need for a jacket in the morning. I probably could have used my warm gloves but decided to let the Sun take care of my fingers. I also didn't want to hurt myself so even though I was out there riding I decided to keep the day short by stopping in Ocala.

I was glad I rode that day. My butt still hurt but the weather was so nice that it made up for it. Florida hills were back again but the tailwind made them seem even smaller than usual.

Riding through Gainesville on a Saturday morning was fairly relaxing. It was acting like another college town. There were lots of other cyclists riding around. One was even a pack of racers in training.

Passing through town I finally headed south. I had made almost all of the eastern progress that I had to. The main task changed to running down the length of the state. With the wind behind me it felt like I could sail south a long ways if it wasn't for my sore butt and nightfall. At least the scenery was pretty. The farms I came across were starting to show signs of money and leisure. It looked like they were growing happy horses. I also started seeing signs of retirement communities. That must be the start of snowbird land.

Another thing that made the day so relaxed was the almost always present shoulder and a place to sit when I took a break. A lot of my breaks across country were spent sitting on the guardrail. It is not luxurious but a lot better than just leaning on the bike. With a guardrail there I could relax a few more muscles and not have to worry about holding up the bike. A lot of the roads in the Panhandle didn't have guardrails. There wasn't any need. Through most the West there was almost always a fence of some sort. Even if it wasn't a guardrail there were things to lean a bike against. I don't know why but there were a few more along the ride that day and I was glad to use them. It was Fall but being in Florida meant that things were as green as Summer would be elsewhere. The occasional overpass gave me the opportunity to look around and see a bit more of the country. It was a pleasant day.

Ocala is a big town. I made it most of the way through before stopping at a motel for the rest of the day. Checking in early made it very easy to get a room. The manager said that the Fall was usually slow so they hadn't noticed the effect of the terrorist attack. He gave me one of the rooms with a bit more floor space so I would have enough room to maneuver around the bike. He was surprised when I asked about where I could work on the bike. Evidently working on the bike in the room was fine by him. Besides, there wasn't a good space outside except for the parking lot. To be safe, I spread out my emergency space blanket as a work area and rotated the tires. The back one was wearing thin like usual but the front looked fine. Why I never thought of switching the front with the rear before I don't know. Maybe it was because some of them were so hard to get off the rim. I felt much more comfortable with a good tread on my rear tire.

It had been one of my shortest days since Pensacola and it was a nice compromise between taking a day off and making progress. I was more relaxed than I had been the previous year. I had trouble sleeping just like at home but I wasn't nervous about it. If I was awake in bed, I would just lie there relaxed. I knew that even with little sleep I could make good progress. The weather forecast promised another day of almost tailwinds. As the road turned east they would be crosswinds but the next day looked to be another short one. After that the road turned closer to true south and better lined up with the winds.

The Weather Channel talked about how it was near the end of the hurricane season. I hoped they were right.

October 28, 2001 Ocala to Baseball City

In lieu of taking one day off I decided to do two short hops. That way I got some rest and used the tailwinds too. One thing that kept slowing me down was a problem with my top gear. The chain would slip anytime I was in top gear and tried applying even a small amount of power. Back in my training rides it wasn't too bad but even with a tailwind in Florida it was very noticeable. I had a bike shop back home look at it before I left. The mechanic assured me that after he removed a link or two it would be back to normal. I was over three hundred miles through Florida and the chain's action wasn't good enough. My normal maintenance schedule is to replace the chain every 500 miles or so. Oh well so much for that. Stopping early also gave me the opportunity to replace the chain in the afternoon. I needed that top gear and I hoped that a bit of work in Clermont would get it back for me.

It was almost a tailwind. Evidently the local weather was a bit different than the forecast. It wasn't a surprise but it was a disappointment. That wasn't much of a help or a hindrance in the morning. The hills kept rolling along. Ten hills of a hundred feet each is like a thousand foot hill. It probably wasn't that bad but it wasn't as flat as I wanted. The more vexing problem was the disappearing shoulder. My stress level climbed and my speed dropped. It was good that I was going to have a short day. The route was getting closer to Walt Disney World. US-27 passes to the west side of the complex so I hoped there would be a lot more places to stay and to eat; though, I realized it probably also meant more traffic.

Orange groves started showing up. So much of Florida's image is tied up with orange juice that I was surprised I hadn't seen orchards earlier. Citrus is a better description because there were all sizes and colors of fruits hanging on the trees. Little signs on the roads educating the passerby about the crop would have been welcome. There was also a lot more emptiness than I had expected. The emptiness looked temporary. Resort housing, snowbird palaces, and more pretty ranches began eclipsing the poorer homes.

The final stretch into Clermont turned enough to the east for the wind to become a real pain. Sometimes it was a headwind. Sometimes it was a crosswind. Dancing with the wind and the random bit of shoulder while in hilly terrain was a chore. At least it wouldn't last more than about eight more miles. Then I would be at the motels, could work on the bike, and let my body relax.

A cluster of motels sat at the top of a hill near a turnpike interchange. They all looked to be big places with their own restaurants and gift shops. As I got closer though the first one looked bad. It had been abandoned for years and showed it. Two of the remaining three were from national chains so they looked to be in better shape. I passed one because I had a poor experience at one of their other locations. The next one only had a convenience store instead of a restaurant so I passed it by. The last one I checked didn't have any cars in the parking lot and had yellow tape cordoning off the lobby entrance. That didn't look good. I backtracked to the first open one to find out what was happening. I don't think the desk manager expected anyone to come through the door. Once she swallowed her lunch she informed me that they did have rooms but that none of the motels were operating their restaurants. The only food in the area was in the convenience store at the neighboring motel which, by the way, wasn't operating as a motel anymore.

I stepped back outside to look over my notes. There didn't seem to be anything else in town and wouldn't be anywhere to stay until thirty miles farther south when the highway crossed another Interstate. It was only about noon and the road looked like it would turn a bit away from the wind but I was tired. The idea had been to try shorter days instead of a long day with a day off. Thirty more miles were enough to make it a long day. The food in the convenience store did not look good enough to make into three meals so I grabbed a quick bite and headed south.

Getting through town first meant getting to town. The motels were on the north side of Clermont. There were a few miles of not much life and a few more hills until I reached the edge of town: The Citrus Tower. At the crest of a hill they had constructed an observation tower. I don't know if it was purely for tourists or if it also had some practical purpose but it was enough of a draw that there were a couple of motels at its base. It had that pastel pink and green color scheme that may just be Florida's official color palette. The tower looked nice but I didn't notice anyplace to eat. The encouraging sign was that there were more motels than my research had uncovered. A hill or two later there was. It was a brand new motel beside a restaurant and I was so glad to see it. I was even a member of their frequent guest program. My relief was gutted as I rolled to the front door. They had a sign up stating "No Bikes in the Building". That attitude is so rare but there was hope. I had finally learned that some motels have such a policy because of bikes with suspension systems. Evidently some of the suspension systems have oil filled shocks that occasionally leak. My bike was so low tech that it doesn't have that problem so I went on in to see if I had a chance. Before I even had a chance to ask I could tell it wasn't good. As the woman came from the office out to the counter she stopped in the office door, leaned against the door jam, and crossed her arms over her chest. The frown she had wasn't a good sign either. After confirming that her answer agreed with her appearance I at least tried to find out if I could park the bike outside. She didn't like that idea either. It was a new motel and they didn't want it messed up. Maybe they should ask all guests to take their shoes off before they enter the lobby.

That put me back out on the road. Finding something so nice was such a lift then losing it was such a crash that the remaining miles looked even longer. At least the wind was becoming more of a help, the hills were abating and the shoulder started becoming more reliable. I was definitely headed into more populated areas. More populated did not mean more places to stay overnight. The tract homes and trailer parks were becoming much more frequent. It looked like suburbia without as many strip malls. Lots of housing and I suspect lots of commuting. That is except for those that were retired.

Eight miles from where I thought the motels were I found a bit of guardrail to take a break on. The day was long and I had started out later than usual because I thought I would only be riding about forty miles. I was beat and the Sun was headed for the horizon. When I got back on the bike, I only made it about a hundred feet down the road and found that I had a flat tire. The rear tire had been punctured by a four inch nail. Even brand new tires wouldn't have survived that so my tire rotation program hadn't made a difference. I rolled the bike back to the guardrail so I would have a better place to work. Despite how tired I was, the tire and tube cooperated and I was back on the road.

From feast to famine, the great emptiness and tract homes yielded up about a half dozen places to stay; and these ones were even in business with restaurants beside them. Half were on the near side of the Interstate. I don't know why but I grabbed the first one on the other side. It was the same company that wouldn't let me in the building earlier in the day and I guess I wanted to prove to myself it was just one surly person and not the whole company that had turned against bicyclists. This time I was welcomed on in and given one of the nicer rooms. I got the room for two nights. I needed the break. Parts of my body were past sore and into the need for recuperation. Some of my clothes were past dirty and in need of a laundry. My chain was past my patience and was going to get replaced. I had a night and a day to do it. That sounded fine. Being so close to a tourist area had its effect. Stocking up on supplies at the convenience store cost $30. Throughout Florida the only grocery I had found beside a motel was when there was a Wal-Mart across the street. Usually convenience stores were the way I got by but this time in particular was pricier that most. So what, I was tired.

There were some logistical hurdles coming up on the road ahead. Again there would be big gaps between motels as I got around lake Okeechobee and headed through the Everglades to Miami. It meant that the next few days on the road would each be long ones. My body needed the chance to rebuild its reserves before I set out.

The laundry and bike repairs went well. The Weather Channel keeps pointing out a tropical disturbance sitting on the coast of Nicaragua that may or may not go anywhere. There's no knowing and nothing to do but be aware of it.

October 30, 2001 Baseball City to Lake Placid

A day off meant getting back on the bike without stiff legs or a sore butt. That would last minutes. The body might complain but the break really was very beneficial. That meant that for one day I had three good meals and didn't burn any of it up. It was like charging my batteries.

Clouds kept the temperature down a bit. That storm sitting on Nicaragua's coast was flooding lots of people down there. It was strong enough that central Florida was seeing high level clouds from it. The low level winds were coming from a completely different direction which luckily gave me a tailwind. Other good news: I had a top gear again. That was a great combination. The terrain flattened out and the shoulder solidified. It looked like there would be a long string of towns to pass through for a day and I was headed for the far end of them. It would be one of the longest days since Pensacola but at least it was through an area with lots of places to stop and even stay if I wanted to pull up short.

Towns in the area had names like Winter Haven and Frostproof. That sounded like a theme. The citrus groves probably liked that and the retirement communities seemed to as well. The area was full of lakes. Straight stretches of road were continually interrupted by the need to swerve around this lake and that lake. That took some of the benefit out of the tailwinds but not by much. It also took some of the monotony out of long straight roads. It was a good day to make good mileage.

By around lunchtime my progress had been good but usually that is something I only roughly judge. I didn't wear a watch and the bike didn't have a computer so I made guesses based on reading the map and watching the Sun. It is a highly inaccurate system but I didn't need high accuracy. It led to the pleasant discovery that I had made it to Sebring, the home of the races, just a little past lunch. That gave me the rest of the day to make the twenty miles to Lake Placid. I was able to fit in a lunch and even had the luxury of finding a bike shop that was right by the road and open. I restocked the bike with a new chain and a replacement spare tube.

One of the more valuable things I acquired was the information about how to deal with alligators. I had no experience with them but I knew that some cyclists came across them. My route was going right through the Everglades and I had no idea what to expect. The shop owner was great. Basically it came down to the same caution anyone should have with any wildlife, usually if you leave it alone it will leave you alone. Don't bug the babies or mom will get mad, and watch out for the big ones. But in general, be really surprised if you see one, at least that time of the season. I don't know if he was right but I felt better about the whole issue.

The next twenty miles weren't as easy as I had hoped. The last miles of the day are always tough but this time the clouds made it tougher. They were thickening and I could see rain falling from the base of some of the clouds that were off to the side. I wanted to get into a motel while I was dry. Passing through Lake Placid I hadn't found the obvious motels right along the road like in other towns. The clouds continued to build as I got to what looked like the edge of the business district. My map showed a couple more places farther down the road but I wasn't sure they would be open. I had seen too many abandoned places to feel comfortable blithely continuing on past the edge of the last town for miles. If I had to turn around it would be at the end of a long day into a headwind with weather brewing. I got out the cell phone and was so glad to hear that the phone number for the motel worked. They had rooms available but because we couldn't pin down my location well enough I had to accept her assertion that I probably wasn't too far from them. That encouragement sounded hollow because I doubted that she was looking at the distance from the seat of a bicycle. A couple of hills later I was starting to give up hope when I saw the hint of their sign beside the road. I was wrong but the next time I saw a sign like that it was for them. I had a place to stay and I hadn't gotten wet.

I did not, however, have a place to eat. They had a restaurant there but it was closed for inventory for the next two days. The vending machines weren't working either and the only other business in the area was a golf course behind the motel and a biker bar across the highway. She didn't mention anything about a restaurant at the golf course and one way I stay out of trouble is by not hanging out in bars that don't have windows. My solution was to call up the local pizza delivery place and order a large pizza, a salad, plenty of fluids and a dessert. The salad and pizza made a late afternoon snack and a dinner. The dessert was part dessert, part midnight snack, and part breakfast. The rest of breakfast was the rest of the pizza. It wasn't an ideal solution but luckily I wasn't, and couldn't be, picky. There had been enough days when I couldn't count on getting supplies that sometimes I would hoard my Gatorade and Powerbars. I was glad that I had. The next day was going to have some long stretches where there didn't look to be any towns or supplies. It was a series of roads that were straight for miles with hard corners that pointed it off in a straight line for more miles. That tends to be the shape of roads passing through nature, not towns.

The storm sat in Nicaragua. It wasn't dissipating and it wasn't moving. The forecasters had no idea what would happen to it. The clouds convinced me that I should be ready for anything but I wasn't going to stay in Lake Placid for two nights in a row. Surviving on pizza for 48 hours was fine in college but wasn't necessary yet.

October 31, 2001 Lake Placid to Clewiston

After a fine breakfast of leftovers I got on the road. The women at the front desk looked upset that I hadn't taken advantage of what they considered to be a fine continental breakfast. They had made sure to provide it just for me. I didn't know about their extra effort until I was checking out and had a hard time spotting what they were talking about. Looking around the small lobby I noticed some cereal, but at this point I can't recall that anything else was there. They felt that it was more than sufficient for a breakfast, even for a touring bicyclist. My hopefully gracious "Thanks but I've already eaten" had no effect. I wasn't going to eat just to appease them and they looked unhappy about it. The road seemed a friendlier place.

My goal for the day was Clewiston. It is beside Lake Okeechobee down where the land was flat. I'd been advised to stop there rather than going the next fifteen miles to a place called South Bay. South Bay looked to be smaller which wasn't a problem in its own right, but some of the locals had described it in less than positive terms. I couldn't get much in the way of details so I just took their advice. It meant the next day into Miami was going to be fifteen miles longer but it sounded like the safer choice.

The clouds stayed with me all day and the wind alternated between almost being a tailwind to almost being a headwind. It wasn't changing direction, but the road was. The road was a series of straight lines that would abruptly change direction every few miles. The straight parts were long enough that the turn was over the horizon and the turns were sharp enough that the wind went through big swings.

Orchards lined the road through the first half of the ride and they gave way to cane fields. The cane fields were nothing new. I had been travelling past some on occasion for days but they became the dominant crop. It was harvest time for both. Trucks full of colorful round fruits went by while the cane fields were being chopped and burned. I'm not sure why they burn the fields but it was obviously not an accident. There always seemed to be a smoke plume somewhere in the vicinity. Unfortunately the smoke didn't always rise straight up. When it blew across the road I got to suck it in.

For the most part the shoulder was excellent. Some of the road fill beside the shoulder was crushed sea shells. How tropical. The area wasn't desolate but it was lonely. There were occasional abandoned buildings deteriorating, for sale, or both. Florida seemed to have more than its share. I wondered if they were all part of a boom that busted or if they were part of a never-ending cycle of ambitious construction and fallen dreams.

The land flattened out and the drainage ditches grew up to be canals. All through Florida I had seen what I took to be egrets: big white birds with big necks and long legs. They were skittish and in greater numbers as I headed south. Maybe I noticed them more or maybe they were easier to spot with all the water around. In any case it became an ongoing event to unwittingly spook some big white flapping thing that was in the bushes or the water.

You know regional cooking has taken hold when the global fast food franchises sell something besides the normal menu. I passed on the opportunity to order fried livers and kidneys. The normal meal was fine for me. I had made very good progress despite the fickle help from the wind. The top gear was working fine though I could only get into it with the wind directly behind me.

The lake looked enormous on the map. I never saw the water but I saw the canals that carried boats as well as just water. The overpass was impressive and the nearest thing to a hill for miles. Clewiston was supposed to be close but it wasn't close enough. At one of the turns in the road I faced into a headwind and the rains came down. I almost pulled into the first motel I saw but thought that if the weather was turning bad I would want to wait it out somewhere better than what I saw on the outskirts of town. The winds of the last few days had helped enough that I was ahead of schedule. I even got back to having four extra days on the calendar to play with.

About the time I found a nicer motel the rains quit. The woman behind the counter was great to talk to. She guessed all of my questions before I had a chance to ask most of them and had no problem putting me into a ground floor room. She knew it would be the best place to store the bike. I dried off the bike before putting it in the room. After I cleaned myself up I went back out to her desk and thanked her. Bicyclists came through there often enough that she was very comfortable with taking care of them. She even knew how hard it was for some folks to think straight after a day on the road. One guy was so tired that even when he had lost his wallet he couldn't deal with any of it until he had showered, napped, and eaten. She took care of his charges and found out where the wallet had been misplaced. A couple inadvertently picked it up and called from the road to get it back to him.

Before I did anything else I went to the local restaurant and got a slice of pecan pie and a glass of sweet tea. That was heaven and gave me the energy to shop for more supplies. It was a fine place to stay. The Weather Channel kept producing hints that staying might be a strong possibility. The storm over Nicaragua was not weakening and was possibly growing. The chance of rain was going up each day and I had seen a bit of that myself. If I didn't stop and things went well I could get to Key West in four days and have four days in Key West. I could afford a rain day if necessary. The next stretch was the longest ride through a dearth of lodging and food joints that I had ever encountered. After South Bay there was nothing on US-27 until it ended in Miami. The recommended route was even longer. It bypassed Miami but supposedly didn't have a place to stay along eighty miles of road. Taking on a ride like that in bad weather was a bad idea. The weather in the morning would help me decide whether to go or stay. My progress would pick the route. If I did well, I'd shoot for the bypass; otherwise I had to drop into Miami. Ending a long day's ride in rush hour traffic in a city that was once know for atrocious bike statistics was not a good choice but it was the only other one available to me. That was a problem for the next day. First eat and sleep.

November 1, 2001 Clewiston to Miami

The morning looked fine. There wasn't much of a breeze and it didn't look like it would rain soon. After an early breakfast where the waitress quietly giggled at my bike shorts, I headed out fed, supplied and hoping that the weather would hold. For the last few days I had been travelling south with winds almost out of the northeast. The farther south I went the more the winds came around to the east. The storm in Nicaragua was gaining strength and was getting upgraded to a tropical storm. The stretch of road I was on would take me from Central to South Florida where there was also a better chance of rain. If the storm kept gaining strength it could become a hurricane just as I got to the coast.

In the meantime it meant that I fought a headwind for the first fifteen miles of the day. Most of that was spent beside and below the levee holding back Lake Okeechobee. All I could see of the lake were signs saying "Authorized Personnel Only" and a line of leafless trees poking up past that. Starting early and riding beside the levees probably kept the winds down somewhat. It didn't take me very long to find South Bay. Granted that it wasn't as big as Clewiston but it looked comfortable enough. It is hard to judge such things until you get there. Oh well, I'm not sure what folks were worried about. It looked fine to me.

South of South Bay the road got tired of silly things like turns. One stretch of road was 27 miles long without a turn or a town. The road just disappeared over the horizon or into the heat mirage over the road. If it wasn't for the wind and roadside debris there wouldn't have been a need for the handlebars. The wind wasn't going to go away though. At the start I headed southeast with a 20 mph east wind. The day looked to be long and a lot of work. Fortunately the few clouds wandering around never collected themselves into something that got me wet.

The area wasn't empty after all. It wasn't exactly packed either but it was busy with more cane fields and, surprisingly, sod farms. The road certainly wasn't empty. It was mostly truck traffic cruising along at top speed. I guess seeing me helped break up the monotony for some of the drivers. I got a few friendly horn honks and a thumbs up. Aside from that, there was nothing else for me to do but put my head down and pedal. Without any towns to mark my progress I had to guess how things were going by watching the Sun move my shadow along. I took breaks at what felt like regular intervals. There were guardrails more often which made that easier. Each time I stopped I would alternate between getting something to drink or something to eat. That was the sort of ride I saved up supplies for.

A few hours of riding and I was on a straight road that vanished over the horizons in front of me and behind me. In an emergency there were farm buildings along the road but there was nothing for the general public. There was one innovative entrepreneur who realized that. One of the folks that sells lunches out of the back of a pickup truck, some folks call them "roach coaches", had found a spot in the road that was a bit wider than most. It was big enough to park about a half dozen tractor-trailer rigs. He set up shop there and pulled in a good business. I couldn't even see him as I rode up. All I could see was the collection of trucks. Finally I caught a glimpse of him when I was right beside him. I couldn't pass up such a good deal no matter how much he charged. The more valuable thing I got though was advice from the truckers. They were very aware of where we were. My progress had been better than I felt, but not as good as I needed. Unless I moved faster I would have to stop in Miami. There didn't look to be enough time for me to go that long route that bypassed the city. They all thought that it was the better route and that I shouldn't go into Miami but they also pointed out that they thought the bypass didn't have a shoulder and they were pretty sure it didn't have any motels along it. One guy thought there was an Indian casino somewhere along there but he wasn't very sure about that. I sucked in their advice, told them a bit about my ride and got back on the road. From what they said I had a long day ahead of me no matter which way I went.

Eventually the road left behind the farms and entered the Everglades. I didn't realize that Everglades National Park does not encompass the entire Everglades. I got to pass through the part that wasn't the park. I don't know what the difference was but I saw a big difference once the farms were behind me. The trees along the road became wild and tall enough to screen some of the wind. It was a welcome relief. The view was a lot more restricted but I don't think I missed much. Whenever I caught a glimpse between the bushes it all looked like one very large mix of grass and water. Building the road through that must have taken an awesome number of dump trucks of dirt.

Dirt and salt covered me by the afternoon. Somewhere off the road was a sand and gravel pit. The trucks coming out of there had covers on their loads but whenever they passed me grit would end down my back. All through Florida road dirt would coat my legs as it stuck to the sweat. In any endurance event my sweat can create a crust of salt around my eyes. That day I had salt encrusting my elbows. Maybe some rain would have been cleansing at that point.

After enough work and enough grit I found myself at the intersection with the roads leading around and into Miami. It was getting late and the nearest motel was at least another fifteen miles away. I called ahead to get better directions but didn't have any luck. One operator was impressed enough with what I was doing that she offered me a special discount if I made it to their motel. Rather than chase down complex directions in a big city I relied upon the simple observation that most airports sprout motels. US-27 headed into Miami and ended somewhere near their airport. It would be harder for me to get lost and my weary body and mind didn't want to have to work too hard. My hope was that someone had built a motel on the outskirts of the city like so many other undocumented motels in so many other cities.

Two hours later I knew that a motel was not going to magically appear for me. The land gave way to housing and lots of signs sprouted up that I couldn't read. Spanish is one language I have never studied. The traffic got heavy and the few motels I saw didn't look safe. They may have been fine but I wanted someplace I could hole up in for days if the storm down south grew much more.

A half hour later I was questioning my decision to continue. The shoulder had vanished and the traffic had thickened. If it was bumper-to-bumper it would have been better than the heavy fast surges of cars that I kept maneuvering beside. Driveway hopping was not an option. I was on the canal side of the road. The driveways were on the other side. I had a curb and sewer grates thrown into the mix. I was tired and on edge. That is when mistakes happen too easily. Airplanes were flying by low so the airport was probably close but I couldn't see any signs pointing to it. Finally I found a small space to park the bike and checked the map. I wasn't exactly sure where I was but it looked like a road up ahead would cross the canal and maybe lead to the airport. As long as it wasn't too bad a part of town or a road with worse traffic I would take it.

Hallelujah I crossed the canal! The bridge and the road were small so I wondered if I was about to get very lost. A hundred yards later the noise level has plummeted, and I found myself in a part of town where I could read the signs. None of them pointed to the airport and I was in a traffic circle of five intersecting roads, but the problem had changed from survival to logistical. A pedestrian gave me a vague hand wave as a hint of the way I should go. There were two roads off that way and I picked one for no apparent reason. It didn't look like it was headed to the airport but it had a bike path and ran under some wonderful shade trees. I was lost but it was nice. The bike path dumped me out into a parking lot where another pedestrian gave me some detailed directions that I couldn't follow. I at least got the impression that I was headed the right way. After a bit of meandering I came to the intersection with a street that ran along the back of the airport's hangars. I was so relieved. I couldn't see a motel but that didn't last long. A few minutes later I was checked into a hotel with an enormous feeling of relief. I made sure that I had the room for at least two nights and that the hotel was not in an area that would have to evacuate. Then I felt secure.

Up in my room I checked The Weather Channel. The storm was intensifying and they expected it to become a hurricane but because it was moving so slowly and was partially over land they had difficulty making forecasts. I wanted to make it to Key West but was glad to know that Miami was a major milestone and a good enough destination. The only milestones left were the Keys and the coast. The weather on the coast was bad so I would probably have a tough time finding a room in a beachside motel. For that night I was just happy with making it to Miami and would worry about the weather in the morning. Ironically, sitting in the city there was no place within walking distance for me to buy supplies. I had used up everything on the ride south and would have to buy things on the road. That night the celebration dinner was in a pancake house. That's the way things go.

November 2, 2001 Miami to Florida City

There wasn't much of a reason to wake up early. If I was going to stay, I could sleep in. If I was going to ride, I didn't want to jostle with rush hour traffic, so I could sleep in. It didn't matter. I didn't sleep in. When I woke up though all I did was roll over, grab the remote and watch the Weather Channel. Since outside Orlando, each day the forecasted chance for rain increased. Miami's forecast was no different. The tropical storm was looking more like it wanted to be a hurricane but it didn't go anywhere. I was only about a day's ride from the first of the Keys: Key Largo. If there was a hurricane in the Keys, people would have to evacuate and I didn't want to be part of that. But if the storm stayed where it was, the existing winds would blow me right down to Key West. I decided to take a small step towards the Keys. The collection of motels down in Florida City was about a thirty mile ride depending on which roads I took to get out of Miami. That would put me within easy striking distance of Key Largo and still in a safe place in case the storm got nasty. Looking out the window it was obvious that the world was cloudy but not very wet. The view out the window also inspired me to leave. Waiting out the storm by looking at the back side of the airport was not an appealing option.

After a nice, leisurely breakfast during which traffic hopefully abated, I checked out of the hotel. The desk clerk looked at my bike in disbelief. The previous day's staff had compared my story with the other cyclists that they had seen over the years. The morning clerk looked shocked to see a bike that wasn't collecting dust in a garage.

My escape route was to find the bypass that had been my preferred route from the previous day. The safest route out of the city was long, but it at least took advantage of the tailwind. After lots of time with the map, it came down to: go west a bunch of miles, go south a few miles, go west a bunch more miles until I found that road again. It looked so easy on the map. The scale threw me off. Miami is a big city and I got to see a lot of it on that route.

I hoped to dodge the rain but didn't manage it. A few miles from the hotel the rain came down. I dreaded the thought of riding all day long in wet windy weather; and I was saved. The rain only lasted long enough for my imagination to conjure up how soaked I could get with windy rain like that. I had rain gear but it can't stand up to hours of being drenched.

Eventually the city fell behind and I became part of the reverse commute. The shoulders returned and the skies cleared off. There was even a nice tailwind. It was much better than sitting in a hotel all day. I was on a divided four lane highway that had a canal along one side. It almost looked like Florida's highway system was designed to have room for cars, trucks, a shoulder for bikes and a canal for boats. It only looked that way. I knew the shoulder could vanish and I know that there weren't many boats except kayaks that would make it under the bridges over the canals.

Getting to the bypass route took a seemingly long time but it was easy riding. I was on the road that headed off into Everglades National Park: Alligator Alley. Bikes are not encouraged to ride on it through the park but I would be turning before I got that far. And there it was, the bypass where I would turn ninety degrees and the tailwind would become a 20 mph crosswind. The other surprise was the brand new multi-story hotel at the intersection. The previous day if I had stayed on the bypass rather than heading into Miami, I would have found what looked like a marvelous place to stay. It was the Indian Casino that the one trucker thought might be there. I couldn't bet my route on his vague recollection but if I had then I would have missed out on a lot of nerve-wracking riding through Miami. I took a break, then headed south.

The bypass was a much better road than the truckers had described. The shoulder was usually fine. They probably are influenced by some of the blind jogs in the road that made their job tougher. I was even treated to enough foliage beside the road to have a bit of a windscreen. The road wasn't nearly as desolate as I had expected either. There were certainly stretches with nothing but bushes and water, but there were lots of nurseries and small farms. Seeing palm tree nurseries was one new event, but seeing the trees stacked and ready for delivery was funny. I had seen them in other places on the ride too and they always looked like monstrous asparagus. Monstrous was typified by some of them requiring eighteen wheelers for shipping. With their tops trimmed and a stubby root ball they looked comical. They looked elegant only after they were planted.

As I got closer to Florida City the shoulder occasionally vanished. It wasn't until Homestead that the traffic began to do so too. Homestead looked like an interesting town. There was artwork on the buildings and even mosaics in the road. It looked like a much better place to be stuck than behind the airport but I hadn't found the motels that I was after. I hoped they were close enough for me to come back. Off to my left I started seeing hints that I was going to converge with US-1. I saw the back of strip malls lining a road that slowly was getting closer to the road that I was on. That was also where the motels were. I decided to stick to the road that I was on and then work my way back up US-1 if necessary. Just before the intersection of the two roads I found a motel that looked much nicer than I had hoped for. I doubted that I would find anything farther south of it on the mainland. My hopes of making it to Key Largo faded as the pains from my carpal tunnel problem surfaced. There had been too many miles of crosswinds. Heading to Key Largo would be another couple of hours without any improvement in the winds. Being prudent I decided to get a room and check out the storm. If it had worsened I would be in a very good place to stay. If it looked like it wasn't moving then I probably had plenty of time to get to Key West. There were only 140 miles to go and a lot of them could be with a powerful tailwind. That was potentially only two days of riding. Hopefully the storm would stand still that long.

I checked in and found yet another desk manager who knew just what a bicyclist would want. She also allayed my fears that the motel would be part of the evacuation. Rather than having to evacuate she pointed out that I was now in one of the places folks evacuated to and that rooms were given out on a first-come-first-served basis and that I was definitely one of the first if it came to that. Once in my room I heard the word from The Weather Channel: the storm was become officially Hurricane Michelle and had a chance of hitting the Florida Keys. I went back out to the front desk and made sure that I had the room for at least two or three nights.

My wrists were sore but it was my shortest ride of the trip. I spent the afternoon doing laundry and shopping for supplies. In the morning I would check out the weather and see if I could get two days of riding in before an evacuation order came through. That was all I needed to get to Key West and I didn't care how wet it was. If the roads were open and I didn't have to fight cross winds and headwinds, then I could sprint to the finish. In the meantime I found one of the best dinners I had in Florida. It was in a place that billed itself as a sports bar but the food was excellent. I had excellent crabcakes and a real beer. That was a nice end to the day.

November 2 to 4, 2001 Florida City

Sleeping in wasn't an option the next morning. I was too eager to ride. Before anything else, I got my bike clothes on and made sure the bike was packed and ready to go. If the weather forecast looked like I would have a chance of two days of riding, I wanted to be prepared to start the sprint early. Breakfast could wait until I was in the Keys. An early start might get me there before the worst of the Saturday morning traffic hit. The first twenty miles would be with crosswinds but they might be calmest around sunup. Then I heard the tropical storm report. They couldn't be sure but it looked like there would be a hurricane watch posted for the Florida Keys. That meant there was a strong chance that they could evacuate all non-residents as early as that afternoon. I did not want to be forced to evacuate on a bicycle. Of course if I was on the road I probably would have hitched a ride back and maybe even lock the bicycle up where I stopped if there was something besides swamp grass around. I didn't know how serious the local authorities took the evacuations. The situation had the potential to be grave and I didn't want to be some frivolous tourist whose self-centeredness got in the way of someone's emergency procedures. I changed clothes and had a leisurely breakfast.

The hurricane wasn't moving very fast at all. I could pedal faster than it was going. At that pace I had to consider the possibility that I would be stuck in Florida City for days. It was very possible that I would either have to spend a lot of money sitting still and pay for a change in my airline ticket, or call it quits and fly out of Miami. There was no way to tell. All I could do was wait and watch what the storm did. In the meantime the weather was a little windy but not rainy. I decided to spend the day exploring a little of the local area and stock up on supplies to stave off cabin fever. Luckily the motel room had a microwave and a refrigerator. After a bit of wandering about it looked like the best place to grab a book or two was the local Wal-Mart. Everything else was too far away and the traffic was picking up. There were a lot of folks headed into the Keys. Maybe they were going to shore up their properties. There were also a lot of folks heading out of the Keys. Maybe they were trying to beat the rush. Inside the Wal-Mart was a zoo. The place was packed and some of the shelves were picked clean. Maybe that is normal for a Saturday morning. Everyone's need to buy emergency supplies definitely didn't make it easier. The chaos in the parking lot had some out-of-state license plates mixed in which probably didn't help. I grabbed munchies and something to read. On the way back I stopped and bought a large deli sandwich that could live in the fridge in case the weather was too wet for me to venture out.

Outside of the motel was a vacant lot that had sprouted some monster off-shore racing boats. Evidently they had been in Key West for the World Championships but the event had been cancelled. The boats were enormous, sleek and colorful. They were big enough to almost not fit on their trailers. There had been 120 of them in Key West and they were all being evacuated. The local authorities had given them a head start so they wouldn't be tied up in traffic. Once they were on their way the mandatory evacuation order for tourists would be announced. Most of this I got through talking to two of the race fans who had situated themselves on a bench beside the road. They were disappointed that the race was cancelled but they at least had a front row seat to what was effectively a parade of every boat in the race. There was only one road out and every boat had to pass by them in review. The ones in the vacant lot behind us had come off first and were trying to decide what to do next. We were surrounded by boats and those guys were enjoying it. I stood there for a while and then headed into my room for lunch.

I ventured back out for dinner but for most of the time I was in the room either reading, watching TV, or analyzing the storm's progress.

Sunday was wet enough that breakfast in the motel lobby looked good and that deli sandwich was just right for lunch. All through the day the storm grew and moved closer. I didn't know that a hurricane could go from being a tropical storm to a Category 4 hurricane so quickly. It looked like Cuba was going to get slammed. Each time they redrew the forecast path it looked like the Keys would be spared by an increasing margin. They would get bad wind and rain but not hurricane force conditions. Just to be safe though, there was a mandatory evacuation of all residents in the Keys as well. Ideally that meant that no one was down there. Realistically a lot of the locals wouldn't leave unless they knew it was going to hit them dead on. It looked like the storm would only brush them so evidently most folks stayed where they were. The motel certainly filled up though. There probably wasn't a spot left in the parking lot.

On Sunday night it looked like I might not get started on the road until Tuesday morning. My flight was scheduled to leave Key West Thursday afternoon. That meant if I didn't change the ticket I would have to do 140 miles with no time to relax when I got there. So much for being ahead of schedule and enjoying the bars and the beaches of Key West.

November 5, 2001 Florida City to Key Largo

Hurricane Michelle really picked up speed and took a right turn to the east after it slammed Cuba. It was east of Key West and heading away quickly. Its closest approach would be near the middle of the Keys and the weather could be bad but the worst scenarios were past. There would be no hurricane weather in the Keys. People started streaming back down US-1. I wanted to get going but I didn't want to jump into the worst of the traffic. I had been warned that US-1 could get very bad for bicyclists. Rather than challenge that notion head on I decided to wait as long as I could before checking out. As usual though I had to find my next place to stay. While everyone else headed south I started calling motels and hotels in Key Largo trying to find out if anyone was open. In the first four phone calls there were two that weren't even answering the phone, one place that would be open in 24 hours and another that wouldn't open for two or three days. Hope was fading until the fifth call got through. Just for the fun of it I called one of the resorts. Normally their rooms were outside my budget but it looked like their Fall rates were possibly low enough. Besides, getting to Key Largo that afternoon meant possibly not having to spend a few hundred extra dollars extending my trip and paying more airline fees so I was saving money, right?

The rain almost quit but the wind did not let up. It came out of the east at probably over 20 mph. At least the temperature was more reasonable than it had been through most of Florida. Getting to the coast meant riding south along a two lane road through swamp, marsh or the outskirts of the Everglades. I don't know exactly what it was, but water played a very big part. I'll never know if I got close to alligators but about a half a dozen times I came across patches of water within twelve feet of the road where there was something large underwater and rapidly swimming away from the shore. Everything was so murky that I couldn't see what was in there, but I know that the ripples were big enough that I didn't want to investigate without lots of help.

I got to see why the road has such a bad reputation amongst cyclists. There is actually a wide enough shoulder the whole way but it has reflectors glued onto it four abreast every ten feet or so. The gaps between the reflectors are only about six inches wide and the attention required to continually steer between the reflectors for ten miles or so is nerve-wracking. Because it is only a two lane road, the shoulder can get crowded when a wide load comes through. I understand the need for some reflectors and rumble strips. Drivers leaving the road would find themselves in water without an effort. There has to be a better way of setting things up though. Staggering the reflectors would help a lot and I have a hard time imagining that four reflectors save many more lives that three would save. There is an alternate road for that stretch. Some cyclists like it because it has a lot less traffic. I was interested in it too until I was told that it didn't have a shoulder.

Perseverance prevailed and I made it through to salt water once again. To my surprise there were two motels sitting right by the bridge that, at least for me, signified the entrance to the Keys. The buildings looked like they hadn't taken any damage. The fisherman with their lines in the water didn't seem to be too concerned either.

Traffic was heavy so with the worst stretch behind me and the winds now in my favor I took it easy and resumed my driveway hopping. In a short bit the road made that a lot less necessary. From a two lane road, US-1 blossomed into a divided four lane highway. I was on Key Largo and looking for my resort. Most businesses had someone outside taking down the heavy metal hurricane shutters and it was clear why lots of places weren't open. By the next day I suspected that enough places would be open that I could be relaxed about where to stay.

When I pulled into the parking lot of the resort I wasn't convinced that they were open for business. The gray and brooding sky didn't help and neither did the lack of cars. There were just enough parked there for my guess at a maintenance staff. They also had some of the flooded puddles in the parking lot just like everywhere else. The place was enormous. The landscaping was full of big magnificent tropical trees and plants growing everywhere. I parked the bike and wandered around until I found the registration desk. That was usually not a task but like I said, the place was big. Evidently I was the fifth person to check in that day. I got room 101. It was the most convenient room for me in the whole place. It was wonderful. I had made it to the Keys and got to enjoy the event in style. There were some minor inconveniences. It had been so long since anyone had stayed there that it took about fifteen minutes and a call to the maintenance staff to get hot water into the room again. In the midst of channel surfing for The Weather Channel I came across a live report of a police chase in progress. Evidently someone was running from the Miami police by driving south into the Keys. The police closed off traffic and had put down spike strips and such to stop him. I missed most of the details but later on I found out that if I had been on the road for ten more minutes the chase would have gone right by me at high speed where there was potentially no shoulder. I think I stopped in the right place at the right time.

Other folks checked in during the afternoon but I felt that I had the place to myself. I wandered out to the beach to officially touch salt water and walked out onto the dock to stand amongst the wind and waves. Supposedly the water is clear down there, but it wasn't the day after the storm. All I could see was opaque. The weather improved rapidly. By dinner, where I was almost the only person in the restaurant, the sky had cleared off and from the third floor restaurant I got to watch the first sunset I had seen in days. It was out across the water with a few scattered islands in front of it and with tropical trees swaying in the remains of the day's winds. I topped off the celebration with a Pina Colada in the bar. Before I left lots of my friends had suggested drinks that I should have when I made it to the islands. If I waited until Key West to drink them all I probably wouldn't remember anything about Key West. Each day I had another drink or two from the list. That night in the bar it was me, a Pina Colada, and a couple of guys from the hotel. I got the impression they would have been supremely bored if they didn't have a customer to talk to.

It looked like I would be able to fly out on time. I had less than a hundred miles to go and the weather was improving. That night I reviewed a bicyclist's guide book that I had purchased back home. It hadn't been very useful because in 700 miles there had only been one bike trail that was in the book and along my route. Oops, evidently I had missed one. It was back at the start of Key Largo. All of that time that I was driveway hopping there was a bike path somewhere nearby. The book claimed that it continued for quite a few more miles so I resolved to find it and use it in the morning.

November 6, 2001 Key Largo to Marathon

The view at breakfast was as nice and as lonely as dinner had been. The clouds had cleared off and I had an unobstructed view of the water all the way to the horizon. I was looking forward to the day. Of the bike paths described in the guidebook, most of them were along the next stretch of road. As much as I wanted to get to Key West, it looked like I could only make it in one day if the weather cooperated and my body was up to it. The town of Marathon looked like a good destination. Stopping there would also allow me to tackle the longest bridge in the Keys early the following morning rather than late in the day. With that in mind I looked forward to a day of riding fifty flat miles through island life.

I was determined to find that bike path that I had missed the day before. As soon as I got out by the main road I started looking around for it. In the median that divided the highway, behind some tall grass I spotted it. All that time it had been within twenty feet of me but I hadn't seen it. Maybe I had been concentrating on the traffic too much. In any case I didn't want to miss out on it again. After a break in the traffic I crossed the highway and got on the path. That was a stress reliever. Within a few miles though it was apparent that I might have missed it for a very good reason. Drainage is poor in the Keys and the bike path was usually lower than the road. About a third of the time it was underwater in some massive puddle left over from the storm. So even though I had found the path I had to abandon it most of the time. Riding through hundred foot long puddles was not going to help me get to Marathon. When it was dry it worked well but I had to keep my eyes open. It won't be long before things are even better for bicyclists. There were miles of bike paths under construction. They weren't any use to me but someday they will make the trip easier and much safer.

The winds weren't lined up with the road as well as I would have liked. There was more of a crosswind than a tailwind. But the shoulder was good and the traffic was a lot lighter than it had been the day before. Luckily for me the wind was coming from my right. That had the tendency to blow me towards traffic rather than away from the lanes. Getting blown towards cars and trucks sounds bad but I preferred it because of the bridges. The reason it is possible to visit the Keys on a bike is because of the bridges linking the islands. With hurricanes coming through the area the road builders were smart enough to build the bridges high enough to allow for some tall seas. Unfortunately for me I am afraid of heights. The prospect of being blown towards traffic was less fearful and less embarrassing than getting blown off the bridge and into the Gulf of Mexico. Besides, all of the other crosswinds had been from my left. It was my right arm that had carpal tunnel syndrome. Winds coming from the right taxed my left arm which didn't have any problem with the task of keeping me in a straight line.

About half of the time I rode on the bridge with the cars and trucks. Every once in a while though there was a bridge that was too old for today's traffic and it had been replaced. Just because cars and trucks couldn't use it didn't mean it was worthless. Some of them had been left for pedestrians, fishermen, and bicyclists to use. Some of them were also so small that I wondered if they were old or actually built just for those of us that didn't have engines attached. As long as they made it all the way across the water from one island to the next I was happy to use them. Not all of them made it all the way across and it was something that wasn't marked. When in doubt I took the main road. They had good four foot shoulders so the alternative was pretty good too. One advantage of taking the foot bridge was the opportunity to stop without having to worry about traffic. Those breaks were wonderful. The water was starting to clear and I could stand there lean on the railing, eat a snack and watch the fish go by. I can see why snorkeling and kayaking in the area would be fun.

When I got to Marathon I was tired. My poor old body refused to acclimate to what it felt were the tropics. Imagine if I had tried riding there in August. I got a room in one of the last hotels before the famous "Seven Mile Bridge". Its name says it all. I didn't know its condition but I had been warned that some bicyclists don't like it at all. Going any farther would not change the fact that I wouldn't make it to Key West until sometime the following day. My room was in the same motel that the network news crews had occupied during the hurricane coverage. It was empty. They had all left the day before. They gave me a room on the top floor so I could see the water. All that day I had seen lots of people taking down their storm protections. The hotel was no different. One of the implications was that their restaurant was out of order for a day. They hoped the bar was okay. I showered up and headed down to the bar for a margarita.

Ah, the island life is nice. They had an open air bar beside the dock for the charter boats. The bartender was in the midst of setting things up again. At least the blender worked. If you recall I am something of an enthusiast when it comes to the stock market. There was a gentleman there who was living that ideal in his own fashion. One of the charter boats was his. His other occupation was that of a trader. He had a laptop set up with a wireless connection of some sort. The whole thing was sitting on one of the counters where he could watch his boat, his screens, and one of the TVs that was tuned to CNBC. What a life. I was happy enough to sit there, relax, write a postcard, and enjoy my drink or two while the breeze came by off the water. Very nice.

With the restaurant shut down and the bar closing at six I decided to have an early dinner at the bar. That idea evaporated when the bartender found that the kitchen's vent hood wasn't working. She suspected that something had been blown into it. She couldn't cook until it was fixed and getting it fixed would have to wait a day. Anyone involved in maintenance was out there taking down storm shutters and pulling things out of storage. The lady at the front desk recommended pizza delivery because there was nothing within walking distance of the hotel. She was probably right but because I wanted to go for a walk anyway I decided I could look around for food too. My walking range is possibly longer than hers. She had forgotten about a restaurant that was right around the corner from the end of the hotel's driveway. I was the only one in the place. Once I got back I told her about where I had eaten. Her eyes popped as she recalled the place. Evidently she usually doesn't recommend the place because she got so sick after eating there once that she had to call in sick the next day. My mind had an image of missing my scheduled flight because I had eaten the wrong food. That is part of the adventure I suppose.

I was eager and anxious. I was within fifty miles of Key West. If all went well I could be there by noon. It was hard sleeping that night. The occasional stomach rumble didn't help.

November 7, 2001 Marathon to Key West

One time near the end of a very long hike a friend reminded me, "No Stupid Mistakes". So often grand journeys can have simple failures near the end from people relaxing too early. I didn't want that to happen. Relaxed didn't describe my attitude as much as relieved with a bit of conscious caution. Starting the day by tackling the longest bridge in the Keys reinforced the cautious side of me.

I had heard a lot about the bridge but a lot of what I had heard was impressions. There were a few factual descriptions of things like shoulder width and such. One thing that I had heard was that there was an old bridge that was a good ride out to Pigeon Key and a new bridge. When I got to the end of the island I was at the start of both of the bridges. There were no signs saying which way a bike should go and both bridges seemed to be open. The traffic wasn't too bad that early in the morning and the wind was coming from behind me on my right. Both bridges had a bend to the left halfway along so the second half of the bridge would be with a tailwind. But I had to decide which bridge to take. The new one had a big hump in it for boat traffic but I knew that it would make it all the way across. I wasn't so sure about the one that went via Pigeon Key. All along the Keys the bridges had signs saying "No Stopping on the Bridge" so my seven mile jaunt would be without a break. I doubt that anyone would have troubled me if I stopped to take a breath but I knew that if I wanted to look in the water I could do so from one of the bike trail bridges. There were probably a few more of them between Marathon and Key West. A big deal was made of Seven Mile Bridge and it is impressively long, but it was just a long relatively low bridge with a hump in the middle. I didn't measure it but I would guess that it goes up about sixty feet. With a four foot shoulder and light traffic the only problem I had was the self-imposed one of deciding not to stop until I was on the other side. It was a good thing I did not take the old bridge. It is almost complete and does make it to Pigeon Key but it didn't have a hump that let boats through. They got through where one of the sections had been removed. It makes sense in retrospect. If the new bridge accommodated boats, the old bridge paralleling it had to be modified somehow too. The cheapest way was to cut a hole in it.

Just getting across the bridge got me 20% of the way to Key West. That wasn't the last bridge because the remaining route was stitched together across lots of little islands. That meant there was lots of water to cross. The wind was my friend and it was nice to relax on some of the smaller bike trail bridges that paralleled the main road. They were probably more appropriately called fishing bridges. Lots of them didn't have paved approaches. I had to maneuver the bike across grass and through guardrails. I didn't care what they were called. They gave me the chance to stop and look straight down into the water. A lot of it was very shallow and I could see small schools of fish and even some fish that were about two feet long and were almost as skinny as the grass they were hiding near. Throughout the Keys I had been seeing a lot more wild birds: cormorants and pelicans especially. It was nice to add fish to the list of animals I had seen.

Another of the bridges had a boat hump in it. I knew I wasn't supposed to stop on it but I saw a passport on the shoulder. I consider passports important things so I stopped to pick it up. One possibility I considered was that it was a play passport like some theme parks issue, but it was the real thing. I put it in with my stuff and got off the bridge to call some official type so I could turn it in. Four phone calls later I got in touch with a police station ten miles ahead of me. When I started calling I knew that I was not in a very busy area but I underestimated how far I was from anyone official. Having a small mission of delivering an errant passport helped break up the day. It turned my focus from Key West to something even more near term: the next police station. A lot of the intervening highway was on islands that were so small that there wasn't much land left after the road was built. Some of them looked so skinny and straight that they could have been manmade for all I knew. A bike path showed up again and I followed it right to where it ended which just happened to be at the police station. It turned out that the passport was expired. Even if I had seen that I probably would not have had the heart to toss it away.

One of the officers told me that I would be pleasantly surprised by how much nicer the bicycling would be up ahead. There were evidently lots more bike paths. He was right. About half the time there was a bike path or the beginnings of one. Even without them though the shoulders were broad enough and the traffic light enough that I didn't have a problem. It was a glorious day for bicycling.

In a short while I was by the Naval Air Station and then I was back in amongst stores and homes. Traffic picked up and I was as busy watching out for myself as I was looking around. There were a couple of milestones to hit now that I had reached Key West: The Southernmost Point monument and milepost zero for US-1. But I wasn't sure I was even on Key West. Even the tiniest Key had a sign proclaiming its name. Maybe I blew past the one for Key West. Finally I came to a T-intersection that looked similar to one on the map. It was noticeable because to follow US-1 south it meant turning to the north. That's when I knew I had made it. I breathed a sign of relief but knew that I had to ride another mile or two to accomplish my other goals.

The bike path became part of a broad tree-lined sidewalk. That meant I didn't have to dodge cars anymore. Instead I had to deal with cracked concrete and duck under untrimmed branches. So what, I was on Key West. The side that wasn't traffic was water. It was pretty neat.

At first the route went past large motels and strip malls. After about a mile though it dove into the old section of town. The streets were narrow and while most folks were riding their bikes on the sidewalk, and there were a lot of bicycles around, I had to jump back out into traffic when the mailboxes and such made the sidewalk so narrow that my panniers wouldn't fit. So I was simultaneously watching out for traffic, looking for room on the sidewalk, watching out for pedestrians, taking in the sights of old houses with lush tropical foliage, and minding the road signs. It was only for a mile or so but it felt like it went on for five. So what, I was on Key West. I found MP0 at a set of tourist shops and a large complex of exceedingly nice lodgings.

Having accomplished that feat I asked a pedestrian who wasn't dressed like a tourist about where the Southernmost monument was. She pointed right back down the road I was on. It was at the other end of the road. Where I had turned north for US-1 MP0, I could also turn south for the monument. After a bit more traffic jamming I ended up at the end of the road. The marker is large. It looks like a twelve foot tall thimble painted black, red and yellow. There isn't a great park around it. It has a bit of a concrete pad at the corner of two roads. A small cloud of tourists hover around it getting their pictures taken and then dispersing. I parked behind it by leaning the bike against it. I touched the south side of it and then laid down on the end of the concrete pad to touch the water. I was done. After relaxing for a bit and looking out at the water I called Kaye and my Dad to tell them I had made it. One of the locals was making a few bucks by taking people's pictures with their cameras. I handed him my camera and he took a shot of me and the bike in front of the monument.

Logistics never vanished. I had to find a place to stay and get ready to fly. It was Wednesday. My flight left in 28 hours. Evidently I had planned much tighter than I had thought. Because I was only going to be in town for one night I decided to get a nice place that was on the water and that had a beach. The Keys didn't have as much beach as I had expected. The shoreline seemed to be mostly plants growing out past the land or marinas harboring big boats. But I wanted a beach. After grabbing a quick lunch I found a nice resort that not only had a beach but was only two blocks away. They gave me a junior suite for no extra cost. I think she liked my story.

As much as I wanted to relax there was one large task ahead of me. My airplane flying out of Key West was too small to carry a bicycle. I knew that ahead of time. Back home I had called around until I found someone who could ship a bike. The resort was about two or three miles from his business, but calling from the resort I couldn't find anyone closer. I took a shower and repacked my panniers. If I was going to ship the bike I might as well grant myself a small luxury and ship some of the luggage home too. I stuffed one pannier and headed back out. Getting the bike shipped ate up some time but it wasn't much of a hassle. I didn't even have to break down the bike. They would do that for me. Without the bike I had a long walk back to the resort.

It was a nice afternoon and I decided to take a small detour and walk through the old section of town. Given four days I probably would have found a fairly cheap place and really explored the town. Just looking at the gardens in people's yards would eat up a day for some folks. Instead I only had a bit of time so I knew I could either breeze through everything or find one place to enjoy for the afternoon. For me it had to be Jimmy Buffett's bar: Margaritaville. That was a long walk after fifty miles of riding but I found it and sat myself down at the bar for one of the last drinks left on my list. It ended up being a banana daiquiri. After telling a bit of my story I found that my first drink was free. So I bought another. Two drinks after being dehydrated by riding in the islands go a long way. It was nice wandering past the stores on the way back. Some were touristy places full of T-shirts, some were very expensive art galleries and a few were for very open-minded lingerie shoppers. Oh yeah and there were lots of places to eat and drink. Halfway back I hailed a pedi-cab. It just seemed a fitting way for me to travel. Now that dude was in shape.

Back at the resort I wandered down to the beach. It was a fine beach and I waded out into the water. It was murky enough that I didn't think that renting one of their kayaks would give me much of a chance to see anything more than I could see from the end of their pier. So I went back up and onto the pier and sat there for a while relaxing. The view was mostly flat water so there wasn't much to look at or describe but it was nice to contemplate everything that I had done. I had started out this whole thing almost two years before. It had gotten delayed once and didn't finally get going until that Fall. Two months of cycling later I had made it to Florida but felt that I had fallen short by turning for home in Pensacola. It was demoralizing to realize that 3,000 miles of aerobic activity hadn't change my weight, waistline or load of fat at all. Over the next year though it really began to sink in that while my body wasn't the shape I wanted, and it wasn't the shape the doctors approved of, and it wasn't the shape I knew I could have, it was the shape that was good enough to let me go out there and see the world slowly go by under my own power. Rather than measure myself on someone else's abstract ideal or by what the medical profession considers statistically nominal, I could measure myself by what I had actually done. What I had accomplished was nothing monumental but it was hardly insignificant. I think it is the sort of thing that lots of folks could do but think they can't because there is so much out there discouraging them. The only way to find out what you can do is to try doing it. Maybe the others are right but nobody knows your own abilities and even if they do, they may not know how much you can change with a bit of practice and perseverance.

Would I like to have a slimmer body? Of course yes. But I am not as worried about that as much now. Now I am more interested in what else I can do and where else I can go. I am definitely going to get a touring bike, but I am also going to do more with hiking, kayaking and skiing and I want get some snowshoes and learn how to sail as well. There is a lot of world out there and we get to go play in it. Sign me up.

ABOUT THE AUTHOR

The author lives near Seattle where he plays outdoors a lot. His favorite spectator sport is the stock market. He has a Masters degree from Virginia Tech and a black belt in Karate. At the start he was 41 years old, 6 feet 2 inches, 185 pounds, with 22% fat.

Appendix

Who Helped

Wow, there are a lot of people to thank. Some are friends and family. Others are strangers I met along the way. A lot of the help just got me through the rest of the day and some of it got me past some amazing hurdles. I am an independent sort so it is sometimes hard to accept help even when I really need it.

The list begins with my wife, Kaye, and goes on to include the bike mechanics that I met (in Pendleton, the Dirt Dart, in Grand Junction, and Jared at Gregg's Bellevue Cycle), the Angel ladies (though they don't call themselves that), a few organizations like AAA, Cascade Bicycle Club, REI, Bike Nashbar, assorted unnamed motel desk clerks, random pedestrians, a few local police and fire officials, the software people at DeLorme and MapQuest, those folks that got me access to the Internet (like a few motel managers and the folks who run cyber cafes like www.futurekansas.com), The Weather Channel, some of the road maintenance crews, and all of the understanding drivers out there.

Kaye really got into the trip planning. Originally I was just going to wing it. I expected to do the route planning as I went. I thought that I would get advice from people I met and from occasional sessions on the Internet. Once I got a few days into the ride, Kaye got very interested in knowing where I was and where I was going. A few days after that, she bought a bunch of software packages and picked up an armload of information from AAA. With so much data available, a large part of our nightly phone call was her analysis of the motels and the terrain that I would probably come across in the next few days. As I got closer to the

Continental Divide that task became enormous. She compared a lot of the routes across the Rockies against each other and then checked how tough they were relative to the rides that we do around Seattle. Normally she worked a nine hour day with a long commute so she only had about three hours to do everything else each day. On the busiest days I think she spent one of those hours doing research for me and one hour talking to me. She had to cram everything else into the one hour remaining. There was a lot of information there and I'm glad she launched into the task. Without her I would have had to add a day or two just to get through Idaho. My choice of passes over the Rockies would have involved a much tougher climb. Besides, it was always nice to know that someone knew where I was, where I was going, and was there to hear all the boring and agonizing details.

The bike mechanics were probably the next most sympathetic group of people that I met. They understood bikes and gave mine the love and attention that I certainly hadn't. I am not mechanically inclined. Changing tires and tubes is not too bad, but I have trouble changing a bike chain. I'm even fairly ignorant of the names of some of the less often replaced parts. In Pendleton one mechanic was kind enough to change out a chain and rear gears while giving me advice about how to climb "Cabbage Hill". In Boise I met the Dirt Dart, a bicycle mechanic that does house calls. For $35 I got an enormous amount of work done and an accurate diagnosis of a problem that sidelined me later. He did all of the work in the parking lot of the motel and didn't quit until he was satisfied that he had done all that he could for me. When I called him the next morning from the road he was nice enough to talk me through the road side fix that literally helped me get back into gear. In Grand Junction I met a mechanic who called around to at least a half a dozen shops to help me find the tires that I needed. He ended up getting the business anyway but that's another story. He was friendly and supportive which was really appreciated because my knees and I certainly did not want to ride all over Grand Junction. The mechanics on the phones at REI and Bike Nashbar were nice enough to listen to me explain my technical difficulties. I didn't even end up buying their products but they delivered some useful advice anyway. I appreciated that. Finally there is Jared and the folks at Gregg's Bellevue Cycle. Jared listened to my story and built me two wheels that same day and handled some other bits of work as well. That fixed the bike so well that I didn't have any equipment problems for the rest of the trip. I hope his ride to Alaska went well.

Ah, let me give thanks for the Angel ladies. They are two sweet women running a small diner and mini-mart part time in the onion fields in Eastern Oregon about 10 miles outside of Ontario. I mentioned them in my logs but they deserve special attention here as well. They gave me an angel to carry along for protection. I got that and a cool relaxing break on an incredibly hot afternoon. All of that was for the price of some potato chips and a Mountain Dew. I hardly spent anything there and they were still kind, generous, friendly, and thoughtful. I wasn't the only recipient of their good graces. The young salesman who came in while I was there should be even more appreciative. They were friendly to everyone that came into the store. What I liked was that it wasn't the sappy friendliness that is on TV or in some high end store. It was a relaxed and honest reaction. They are wonderful role models for all of us.

The AAA may be there for automobiles but, except for one of their employees, everyone Kaye and I dealt with was happy to help a bicyclist. Their maps showed where I could find food and lodging. That made eating and sleeping much easier. What can be more basic than that? The one individual I want to especially thank though is the woman who works the office in Pendleton, Oregon. The bike mechanic in town devoted great energy to warning me off from the next piece of Interstate. Unfortunately I was so tired that I couldn't remember his directions for the alternate road. When I phoned the AAA office it was apparent that I couldn't make sense of her directions either. Because it was so late and I had doubts about finding the AAA office before they closed for the day, she made a special trip over to the motel and left a map at the counter with the route highlighted. That was special service.

Cascade Bicycle Club had no idea that I was doing this trip. I am not a member and if any part of their organization heard about it, it might have been as some tidbit in a conversation. So why thank some organization that wasn't even involved? Two very important reasons: what they have done for me and what they have done for the Puget Sound area. Over the years I have taken part in more than a few of their organized rides. Every year they organize the Seattle to Portland ride. That ride gave me the chance to find out that I can ride 200 miles in a day if someone else is handing out the food and carrying my gear. I don't think I could have contemplated any of my other bike tours without the confidence that I gained on those rides. As for what they have done in the Puget Sound area, I can not point to anything in particular, but I know that they are very active in advocating for bicycling causes in and around Seattle. While I have always enjoyed the results of their efforts and been aware that they were somehow involved, I didn't really appreciate them until I came across other large cities where there was no such support. It amazed me to realize that in cities like Boise and Salt Lake City there were great opportunities to have nice, flat, roomy bike paths and yet I couldn't find any. What really surprised me was that the local bike shops and tourist offices weren't aware of any either. Around Seattle it is fairly hilly and wet and yet I have my choice of bike routes, bike lanes and bike paths. The only place that came close was the state of Colorado. When I look at all of the places that I traveled through I realize that I would not consider moving to many of them because I would be comparing them to Seattle. From this cyclist's point of view, this area is hard to match and much appreciated. Cascade doesn't get all of the credit but I know they are key to it, can act as surrogates for the others and I thank them all. (Florida note: The bike path work there has great potential to be on a par with the best of the states that I saw.)

So many of the motel desk clerks deserve small awards for their patience in dealing with a tired bicyclist who dragged himself into their lobby. Riding for over half a day usually wiped me out. By the end of the day it seemed that I couldn't think straight until I had stretched and had a shower. In the meantime they dealt with all the little questions that I handed them even when I asked the same one two or three times. I especially liked the way most of them handled the faxes that Kaye would send out.

While making my way through some of the towns I would put some pedestrian on the spot by asking for directions to whatever I was hunting for: the next intersection or a motel. People always tried their best to give me directions that were useful and none of them treated me poorly despite how much I upset their sensibilities by looking and acting different.

The best source of information and help were the local police and fire officials. Whenever I needed help and could find a police officer, the resulting information was invariably the best. They usually also delivered some insight or bit of news that I wouldn't even have thought to ask about. In Aspen, one was able to tell me details about the road ahead that weren't even on the map. The fact that the road went down to one lane in a couple of places was nice to know ahead of time. The fireman who directed me around the accident right at the beginning of the trip was definitely key that day. He could have just as easily told me to wait in traffic like everyone else. Instead he went out of his way to show me a way through the bushes that got me around the accident. The path was nasty but it got me past the wreckage on a day when even a small detour could have cut the day's progress short by tens of miles.

The road crews were everywhere. The ones that helped the most were the ones that let me ride on the freshly paved lanes that were still closed to traffic. Usually that would be a dramatic shift from being squeezed by traffic through the construction zone to having the luxurious experience of being the only vehicle on the smoothest road around. The guy that caught up to me in the pickup truck to invite me to my own lane is the most memorable. What a nice way to travel.

I couldn't count on logging onto the Internet, so the DeLorme topographic and Atlas software were a great help. Kaye was able to find motel and route information that gave me a lot more confidence than I would have had otherwise. Now if I could only get that in a lightweight, cheap, sturdy bit of hardware it would have saved Kaye a lot of trouble and made the logistics a heck of a lot easier. Given the speed of technological development, it probably existed and I just didn't know it.

Where would I have been without the Weather Channel? Nowhere different actually. I didn't change my route due to weather. Without a doubt though, the information I got there was some of the most valuable to me every day. How else would I know that I was in or about to be in record setting heat or cold? Their descriptions of which way the wind was going to blow even made me start wondering if it would be fun to do a bike trip based on what would essentially be a tailwind forecast. I was bummed when I checked into a motel that didn't have such good local weather coverage. Forget the stocks and the news. Just tell me the weather. The side benefit was that I could track my progress by watching their maps each night. Not that I didn't have enough maps already but it felt different watching them describe places I had been through, or were heading to. It helped place me.

To an Internet junkie like me, finding a computer tied to the Internet was like finding a water fountain in the desert. The majority of the time was spent typing up the trip logs that I sent out via email. The motel managers and clerks that let me use their machines never pressured me to get off the machine. They treated me as a responsible user. Some of them apparently did so at some small risk to their job. I hope there was no trouble. The individuals running the Internet cafes are pioneers. They all seemed to be enthusiasts who were operating the business primarily as a public service. I am sure they wouldn't mind making money at it, but their primary motivation seemed to be that they wanted to get folks excited about technology and what it could do for their lives. They were quietly noble.

The people that are impossible to thank directly but were the most important are all of those drivers who didn't hit me. Let's get right down to it folks. That would have ruined my whole day. Seriously, while I would provide as much room as I could, I would still exercise my right to travel on the roads. Sometimes as the shoulder narrowed, that would make it more difficult for the traffic to pass me. I am a driver too so I appreciate this. (Frequently people forget that bicyclists own cars too and talk about bicyclists as if the bicyclist doesn't know what it is like to drive a car. It is too easy to judge a person by one aspect of their life and forget about the whole.) Out of 3,000 miles I can only think of about three close calls and they were when everything stacked up wrong all at once: heavy traffic, narrow roads, and not enough shoulder. Even in those cases, the vast majority of the drivers acted responsibly without any hint of road rage. I particularly came to trust the long haul truckers. They were excellent at knowing where the edge of their truck was and drove sanely and predictably. Hearing them behind me on the Interstate was much better than hearing normal traffic in town. They drive well and I am thankful. Oh yeah, and the honks and waves as I climbed the hills helped my morale. I guess they appreciated what I was going through. I gained an appreciation for horsepower, air conditioning, a comfy seat and cruise control. Maybe I'll use them next time.

What I Carried

Let me preface this section with my philosophy on packing. Nitpicking weight doesn't make a lot of sense to me. It is easy to convince yourself that every ounce counts, and it does. Physics says so. But if weight is that important, then you should weigh the food and water that you carry. Food and water are much denser than everything except you and the tools you carry. Shaving pounds is good, but shaving ounces is going a bit too far for me. Besides, if you manage to lose some weight on the trip, it will more than make up for an extra ounce or two. The reduced weight may let you go farther or faster, but it probably won't change your evening's destination often enough to warrant the time and energy spent agonizing over every item in your panniers.

The gear sounds like something that is decided by the trip and how you plan on riding. That is only partly true. I guess it is totally true if you go out and buy everything just for the ride. That's expensive. For me, it was mostly a case of using what I had and making it work for what I had in mind. That would probably be true for most people.

The bicycle

Originally I was going to take my road bike. It is a mid 1980's Trek 510. That's old enough that it only had 12 speeds. This good idea got thrown out very early. When coming home from a tiring training ride I forgot to take the bike off the roof of the car before driving into the garage. Poor thing. Stupid, tired driver. The frame was irreparably bent in two places. That left me with the option of buying a brand new bike or refitting my mountain bike to take the place of the road bike. The mountain bike had worked well enough during our trip to Austria so I knew that it could do the job. It is heavier and slower than a road bike but it is also sturdier and more reliable. Really the only modification required was to replace the knobbies with touring tires. That ended up being a problem on the road. In the smaller towns the bike shops are working hard to not carry a lot of expensive inventory. Most of the stores only carry mountain bikes for riding on dirt and therefore they only carry knobby tires. If they are a big enough store to carry touring equipment, it is usually only for their road bikes. An odd beast like mine just did not fit into a nice niche so no one seemed to carry the necessary equipment.

In the end the mountain bike was a good enough way to go. I sacrificed some speed, carried more weight, and had a tougher time in headwinds, but I felt that I had a more dependable bike. If there were smooth bike paths along the entire route then a road bike would rule. I encountered rough shoulders and much more road construction than I had expected. It was reassuring to know that if I had to, I could just ride off into the dirt and not break the bike. Of course there was no guarantee that I wouldn't break. I was especially glad when I had to hit rumble strips while screaming down some steep grade at over thirty miles an hour. Even if a road bike would have sufficed, I was more confident on the sturdier equipment. That confidence can mean a lot for morale and attitude.

The tires are hopefully the only part of the bike hitting the road. Because of that, they are very important. To me, puncture resistance and a good touring tread were very important. I wasn't concerned with that amount of extra weight. To typify the need for puncture resistance, one bike shop that I visited charged $24 per hour to remove cactus needles from tires. The needles are evidently very easy to pick up and you tend to get them in quantity all at once. I think that is what happened between Price and Green River. I thought I would be immune to such because I stayed on the pavement. Those needles had to come from somewhere though. A good touring tread for me is one that has some channels or grooves for releasing the water and good tread thickness. The slicks that I saw out there were too slick, tended to have less tread than I like, and seemed to have thin sidewalls. The tires were nice and light but I didn't want to trust them on the open road. The extra thickness helps the puncture resistance and takes longer to wear out. The nice tires that I started out with lasted about 2,500 miles including some training rides. So even if they were brand new at the start of the ride, they would have to be replaced somewhere along the ride. In retrospect I should have lined up some good bike shops before I left so I would know where to get such good equipment.

About the only other noticeable change I made to the bike was the addition of some aero bars that I used as very long bar ends. I had intended to fit them on as aero bars to help in headwinds and to give my hands a break. Unfortunately I couldn't get them to fit in and around the existing hardware on the handlebars. I could only mount them as bar ends. That gave me some more hand positions and allowed me some moderate streamlining in windy conditions. They ended up in a spot that wasn't nearly so sporty. Of course even at their best they didn't have a chance of turning a mountain bike into a streamlined marvel. The help was appreciated though.

Lest one think that this ended up being some fancy setup, keep in mind that this was a circa 1992 Trek 8000. It is also know as a hard tail. There is no fancy suspension or cantilevered seat. This made for a harder ride but still one that is softer than a hard tail road bike. It also left me with a bike that was simpler. Fewer components meant fewer things to go wrong. Besides, some of the suspension bikes leak oil, which is immensely frowned upon by motel staff and has meant that some places won't allow bicyclists to store their bikes in their rooms.

Tools

Here's the list of the tools I used:

Tire irons

I started with one set of plastic ones. One of them broke when I tried to get a tire off the bike. That's the downside of the sturdier tires; they tend to be a pain to get on and off. I bought a second set of steel tire irons on the road.

Crescent wrench
Its main use ended up being for pedal removal when I was getting the bike ready for shipping.

Hex key set
These were necessary for adjusting the bar ends and for the breaking the bike down for shipping.

Tube patch kit
I carried some of the newer ones that don't require a separate tube of glue. Around home I might patch a tube many times over. On the road I want reliability so a patched tube was replaced at its second hole or when the tire was off for some reason.

Pressure gauge
Hit a few rumble strips and watch your blood pressure rise and your tire pressure fall. I don't know if that was the cause, but I used it as a scapegoat.

Spare tubes (2)
This number would vary but I always carried at least two if I could. I wanted to be prepared in case both tubes blew accidentally or due to mischief.

Leatherman
The screwdrivers were handy for adjusting the gears and adjusting the panniers.

Swiss Army knife
Isn't this a required piece of equipment? This is a very handy little item that got used for clipping toenails, tuning the derailleurs, and who knows what else. I carried a big one and a little one and used them both.

The list of what I carried and didn't use:

Vise grips

Spare spokes

Spare tail light

Spare chain and a chain removal tool
Whenever someone was working on the bike I had them change the chain if the old one had more than 500 miles on it. My lack of mechanical aptitude is reflected in the stuck links I tend to create whenever I change a chain. It is better that someone else replaces it. (Florida note: I did manage to successfully change a chain in Florida.)

Spare pannier hardware
It is one of those little plastic packages that was in the box and I still haven't figured out what it is there for. Might as well bring it along.

Spare cable
The cable came along and I can't remember if it is for the brakes or the derailleurs. I should have carried a full set.

Bike lock
I carried a combination cable lock the whole way and only used it twice. (Florida note: And I used it once more in Florida.) By using a combination lock I didn't have to carry any keys. That was one less item to keep track of. The cable lock made good sense because the U-locks that I like better are best used in cities around pipes and bike stands and I was usually far from the land of bike stands. The cable could wrap around a tree much easier. The lock wasn't used much though because I could usually park the bike where I could see it. It also seemed that most folks wouldn't know what to do with the bike if they did take it. Being able to keep it in the motel room helped a lot too. In all the time

on the road, I don't think anyone attempted any mischief or even poked around it. It was too big, odd and cumbersome for just anyone to try carting it off. Like I've said elsewhere, there are a few bozos out there but there are far more folks that you can trust.

Food

It is easiest to just say that this varied day to day. Elsewhere there is a description of my daily eating habits. For this section though I will concentrate on what I actually carried. Typically I would try to carry enough food for the ride plus some extra for emergencies. I rarely ate everything that I carried even though it should have happened more often. It was usually a few bottles of sport drinks like Gatorade and a few energy bars like Powerbars. When I was lucky enough to get a chance to shop in a grocery store I might also pick up some cheese, bagels, bananas, or beef jerky. Sometimes my choices were limited to what I would find in a poorly stocked mini-mart. In that case I might end up with just water and some cookies. The sport drinks were usually anywhere from one to four of the 32 ounce plastic bottles depending on how much support the road ahead would provide and require. I always tried to have at least four of the energy bars along though on occasion I ended up with as many as eight of them in the pack. The bagels held up well but took up a lot of room and could be hard to swallow. The beef jerky was easier to pack but even harder to swallow. I carried cheese sometimes but I couldn't find it as often as I would have liked. The two water bottles were only used for water. I didn't want any sugary buildup attracting dirt and bugs. Luckily the bottles of sports drinks never leaked despite the abuse they encountered in my panniers. They would get filled with water if I ran out of the sweet stuff and it looked like I would need more fluids that day.

Luggage

I only had three pieces of luggage: two rear panniers and a fanny pack that can be strapped to a bike rack. Conventional wisdom holds that you should distribute the weight evenly fore and aft and maybe have a handlebar bag too. I decided that I would rather have fewer things to have to deal with. This is where I spent some good money and bought the sturdiest and most water repellant panniers that I could find. I bought two Ortliebs. They have lots of adjustments for fitting snugly to the bike rack and proved to be stout enough. Some of the bumps I hit would have dismounted my cheaper set. I don't like having to chase luggage in the midst of heavy traffic. I am also glad that I did not overstuff them. During the hotter, drier and lonelier parts of the ride I would have the most clothes in the panniers and would have to rely on the water I carried to get me through the day. Some days that meant carrying at least a gallon of Gatorade. That can take up a lot of space in the panniers. By the way, because I was almost always storing the bike in my motel room, it also meant that the panniers usually stayed on the bike. The bike ended up being my luggage carrier. I used this imagery with some of the motel managers when they were wondering about allowing me to store the bike in my room. When I joked about it being an expensive luggage rack they seemed to relax a bit.

The fanny pack was handy for those times when I took a day off and was just running around town doing small errands. It was such a treat to ride around for a while without all of that dead weight in the rear. It was also handy for carrying the small important stuff like my wallet, cell phone, maps, and snacks.

By the way, I never weighed the luggage and everything in them. That data point would only be demoralizing and would not have helped me get there faster. (Florida note: Kaye snuck a peak at the baggage scale at the airport which registered 34 pounds.)

Clothing

What a fashion statement a bike tourist makes. Two panniers contained all the clothes I needed to get by for weeks. One pannier was mostly emergency gear and foul weather gear. So, I almost could have fit all of my clothes into one pannier. It is amazing to compare that against how much stuff I have in my closet at home. You, actually I'll just speak for myself here, really don't need much to get by. It also helps that because almost every night was a different town, no one could tell that I had worn the same clothes to dinner for the last few weeks. I had some variation available to me but it was not much. Here's the list:

Bib tights

My one pair of long legged black bike pants with suspenders came along because they are good for cold and wet weather. Unfortunately they are unpadded. (Florida note: I left them in Seattle.)

Bib shorts (2)

The bib shorts are just like the tights but they only go to the mid thigh and are padded and good for hot weather. Kaye custom made one of them for me. I put a hole in the store-bought pair by sitting on a concrete barrier during a break. The hole never got too big but I was more careful where I sat after that. (Florida note: I ended up having to buy a pair before I left. The tiny tears from the earlier trip had grown and ruined my other shorts.)

Zippered cargo pants

These are the sort where you can take the legs off and wear the pants as shorts. Their primary purpose of being worn at dinner. The shorts could be biked in if necessary. They were part of my conservative backup attire for areas that aggressively didn't want to see a grown man in skintight shorts.

Beach shorts

I could bike in these too if necessary. I mainly carried them to have something to use in a pool, hot tub, or if I made it into the ocean. This gave me two pairs of shorts so I could wear one while washing the other. They also packed down well.

T-shirts

I had two cotton T-shirts: one long sleeve, one short sleeve. They had a fun graphic on them. We made them up like some rock group's tour shirts listing all of the places they'll be stopping. In my case we labeled them "Trimbath's USA Tour Fall 2000". I annotated the long sleeve one as I passed through the towns. That was fun though after a few washings and sweaty days it was hard to read.

Polypro turtleneck

It gets cold in those mountains and some days I wished I had packed a thicker one. (Florida note: I left it in Seattle but could have used it one morning.)

Polo shirt

This was my dinner wear though I could have worn it riding if necessary. It was nice to have something along that was not specifically for riding.

Sweatshirt

I had carried this as an extra layer and as something to relax in. I ended up leaving it at home after my Intermission. A cotton sweatshirt is not good for much when extra layers are needed and I already had enough to wear to dinner because of the T-shirts and polo shirt. (Florida note: I left it in Seattle.)

Micro-fleece jacket

This was my first layer over any shirt that I would wear. It was light enough to take the chill off and heavy enough to act as a mild windbreaker. It was bright orange. Again I chose functionality over fashion. (Florida note: The zipper on the orange one broke so I bought and new blue one and didn't feel as visible as I would have liked.)

Yellow rain coat

Besides being rain protection, this was a good top layer on cold days and because it was my best wind protection. The hood helped me stay warm too.

Yellow rain pants

These were another custom job from Kaye. She built them with suspenders and ankle straps. She made them when we had trouble finding rain pants that weren't black. It was amazing that the bike clothing catalogs would sell dark foul weather gear. Any nut willing to bicycle in foul weather should want to be seen. Hiding the dirt with some dark fabric is way secondary to me. (Florida note: I left them in Seattle figuring that Florida would have warm rain. It did but my legs got messy from the road dirt.)

Socks (4 pair)

For the most part there is nothing fancy here. Two pair were nice Nike ones that my Dad got me for Christmas and one pair was very short for those hot days. The one fancy pair were some Gore Tex socks that I got for riding in the rain. They weren't as good as booties, but they weigh less and do a good enough job for me.

Shoes (2 pair)

I had one set of old touring bike shoes without cleats. Some places won't let you walk around in cleats. They like their floors the way they are thank you very much. I also had a pair of boat shoes for after the ride. I wanted to be able to let the bike shoes air out and dry out each night. Besides, the boat shoes could act as an emergency pair and they didn't take up much space.

Gloves (3 pair)

I started out with the requisite fingerless bike gloves and added a lightweight pair of polypros for colder days. I ended up replacing the bike gloves when they wore out. They were old at the start of the ride.

I also ended up buying a pair of lined work gloves in Kansas on one of the coldest and dreariest days of the ride. My polypros weren't helping much because they had gotten wet. The weather wasn't going to let them dry out so I stopped in a grocery store and bought nice warm gloves. Such luxury. I appreciate little things like that much more than fancy hotels. Next time I will carry work gloves to work on the bike with. Instead I ended up trashing one pair of polypros while changing a tire. (Florida note: New, cheap work gloves made the bike maintenance much easier.)

Hats (2)

I always had one bike hat though I had to replace it on the road. The brim gave out. For cold days I carried a lightweight balaclava that I could wear under the hat. A heavyweight one would have been warmer but it wouldn't have fit under the helmet as well. (Florida note: I left the balaclava in Seattle.)

Underwear (3 sets)

I started out with one set of regular briefs but had two along for the second half. I'll leave the details to your imagination. For the entire trip I carried along one set of padded underwear. This was necessary for the unpadded bib tights but it also allowed me to ride in regular shorts should I be forced to because of local culture or because the bibs were out of commission.

Bandanas (5)

I only expected to carry 3 but I kept accidentally packing more and lost track of how many I had. They were good as handkerchiefs, headwear, and as shop rags. They are quite versatile.

Eyewear (2 pair)

Until recently I would have been carrying two pair of prescription glasses but since the Laser surgery I have been able to buy cheap sunglasses. I considered the fancy ones like Oakley and Smith but decided that I would rather have something that wouldn't be a problem if they were stolen. I started out with one pair of dark $10 Foster Grants and added a clear pair for cloudy days by picking up a set left on the side of the road. Thanks to whoever left them behind. Did you forget them or discard them because of the scratch? (Florida note: I switched to some Smiths that I got for Christmas.)

Toiletry kit

I carried a lot more stuff than I needed. The stuff I used most were things like a toothbrush, toothpaste, floss, and a razor. If you run out of something without a store nearby, the motel might have a small supply for you to pick from. By the way, carry along one of the hotel shampoos for those motels that only supply hand soap. Q-Tips were handy for me and for the bike. Local barber shops helped with the trimmings and such. Keep it simple. No one expects you to look good and I never really got very odiferous. I'll make that more personal, no one expects me, Tom Trimbath, to look good. You get to lead your own life.

Journal

I carried a half sized zippered three ring binder. There is so much going on that I wanted to spend some time each night recording a bit of what happened each day. This was a bit different than what I published in the emails. It is good to have some place to record more personal moments, insights and feelings. The binder also ended up being a good place to store maps, a calendar, business cards, a floppy that was never used, and my receipts. By the time I was done it also carried a pencil, pen, permanent marker, and a highlighter. It was a handy package to take to dinner where I could do some trip planning while I waited for my meal to arrive.

Envelopes

I carried both paper and plastic envelopes to help organize my receipts. The plastic ones were good for protecting maps and stamps.

Camera

Kaye was nice enough to let me run off with her point and shoot camera. I left my big SLR at home. Between rough roads, possible accidents, and possible theft, I wanted to carry a camera that was easier to replace than my ancient SLR. The digital camera didn't come along because I didn't want to have to worry about batteries and storage media. The new Advantix cameras would have been useful for the panoramas but I didn't want to buy a new camera just for this trip. For me, conventional equipment is the easiest to maintain and use. Having said all of this it was ironic that when I finally got to the Gulf Coast, the reliable little camera died. The batteries gave out and I couldn't find fresh ones on a Sunday night in Mobile. I only shot two rolls of slide film. Slides don't have any great advantage; it is just a habit of mine. I love to take photographs and the areas I went through could be photogenic but it was hard to compose a shot that didn't have some distracting feature like the road, power lines, or the guardrail. The lighting wasn't very kind either. Some of those places probably looked marvelous if you could get off the road and catch that good light at dawn or dusk, but those were the times when I was either intent on getting ready for the day or busy recovering from it. (Florida note: I switched to disposable cameras. They weren't as nice but I didn't have as much to worry about either.)

Books

The most useful books were the AAA guides. I only carried them on occasion but when I did, I found them to be useful. I sliced them up as I went and left the useless parts behind. I may not scrimp on weight obsessively, but whenever I sliced off a part of a map I felt that I had made progress. I don't think I carried any other guide or travel information that was worth its weight.

Television is everywhere and good books are not. This can be a bit of commentary on our society but suffice it to say that if you like to read books, take a couple along. I left them behind as I finished them and would pick up fresh ones as I could. Used books are best for this. Most of the time I was in towns that didn't sell books, magazines or even newspapers. Some of the newspapers only had about twelve pages most of which were ads. I really appreciate bookstores of any size when I walk into them now.

Credit Cards

I carried two Visa cards and only had to use one. There was a problem though. Doing a trip like this results in charges showing up in a wide variety of locations. This triggered something in the credit card company's software, which made them suspicious. Don't be surprised if you have to talk to Customer Service a few times to tell them everything is alright.

Emergency Stuff

Deciding to stay in motels rather than camping in a tent was probably the biggest gear related decision that I made. By relying on motels and restaurants I eliminated most of the need for a tent, sleeping bag, cook kit, cook stove and fuel. To be prudent though I had to have at least some of that functionality along. Accidents happen. Weather can catch one by surprise. Bikes break down. I could get lost. If any of these things happened near the end of the day on a road where for some reason the traffic wouldn't stop to help and where the cell phone didn't work, then I had to have some way to get through the night. You can always hope for luck and leave those things behind, but I don't hang it out there like that. Expecting the unexpected helps keep you alive. I decided to take along a first aid kit, a hybrid hammock that has a rain fly and bug netting, an emergency "Space Blanket", and a sleeping bag liner.

As it turned out, I was lucky enough to never need any of it. I helped make that happen by riding conservatively. At each town I would guess what the weather would do between where I was and the next motel. If the weather looked too bad and the next leg was over thirty miles, then I would probably stay where I was. I also always allowed myself a two hour grace period at the end of each day. My final destination was chosen such that when I got to the motel I would still have about two hours of daylight left. That would give me one hour to fix whatever problem was occurring and one hour to try to get a ride into town in case I couldn't resolve the problem. Riding solo meant that I couldn't rely on getting help quickly. Conversely, riding with someone increases the chances of a failure because there are more bikes involved.

First Aid Kit

This is largely determined by your own special needs but I can point out what I ended up using. I used lots of Advil, but then again I am over 40, have worked my joints hard, and have a bad back. When I got a cold I grabbed some decongestants. The better I breathe the farther I can travel. Various bandages got used but I didn't need very many of them. While some folks consider sun block and lip balm to be toiletries, I considered them preventative medicine to stave off severe sunburn and cracked lips. At one point my lips got so cracked that I couldn't open them wide enough to eat a Whopper. They got better. In a similar vein I used lubricating gels in various places. There was a whole lot of rubbing and chafing going on and that was one way to fight it. I used baby powder after each ride to dry things out. I'll leave the details to the imagination of those who are most interested.

Cell phone

I never had a cell phone until this trip. We don't have kids and it seems that most of my friends are using them to figure out who has taxi duty at any given time. For a ride like this, and especially for a solo ride, I decided to get one. That and the fact that Kaye, my family, and all of my friends probably wouldn't let me go out there without one. As Kaye pointed out though, people have been doing rides like this for years before cell phones came along. So it is not a necessity but in the last few years they have gotten to be so small and work so many places that it is a very handy resource to have along. Their use in emergencies is the main reason I carried one.

I investigated the various options and ended up with a fairly conventional solution: one of the Motorola Star-Tac phones through Verizon. I picked the Star-Tac because when it is closed, the display and keys are covered. I am a klutz and wanted something that would be harder to mess up. It is still working so it must have been good enough. The ear bud headset was very useful. I occasionally talked to someone while juggling maps and travel guides and needed both hands free.

Verizon almost worked as well as I had hoped. The service covered almost my entire route but the features would change as I went from region to region. If I was less of a cell phone neophyte it might have gone smoother.

The next step up was to go with a satellite phone. Globalstar was the most readily available and I almost went that route. The plans available when I set out could be very expensive but at least it had the most coverage. I thought it could still be blocked in some of the deeper canyons that I rode through. What kept me from using it was that the cheaper system would provide most of the same coverage. Therefore the satellite option would only make sense if all the odds lined up against me. I would have to have a critical failure of some sort and the failure would have to happen where a regular cell phone wouldn't work but not where the satellite could be blocked. I guessed that the odds of all those things happening simultaneously where I also couldn't flag someone down were too small to warrant the extra cost. By the time you read this, the technology will have probably changed all of these parameters.

Flashlight

I carried a small Petzl headlamp in case I had to ride at night. I have a much brighter bike headlamp, a Nightrider, that I left at home because its battery charger weighed so much. I didn't plan on riding after dark so a lighter backup was a fine option. I don't think it ever got turned on during the whole trip. I'd still carry it just in case.

Bad emergency equipment choices

As it turned out, I took the wrong emergency arrangement. The hammock that I carried would not have worked for more than half the trip. Trees near the road were not available through lots of Oregon, Idaho, Utah, and especially through Kansas. Even where there were trees, they were frequently on the other side of barbed wire fences. A bivy sack would have been a better choice. The other item, which was probably not up to the task, was the bag liner that I carried in lieu of a sleeping bag. The liner is claimed to make a difference of about five or ten degrees. Maybe it would have made the crucial difference but I had very little confidence that it would have helped much during the freezing nights I met in Colorado and Kansas. If I had carried my light weight sleeping bag I would at least have had something that is supposedly good down to about 40 degrees. Throw on the rest of the clothes that I had and I would have been warm enough to make it through the night. It might not be fashionable but it would be survivable and that is the main criterion.

Stuff I Didn't Carry

A few items that some folks have been surprised to find that I didn't take along were a GPS system, a laptop, and fenders. I stayed along major roads so I figured any reasonable road map would give good enough detail for showing me where to go. For the most part I was right but where the road map was insufficient, the GPS may not have been useful either. Knowing my exact latitude and longitude may not help me find a location that I know only by some pedestrian's vague directions. A laptop could have carried all of the necessary reference data but I didn't trust one to survive the trip and be small enough and light enough for my tastes.

Fenders would seem to be a good idea but if I really needed them it would be because it was raining. If I am out there in the rain for six or seven hours, fenders aren't going to make a difference. A fender doesn't stop the splashing you can get from cars. Of course if you are not riding solo, your bike partner might have a different point of view.

I also didn't take a bike computer. Constant streams of data are more distracting than anything for me and it was something else that could break. I figured I eventually would ride a far chunk with it off or leave it on all night. In either case the data wouldn't be much better than what I could provide through the post processing of the route through the software we have at home.

Many people rely on bike mirrors. Usually these are mounted on the handlebars, helmet or eyeglasses. I probably could have used them but never have so I didn't even think about it until someone pointed out the possibility after I was done with the ride. In retrospect a mirror would have been handy but I don't know that it would have made any of the very hazardous incidents any less so. For someone else a mirror might save their life.

Stuff I Should Have Carried

Bivy (bivouac) Sack
> This would have been a much better idea than a hammock and lighter than a tent.

Sleeping Bag
> A small light sleeping bag would have been wiser than the sleeping bag liner I carried. I actually shopped for something like this while on the ride but couldn't find anything small enough. I did consider buying a good synthetic blanket as an alternative.

Brake and Shift Cables
> (Florida note: I carried them and didn't use them.)

Work Gloves

The fingerless gloves weren't the best for working on the bike. Something with full fingers that could be used for the messy jobs would have kept the bike gloves cleaner. Because I would wipe my brow while riding, the cleanliness of the gloves was noticeable. (Florida note: I am glad I took some along.)

Email Device

I don't think there is an easy and cheap solution to this one yet but eventually there will be.

These are just my reasons and rationale. You'll undoubtedly have your own unique situation to deal with. Good luck.

How I Picked the Route

Folks wanting to bicycle coast to coast in the United States have an amazing variety of routes to pick from. From what I've heard, there are lots of established routes generated by the multitude of touring companies out there. I didn't realize how many there were until after I got back. There are lots of ways to approach it: coast to coast, corner to corner, or some smaller chunk out of any of these. Everyone's likes and dislikes will change their route. The only thing I intend to do here is show how I chose my route.

The corner to corner option came to mind for me because I live in the upper left hand corner of the United States. That's all the more complicated that choice was. We get to see quite a few transcontinental cyclists around here. We live about a mile from Interstate 90 and a lot of cyclists pick this route for heading over Washington's Cascade Mountains. On occasion I can display a purist's streak and that drove me to considering the extreme corners. There are lots of ways of interpreting the extreme corner. I decided that by starting and ending beyond the coast was a fine approach. There are islands off the Washington coast, the San Juans, and islands off Florida's coast, the Keys. I got a vote of confidence during one of my training rides when I encountered a cyclist who told me about his nephew's trip. Evidently his nephew went from Cape Flattery on Washington's Olympic peninsula to Key West in 31 days. I was told that he averaged 150 miles a day. Now that is some easy math. If so, he rode over 4,500 miles. There are some awesome individuals out there. His route used I-90 as I had planned to do, but he stayed on it into Montana, then headed south through Wyoming and Nebraska. I didn't get any more details beyond that except that rather than use a tent or motel he was invited to stay in people's houses. That suggests that there is a lot of largess out there.

The first sanity check that I conducted was to grab some mapping software and get a rough idea of the distances involved. I expected the route to be about 3,000 miles. Flying a straight line, actually a great circle route, would take about 2,800 miles. Picking a continuous set of roads upped that to about 3,800 miles. In the meantime I also found out that some of the more established coast to coast routes were about 4,200 miles. I had a long ride ahead of me.

I actually did consider some of the other routes but for one reason or another I decided against them. The west-east routes down south looked very hot. The purely northern routes looked cold and entailed maneuvering around some very crowded cities in the east. The middle route, say from San Francisco to Washington D.C., is a nice compromise but there is still quite a bit of desert east of California. In retrospect on that route I probably would have seen conditions similar to what I came across anyway. The Southern California to New England route could spend a lot of time in the desert early on and seemed to maximize the amount of time spent in east coast cities. Now, I grew up riding around Pittsburgh and its steel mills so I know I can navigate traffic, but it just didn't appeal to me. Logic isn't the only criteria here. Desire is important too. Going from Washington to Florida gave me the chance to see more of the state that I have lived in for twenty years, and also meant that I could use the first small portion as a shakedown ride.

I am sure that some folks would do detailed planning of motels and roads so there was no doubt where they could go, stop and stay for every day of the trip. Just trying to find out each state's laws and attitudes towards bicyclists was enough to keep me busy. First I drew a straight line on a map and looked for roads that kept me close to it. I checked the states to see where there were big gaps between cities and left the details until later.

There were a couple of pieces of geography that were going to determine how I traveled. The Rockies and the Mississippi are hard to ignore and also hard to deal with. The Rockies and the neighboring mountain ranges are only crossable in a few places. For the most part these are Interstates. I can go on about riding myths and one is that you aren't allowed on Interstates. Not so, or at least it varies widely from state to state and police officer to police officer. Anyway I started with the assumption that the Interstates were fine. Simply put, there is I-90 in Montana, I-80 in Wyoming, and I-70 in Colorado. Already the route selection started to simplify. I had already driven the I-90 route by car a few times and wanted something different. Besides, I-90 seemed awfully lonely when I drove it. Because I would be riding in the Fall I also wanted to get south sooner. The longer I stayed north, the greater my chances of running into an early Winter storm. That left the other two routes.

To get a quick overview of how hilly the routes would be, I opened a nice low tech Atlas. I love these kinds of books. Anyway, just looking at the color contour maps helped me a lot. The route through Wyoming spent more time above 7,000 feet than the route through Colorado but seemed to be flat once it got there. Meanwhile, Colorado started down around 4,500 feet and climbed up over 10,000 if not 11,000 feet. Wyoming was also closer to my straight line route, which was even better. The choice of whichever way was better would have to wait until later.

The next hurdle was the Mississippi. I knew it was crossable but I also figured that such a large river would have few opportunities for bridges. Because I was willing to accept even the smallest bridge, I needed to get some detailed maps. Software is wonderful for this sort of thing. It isn't infallible but it did allow me to look at things in remarkable detail. Even doing that I found that there are very few places to cross. Crossing in Tennessee seemed to take me into hilly terrain. Going as far south as Louisiana started taking me farther from that straight line route. The Arkansas and Mississippi border had two viable routes, which was good enough for planning purposes.

Essentially I had two endpoints and two or three intermediate points as well. There was still some doubt about Colorado and Wyoming but the states that I needed information on were becoming much clearer.

The next step was to get out there on the web and on the phone trying to contact each state's transportation or tourism department to find out more detailed information. Someday each state will organize in some standardized or at least searchable fashion. That was definitely not the case when I tried. Information on bicycling can be under highways, tourism, transportation or non-existent depending on the state you're researching. My big concern though was the myth of the Interstate; could I ride on them and how would this affect my route? I started with Wyoming and Colorado because they were critical to getting over the Rockies. I already knew that Washington usually allowed cyclists on the road except in and around large cities. Oregon was probably the same way. I would check on the other states later.

Luckily both Wyoming and Colorado published bike maps showing the good roads, the bad roads, and the roads bikes weren't allowed on. So much for that nice route through Wyoming. It was on the list of roads excluded from cyclists and the alternates went every which way. I couldn't find a very good route through the state. I called and checked and they confirmed that they wouldn't allow cyclists on the Interstate but I was welcome to use the other roads. No thanks. Colorado, on the other hand, not only allowed bikes on their Interstates, but they also provided bike paths if there was a problem. Their bike map also showed at least three other routes and they also published a very detailed series of maps for the route that used the Interstate. The detailed maps were large enough that each one covered about one day's bike travel and included detailed descriptions of road hazards, where to find food, where to find lodging and where to find a mechanic. This was good stuff. If it wasn't for those dang mountains in the middle. Well, at least they looked pretty.

From the Colorado map it was clear that there was really only one good way into and out of the state: Grand Junction on the way in and Lamar on the way out. There were other roads, but there wasn't always other lodging. The details of the middle of Colorado I could leave to as late as when I got to Grand Junction. At worst, there I would find the local bike shops and get their advice before proceeding.

The pre-trip planning was largely done at this point. I checked out the other states for bike maps and came up empty. I was surprised to find that Washington didn't have one. Since then I've come across at least a reference to one. There are lots of them in and around the cities, but I could find nothing statewide. Oregon has an excellent map that I couldn't find online but was able to stumble across at one of their visitor centers. Kansas has a map online, which seems to be based purely on traffic patterns. It looks good to start with but I couldn't find enough motels along their suggested routes. None of the other states had much of anything. Florida did have some information but it was only good for small regions and was too discouraging and vague for my tastes. (Florida note: One year later I found more but I don't know if it was because I dug deeper or because more stuff was created.)

The details of the trip planning then were left largely to during the ride itself in the evenings after I got to a motel. I would generally check about four days ahead and have an idea of where I expected to stay. Circumstances changed often enough though that I frequently ended up using the contingency plans that I had in the back of my mind. Kaye was the biggest help through all of this detailed planning. She used the AAA and software as references. I used the maps I had collected from the various hotel chains. Most of the hotel chains publish a directory of all of their properties. Somewhere inside there is frequently a map showing their properties. Those dots were enough for me to plan with. If I doubted that I could find one of them as I came into town, I would call the chain's toll free number for directions or for the motel's phone number and get directions from them. The folks on the toll free number couldn't be very helpful though because they couldn't be familiar with every small town in the US. The only time I made a reservation was when I thought that there would only be one motel in town and nothing else within about twenty miles, or if I thought the town might be having a special event. Friday and Saturday nights in college towns during football season can be tight. Sunday night was always the easiest.

I have more details in my logs but hopefully this conveys the basic idea of how I did it. It took a lot more work than I had expected and I am glad that I didn't try to do it all in advance. In the end the route through Wyoming was closed for a week due to snow. It was a good thing that I went south. The route through Colorado was in question for quite some time, and the whole southeast portion got rewritten as I realized that I was running out of time and money. I only wish that my body was as flexible as my plans had to be.

What I Ate

Food is the fuel that gets you there. While I had set out to eat less and exercise more, I also had to keep in mind that I would be riding about seventy miles a day. That energy had to come from somewhere. I had a basic idea of what I liked to eat on the road based on my other long rides. I also knew that I would have to work with what was available. If the only thing available for the next thirty miles was a bacon double cheeseburger, then that was the best thing to eat. What I wanted to get by on were large sit down breakfasts, followed by bagels and energy bars with maybe a sandwich and a banana for lunch, and a dinner with a bit of variety. I figured dinner was the best time to check out the local food, though I also realized that I would gravitate to pasta or rice dishes with maybe some room for dessert. I wasn't wanting to obsess on keeping it low fat. I figured that many miles would allow me to relax and enjoy eating somewhat.

What I found is best typified by as standard American fare: burgers, pizza, and fried chicken. I couldn't find breakfast in every town, which surprised me and threw me off right there. Most, but not all of the towns had a mini-mart and most of the mini-marts had Powerbars and Gatorade or their equivalents. Bagels and bananas were harder to come by because grocery stores were hard to come by. Every once in a while I would stock up on bagels. They kept reasonably well for a few days but were bulky. Bananas and fruits were good for the first day and not much else. The record heat may have had something to do with this. Lunches happened only about half of the time. I guess they could also be said to have happened every day. On about half of the days there was a place to grab a sandwich or at least a hamburger. The other half of the days ended up being a series of snacks based on whatever I carried. About the healthiest lunches that I had were probably sandwiches from Subway. They seemed to be the easiest chain to find. At least dinner was an everyday event. Even then though, there were a few towns where there was nothing near my motel or if there was, it was a fast food restaurant. I swear that some states outlawed pasta because I couldn't find any for long stretches of road. I could always find a burger or some fried chicken, and most of the other reliable local food were large steaks with a monster potato, or pizza. One place advertised a 44 ounce steak. That actually sounds painful.

What really surprised me was my appetite. I had expected to be ravenous at the end of each day. Instead I found myself having to convince myself to get up and go out and eat. Most breakfasts were left unfinished and I didn't have nearly as many desserts as I had expected. I didn't eat as much during the day because I would get into a rhythm or groove where all I wanted to do was eat up mileage. This was ironic because it was especially true on those days where I was forced to make large jumps between motels. Just when I could use the most fuel was when I would tend to skimp on the time available for eating.

I really didn't get to eat much of what I would call local cooking. America has become homogenized to the point that for the most part, restaurants are all serving the same stuff. It wasn't until I started getting south of Kansas that I started seeing grits for breakfast and gravy on everything. In one restaurant when I asked for the meal to have no gravy the waiter took pity on me and offered me a side vegetable. I suppose he thought I was ignoring one of the major food groups.

To be more pedantic about it: Breakfast was typically an omelet with hash browns, toast, a side of bacon and a large orange juice. Pancakes and waffles didn't get me as far through the day and cereals and oatmeal didn't sit well as I rode. The fallback plan was usually a fast food breakfast sandwich. If I sat down to lunch, it was almost always a burger or a sandwich and the largest drink they had. Almost everything comes with fries but for some reason they weren't appetizing so I didn't eat them. I don't recall getting anything fancier than that for lunch. Dinner was a bit more varied: spaghetti with meatballs, lasagna, meatloaf with mashed potatoes and veggies, and rice dishes like stir fry. I particularly like the Jambalaya I had in Hattiesburg, wild game medallions in Buena Vista, and the breaded veal in Snowville. Fairly often though I ended with a pizza or a burger. Mini-marts may be driving mom and pop stores out of business, but they usually have something that approximates a meal as long as you aren't too picky. During the day I typically carried about four sports bars, and a couple of water bottles augmented by at least a quart of Gatorade. In drier climes or on longer stretches I packed up to a total of four quarts of Gatorade.

If I had been tent camping, I probably would have eaten simpler and better. Unfortunately, much of the food was either deep fried, dripping in oil or butter, or mothered in gravy. Compared to what I saw, my diet back home is exemplary. At least with tent camping I would have ended up with a lot more rice or pasta and a lot less fat. Of course that means there is more to worry about doing every day. Shopping, cooking and cleaning take time.

One thing that kept me from drinking more on the ride was the lack of rest rooms, rest stops or even trees. I have to admit to some prudishness about relieving myself at the side of the road where there are no trees or facilities but lots of traffic. That is one advantage that side roads have over the major highways. At least there might be a break in traffic when no one will see you. I was also skittish about heading to the bushes once I noticed rattlesnake road kill. What an embarrassing way to get bit. I should have had more to drink but I still can't figure how to hold it that long. Maybe a more detailed map showing all of the rest stops coast to coast would be handy.

Where I Slept

The short answer is that I frequently stayed in the best place in town, which frequently was the only place in town and wasn't all that nice but was much better than a tent.

The longest answer is to go through every town and mention every place that I stayed. Not only would that be tedious, but I would rather not nitpick each place. Besides, my experience may have been unique because that manager or I may have been having a bad day or a good day.

When I planned this trip I decided to stay in motels rather than a tent. I call it Visa card camping. As I have said elsewhere, I wanted to keep this trip simple. Staying in motels eliminated the need for carrying a tent, sleeping bag, cook kit, cook stove and fuel. It is limiting though in that I had to hop from motel to motel. By the way, motel was a much better description of the places I stayed rather than hotel. There aren't that many hotels along the route and even where they existed, the motels were usually easier to find and deal with.

There can not be one major rule governing where I stayed. In a lot of the towns, there was only one motel and therefore no choice. Actually there was always the choice of going on to the next town. A lot of times that next hop was usually just too much for me. Most of the places I encountered were there for the people who were travelling on business and for the few folks visiting family. They weren't there for tourists. Some were also occupied by temporary workers who were busy in the area for a short job but reasonably setting themselves up with a bit of home. Such a clientele works out well for the travelling bicyclist. The motel staff is not expecting any special dress code and might be very relaxed about things that fancy hotels might be a bit picky about. Almost every motel let me keep the bike in the room, though sometime I had to reiterate that it was a bicycle, not a motorcycle. Enough desk clerks asked about that to make me realize that some folks must be trying to park their motorcycles indoors.

The downside of this type of clientele is that many of them are up early or coming in late. Life is a bit noisier that way. It was never any worse than any college dormitory I had stayed in, but then the college dorms didn't have big diesel pickup trucks firing up before dawn right outside the window. Light sleepers might want to ask for rooms on the side of the motel away from the street. Don't be surprised if all the rooms face the street or if the rooms on the other side faces the railroad track.

Given the choice between a motel run by a national firm or a local proprietor, I usually picked the national motel. The local tends to be more relaxed about a lot of things and may be cheaper, but the national can be held accountable for their actions if I had cause to complain. That never was an issue but it was an easy advantage to have. The nationals were also more likely to have a restaurant on the premises. That was not always the case, but I found it to be very useful. Convenience was more important than culinary excellence and leaving the premises was certainly no guarantee of any improvement in the cuisine. Room service was a real time saver but the staff frequently seemed unused to people actually availing themselves of the option. The food or the bill was usually a bit different from what I expected. Despite that, room service was very handy on those days where I was wrung out from putting in lots of miles.

I always asked for a room on the first floor. That way it was easy to walk the bike into the room. Storing the bike in the room was safer than locking it outside and I didn't even have to take the panniers off. It did take up a bit of floor space, but I always had enough left over to do my stretching exercises, so it must not have been too bad. Two people in a room with two bikes would be a problem in some of those places. It was also handy having the bike inside for maintenance, though I was always careful to keep the room clean. Anything really dirty got done outside.

Getting a room on the first floor may be convenient but it frequently meant having to take a smoking room or some other odd room. It didn't bother me but some people might gasp a bit in some of those rooms.

The ideal motel room would be along the road, with a full service restaurant, room service, the Weather Channel, ground floor rooms where I could bring the bike in, a guest laundry with soap, easy participation in a frequent lodger program, approved by AAA, quiet, friendly, cheap, and have a room available for me. What I usually went for was more determined by how far I had traveled that day. If I had some miles left in me, I opted for the motels on the far side of town. If I was tired I might drop into the first motel I came across. Part of the problem was knowing exactly where the motels were in town. I might know that there were three of them, but they might be scattered over a few miles. Sometimes I expected a little cluster of lodgings at an off ramp only to find out that one was two miles to the north, one was two miles to the south, and the other was miles down the road. This is not a problem in a car but it is hard to comparison shop on the bike. In those cases I called the one farthest down the road and see if they had rooms available. If so I'd make a reservation and head their way. Otherwise I would start calling the others, and once I got a reservation, I would get detailed instructions on how to get there.

Luckily for me I am used to camping. When I checked into a motel I was usually measuring it against what it would be like to be in a tent. I like tents, but I really appreciate a bed, heat, air conditioning, and indoor plumbing. Others might be pickier. Being pickier might make the logistical side of things tougher. Each cyclist gets to evaluate that for themselves.

By the way, the frequent lodger plans that allowed for lower rates were more useful to me than the ones that promised awards in the future.

Statistics

2000 Washington to Florida			**2001 Florida**	
total miles	3030	from map software	840	
total dollars	$9,867	from my poor records	$2,975	
total days	55	from the calendar	17	
total riding days	43	it seemed like more	15	
average miles	55.1	including breaks	49.4	
longest break	7 days	back to Bellevue	2 days	hurricane watch
priciest hotel	$109	not the nicest stay	$ 160	almost the nicest
cheapest motel	$26	not the best deal	$ 43	one of many
cost per day	$179	flights included	$ 175	
cost per mile	$3.26	flights included	$ 3.54	
initial outlay	$1,461	cell phone and gear	$ 145	
lodging	$3,067	includes some food	$1,279	
food	$598	lots of mini-marts	$ 815	
repairs	$535	not bad considering	$ 22	
planes and cars	$2,196	the flights added up	$ 414	I got a deal
cell phone	$775	buying it and using it	$ 200	
miscellaneous	$1,400	bits of everything	$ 100	
most miles	114	thanks to a tailwind	93	leaving Perry
fewest miles	27	thanks to a bad rim	29	Key Largo
shortest day	3:00	the breakdown day		Oops, I forgot
longest day	9:30	Provo		"

What's Next

Now that I have finished the ride from Roche Harbor, Washington to Pensacola, Florida thoughts of other rides come to mind. Already some of my friends are talking about doing the rest of Florida and there is talk about trying the Pacific Coast. All of those alternate routes I came across during my planning inspire other trips I might take. Kaye did a chunk of New England and that sounds pretty. After looking at the map I realized that because of this trip I have visited all but 8 of the 50 states. New England would account for a few more. Alaska might be only one state, but there is enough land and maybe enough roads in it for a ride or twelve.

This ride can become a backbone on which I build future rides. I could end up with a spider web of rides starting from this first thread. Maybe I'll fly back to Wichita and head north some Spring when the wind is out of the South and the snow has melted out of the North. I could start in Mobile and head west along the Gulf Coast. It would be fun proving to myself just how good the food in New Orleans can be. Continuing on into Galveston and Brownsville would get me to the Mexican border. If I hit the Canadian border on the ride north, then I would have gone country to country. Hmmm, that is intriguing. The ride up along the Eastern Seaboard would be great for historical markers and lots of neat places to stay. I think I'll skip New York City though. That is a bit too big for me. Upper New York sounds nice. Maybe I'd travel along the Hudson. I hear there is a Northern Tier route that is 4,250 miles long. I might want to do pieces of that. Doing the whole thing solo sounds tough.

With this big chunk taken care of, most of these routes could be done as shorter rides. The timing could be easier to deal with because I wouldn't be as likely to change seasons during a ride. That should also make it easier to find people to ride with. They wouldn't have to take as much time off from work or such. I hope I still have the freedom that I have now.

Having dealt with so many logistical issues I know that I could do it again. There are areas with less support than where I went but given the right conditions I might be able to manage those too. One thing is for sure. Even though I am capable of doing this all myself, riding with a tour group definitely has its appeal and I'd like to try that out. Having someone else handle the logistics and being part of a group can be fun.

In the meantime I am back to saving up my money for the next trip. Every year I do something arduous and aerobic. Bicycle touring is just one of the challenges I set for myself. In other years it has been cross country skiing, mountain climbing, backpacking, marathon running, and one year it was my black belt test. Each of those are whole other stories. I'll just have to see what happens year by year. Is the money there? Does someone else have an itch to do a chunk of the country? Can I make the time? Aside from that my goal is to stay in shape. I want to be able to keep doing all of these things for a long time to come. I may not be the best but that is not the goal. Doing it faster or leaner than someone else isn't as important as being able to do it again and again. Here's hoping that I can and that you can to.

(Florida note: A short ride to Canada is probably next, but I want to devote some time to the other stuff I do. The world is so intriguing and there so many ways to see it. See you out there.)

0-595-22100-9

Printed in the United States
39250LVS00006B/115-120

9 780595 221004